FRUITY STORIES

Dr Joanna Readman is a freelance television producer, lecturer and writer, specializing in horticulture and botany. She has worked on many programmes for Channel Four, including 'Muck and Magic', 'Garden Club' and 'Fruity Stories'. Her previous books include *How to Know and Love Your Weeds*, *Soil Care and Management*, and *Muck and Magic: An Organic Gardening Guide for Children*, which won the Peter Kent award for the best children's book on conservation.

Patricia Hegarty and her husband John have run the Hope End Hotel in Herefordshire, which is renowned for its traditional English food, for twenty years. Much of the fruit and vegetables she uses are organically grown in their traditional walled kitchen garden, including many old and forgotten varieties. She is the author of *An English Flavour*, a collection of recipes devised in the kitchen at Hope End.

FRUITY STORIES

All about growing, storing and eating fruit

JOANNA READMAN

with recipes by Patricia Hegarty

Technical editor: Harry Baker

BⒷXTREE

in association with Channel Four
Television Corporation

First published in Great Britain in 1996 by Boxtree Limited

Fruity Stories is based on the television programme of the same name produced for Channel Four Television Corporation by Hourglass Pictures Limited

Designed by Geoff Hayes
Printed in Great Britain by Bath Press Colourbooks, Glasgow
for
Boxtree Limited
Broadwall House
21 Broadwall
London   SE1 9PL

A CIP catalogue entry for this book is available from the British Library.

ISBN 0 7522 1037 8

Front and back cover photographs by Jacqui Hurst

Picture acknowledgements
Photographs were kindly supplied by the following people:
pp.69, 140 © Fiona Birkbeck; p.33 Channel Four/© Chris Chapman; p.133 Channel Four/© John Harris; p.121 Channel Four/© Jayne Tipper; p.96 Channel Four/© George Wright; p.148 Common Ground/© James Ravilious; pp.80, 100 © Eric Crichton; p.116 © Simon Everson; p.21, 52, 120, 132, 145 © Georgia Glynn Smith; pp.12, 20 Horticulture Research International, East Malling; pp.25, 45, 65, 89, 109, 125, 141, 161 © Jacqui Hurst; pp.29, 32, 40, 49, 60, 81, 92, 104, 136 © Joanna Readman; pp.8, 156 RHS Wisley Photographic Collection/Michael Sleigh, © RHS; pp.48, 74 Scottish Crop Research Institute.

Line drawings were supplied by:
Tony Payne © pp. 30, 38, 54, 72, 114
Chartwell Illustrators, © Boxtree Ltd: pp.13; 14; 15; 19 (after Savigear, *Garden Pests and Predators*); 34; 36; 37 (after Baker, *Fruit, RHS Encyclopaedia*); 41; 47; 52; 56; 57; 76; 77 (after Baker, *Fruit, RHS Encyclopaedia*); 82; 91; 93; 97; 104; 113; 118 & 119 (after Brickell, *Pruning*, RHS Encyclopaedia); 121 (after Baker and Waite, *Grapes Indoors and Out*, A Wisley Handbook, RHS); 128; 129; 134 (after Baker, *Fruit, RHS Encyclopaedia*); 138 (after Baker, *Fruit, RHS Encyclopaedia*); 155; 156; 157; 158.

CONTENTS

Acknowledgements

I would like to thank the following people who took part in the programme, helped with the book and all in all told me their fruity stories.

All at Brogdale Horticultural Trust, the Royal Horticultural Society, Wisley, Horticulture Research International, East Malling , the Scottish Crop Research Institute, the Gooseberry Show at Goostrey, Charlton's Orchards, Hope End Hotel, the Somerset Cider Brandy Company, Read's Nurseries, Scott's of Merriott, Syndale Valley Vineyards, Common Ground, and all the following:

Jonathan and Paula Abbs, Jim Arbury, Gaetano Amatruda, Harry Baker, Imogen Benetto, Peter Brice, Fred and Joan Bromley, Peter Butt, John Cannon, Jeff Clayton, David and Rosalie Colledge, Leonard Cox, His Grace, the Duke of Devonshire, Willie Duncan, Matthew and Wendy Freudenberg, Meg Game, George Gilbert, Marcus Govier, Michael Haines, David Heath, Patricia and John Hegarty, Derek Holt, Dr Derek Jennings, Dr Nigel Kerby, Clare Maree Leighton, James Link, David Lloyd, Thomas McCartney, Peter McKay Blackwell, Dr Ronnie McNichol, Joan Morgan, Mervyn Ellison Nash, John Nelson, Tim Parnell, Dr David Pennell, Terry Read, Charlie Readman, Dave Readman, Jake Readman, Keith Richards, Steve Scriven, Dr David Simpson, Avtar Singh, Duncan, June and Robin Small, Tim Smit, Dr Mike Solomon, Phil Stone, Michael van Straten, Captain Bill Swinley, Mr and Mrs Tait, Julian and Di Temperley, Ray Waite, John Wallis, Miho Watanabe, Ron Watts, Ian Webster, Haden Williams, Ray Williams, John Willis, Jack Woodward, and all the other contributors to the programme and the book.

A special thank you to Harry Baker for reading and advising on the text, and to all at Hourglass Pictures Ltd, including Fiona Birkbeck, Robert Carter, Jacqueline and Martin Chilcott, Simon Everson, Mike Pavett, Tony Payne, Olivia Slot, Su Webb and Steve Warner.

INTRODUCTION

If the marketing lobby could invent a product that tasted wonderful, came in an edible package, reduced heart disease, cleaned your teeth, and was available in a wide range of colours they would make a fortune.

But nature has beaten them to it: the apple and a wide range of other fruits have been with us for thousands of years. However, only one garden in three grows fruit, and statistics show that in a one-week period only half the adults in Britain eat an apple or a pear, and only a quarter of the adults eat citrus fruit. What has happened to our nation of gardeners? There is a myth that growing fruit is difficult and time-consuming, and that it takes up a lot of room. Here are a few fruity stories to dispel that myth and show you how you can easily grow it, what you can do with it once you have grown it, and what it can do for you.

Fruity facts

• Fruit is easy. Once established, a fruit garden takes far less effort than vegetables.

• Fruit fits into small spaces. Using old skills and new varieties, a wide range of fruits can be grown even in a pocket-handkerchief-sized garden.

• Fruit is beautiful. White and pink fragrant blossoms in the spring, fruits of every hue and colour in the summer and autumn, and beautifully shaped trees and bushes all year round.

• Fruit is good for you. 'An apple a day keeps the doctor away' is a phrase coined in 1904 by J.T. Stinson, Director of the Missouri State Fruit Experimental Station. He lived to be ninety-two!

• Fruit is fast. As a fruit grower in Kent recently said: 'Fruit, the ultimate fast food, pick it and eat it. What could be easier?'

1
FITNESS AND TRAINING

Fresh fruit, picked straight from the garden, is one of the healthiest foods in the world. However, if you want your fruit to be good to you, you need to be good to your fruit – you are its mother, its trainer and its doctor. Plant it in the right place, feed and water it, protect it from pests and diseases and you are nearly there. It's much easier to grow than you might think, and can be grown in far more places than you might imagine.

STARTING A FRUIT GARDEN, RECOMMENDATIONS AND REALITY

Before you start, look around you. If other gardeners and growers are successfully growing fruit in the area, so can you. If you have a choice of site, go for something south-facing, sheltered from winds and not in a frost pocket. Choose the sunniest position for the dessert fruit trees and one that has at least

The fruit garden: fit and well-trained

Against all odds

Ampleforth Abbey, on the North Yorkshire moors, 400 ft (120 m) above sea level, boasts one of the highest and most northerly commercial orchards in Britain. Fortunately it is on a south-facing site, and is sheltered by windbreaks to keep out the strong southwesterlies. The orchard, which has 2,500 trees, covers 15 acres (6 ha) and was originally planted to provide fruit for the abbey over 100 years ago. Some of the original trees are still standing and new ones continue to be planted. Varieties were chosen that could cope with the location and provide continuity throughout the season. Stuart Murfitt, who now runs the orchard, tries out as many apple cultivars as possible so that he can advise local people on the best apples to grow in these adverse conditions.

Successes include many old varieties, including the cookers Howgate Wonder, Lane's Prince Albert and Bramley's Seedling, the dual-purpose varieties Belle de Boskoop and James Grieve and the dessert varieties Egremont Russet, Beauty of Bath and good old Court Pendu Plat, nicknamed 'the wise apple' because it flowers late and escapes spring frosts. Of the newer varieties, Fiesta has frost-resistance and is less prone to disease than Cox, and Jupiter has proved scab-resistant in these harsh conditions.

half the day's sun for soft fruit, but if you don't have a choice make the most of what you've got!

Harry Baker, retired fruit officer from Wisley, is a very experienced fruit gardener. He lives in the south (so far so good) but the garden soil is practically pure sand, very acidic, and the fruit garden is in a frost pocket. However, by feeding the soil, choosing the right varieties and paying attention to cultivation details he successfully grows a wide range of top and soft fruits from apples to cherries, blackcurrants to blueberries, and peaches to figs.

If you don't have the ideal soil (a well-drained, slightly acidic (pH 6.5) medium loam), you can fix it with the fairy godmother, organic matter. This adds food and gives water-holding capacity to sandy soils and helps drainage on clay soils. On really badly drained soils extra action is required. Breaking up the subsoil may help but if the problem is severe you may need to put in a drainage system. Peaches, sweet cherries, raspberries, strawberries and some dessert apples such as Cox's Orange Pippin need good drainage to prevent problems with disease.

If your soil is too acid, add lime. Follow the recommended doses, as it is very important not to overdo it. If it is too alkaline, add flowers of sulphur or an acidic bulky organic material.

If your soil is totally hopeless, grow fruit in pots. Container-grown fruit is very productive and very underrated. Because the roots are restricted the plant puts more effort into fruit and less into vegetative growth. One of the beauties of containerized fruit is that you can grow it even if you haven't got a garden, on a patio, in a back yard or even on the balcony of a high-rise block of flats. Pots are also mobile, so can be moved around to make the best use of the sun and taken in over the winter to protect the plants from the cold.

Fortunately you don't have to live south of the Watford Gap to grow fruits outside. Hardy fruits such as apples, pears, plums and most soft fruits are grown in nearly all parts of Britain, from the Scilly Pearl apple in Cornwall to the Hessle pear and raspberries in Scotland. Soft fruits are said to taste better the further north you go, as they mature more slowly. Less hardy subjects, such as peaches and figs, which are grown outside in the south, do need protection in the north. One gardener is successfully growing a lemon tree in the Hebrides! He has to protect the greenhouse as well as the lemon – the structure is tied down with ropes to prevent the gales blowing it away.

The determined fruit fanatics go against all the rules. Commercial growers say that most fruit trees grow best below 400 ft (120 m) but amateurs are growing apples at 600 ft (180 m) or more. Wind is a major factor at high altitudes. Windbreaks are well worth planting or erecting. A 6 ft (1.8 m) hedge can break wind for up to 40 yds (36 m), if you will pardon the expression.

Frost is a killer. It scorches young growth, causes blossoms and young fruits to drop off, increases russeting and cracking of apple and pear skins and makes the middle of strawberry flowers turn black. If frost is forecast, cover fruit with polypropylene fleece or a double layer of netting. This may not look very effective but can keep off several degrees of frost. Cane fruits can be bundled together and smaller plants such as strawberries, step-over apple trees and horizontal raspberries can be put under cloches. If you live in an area prone to frost it is wise to plant late-flowering varieties to save a lot of heartache. Commercial growers sometimes spray the blossoms with water throughout the period of frost. As water freezes it releases latent heat around the buds, which stops them from getting damaged by the frost. It all sounds back to front but it works.

Rain as well as cold can cause problems. Growing fruit trees is tricky where annual rainfall exceeds 40 in (100 cm), because of diseases such as scab, canker, brown rot, and botrytis, many of which love a bit of humidity. As usual some growers have battled on by using resistant varieties and some even grow their trees under glass. In Kent, dedicated growers put plastic sheeting up above their cherries to keep the rain off, which stops them splitting.

Birds love fruit, and British gardeners love birds. Herein lies a problem. The solution: use a cage to keep the fruit in and the birds out. It is comforting to know that the majority of fruit gardeners in this country are willing to spend time and money on a fruit cage rather than harm their feathered friends. A word of warning: remove the top net if snow is forecast. Snow is very, very heavy and can easily wreck fruit cage poles. At blossom time put the top nets on and take the side nets off, because bees and other pollinating insects find it a little tricky negotiating the holes.

Now that you know you can do it, it is time to plan and plant. A plan for the model fruit garden is given in Chapter 8, on page 158.

The Woodwards

The name Woodward was well known in the seventeenth century when Cromwell's agents called for 'fruiterers' or 'woodwards' to enforce the planting of fruit trees in every part of the country. The Puritans were keen on fruit trees because, unlike the things they were opposed to, fruit trees reproduced asexually, were not greedy or temperamental, and could be grown and eaten by the rich and poor alike. Although the scheme was never fully enforced, it did encourage the planting of many orchards.

Today Jack Woodward has over seventy apple trees on his allotment and continues to plant more each year. Jack has grown fruit all his life – it's in his genes. His grandfather was a fruit grower in the Vale of Evesham before 1900 and Jack was the ADAS fruit adviser for the south-east of England. Now retired, Jack has returned to the Vale and grows fruit on the very same plot that his ancestors managed nearly 100 years before. He eats his own apples from August to March and gives away the surplus to friends and neighbours.

PLANTING A FRUIT TREE

Before you plant, make sure there has not been a similar type of tree on the site before or your fruit could get the dreaded SARD (specific apple replant disease) or its equivalent. Get a healthy tree with roots at least 8 in (20 cm) long and no evidence of damage; if bare-rooted, keep the roots covered at all times until planting to prevent drying out. Plant between November and early March if possible, the earlier the better, because roots benefit from warm soil – never plant in frozen or waterlogged soil.

Dig over an area at least 3 x 3 ft (1 x 1 m) to loosen the ground, especially if the soil is heavy. A smaller hole in hard ground acts as a sink which will fill up with water as soon as it rains; trees are often killed in this way. Next, dig out a hole to accommodate the roots and fork the base to break up any panning. The tree should be planted at the same depth as the soil mark on the stem and the graft union should be well above soil level. Before the tree goes in, bang in a stake on the windward side, putting a third of the stake under the ground to prevent it rocking.

Finally, plant the tree. The graft union should face away from the stake and the branches just clear it to prevent rubbing. Gently shake the soil around the roots by jiggling the tree up and down, then firm it in well. Fasten the tree to the stake with a tie.

As with all things, there are various ways of achieving the same end. Some gardeners add a handful of general fertilizer to the planting hole and to the soil that came out of the hole, mixing it thoroughly before putting it back. Some put the topsoil and subsoil in different piles. The topsoil goes back in first around the tree roots and the subsoil on the surface. Subsoil is less fertile than topsoil and when put on the surface will discourage the growth of weeds. Others discard the soil from the hole altogether and plant the tree in a special mix of one part loam, one part peat and three handfuls of bonemeal per barrowload. This, incidentally, substantially reduces the effect of replant disease.

FEEDING FRUIT

The saying 'You are what you eat' applies to plants as well as people. If they are fed a well-balanced diet they will be healthier. Organic matter is essential. It provides nutrients, cures many soil problems, and improves soil structure so that the roots can get right down to tap more nutrients, water, and air. Dig in half a barrowload of well-rotted compost or manure before planting and apply an organic mulch annually in March to a warm, moist soil to keep it that way. Mulches also keep weeds down, reducing competition to leave more food for the fruit.

On fertile soils organic matter is all that is needed, but many fruit growers also add fertilizers in late February or early March to put back in what has been taken out.

Nitrogen

Required for shoot growth. Pears, plums and blackcurrants need nitrogen to encourage new shoots. Apply a slow-release nitrogen fertilizer such as hoof and horn annually: 3 oz/sq yd (100 g/sq m).

Dessert apples, raspberries and strawberries need less nitrogen in order to prevent too much vigorous growth at the expense of the fruit. The nitrogen in the organic matter should be sufficient, but if plants are slow-growing apply hoof and horn.

Phosphate

Required for root growth. Soils usually contain a lot of phosphate so it usually needs to be applied only once every 3 years.

Apply bonemeal; 3–4 oz/sq yd (100–125 g/sq m).

Potash

Required for fruit colour and flavour, development of fruit buds and protection against frost and disease. Potash should be applied every year. Use sulphate of potash: ½–1 oz/sq yd (15–33 g/sq m) or seaweed meal: 3 oz/sq yd (85 g/sq m). Seaweed meal also acts as a soil conditioner. Potash can be applied as a liquid feed and strawberries are often given 3 potash liquid feeds a year at 2-week intervals during the growing season. Many fruits, for example red currants, develop a red edge to the leaves when they have a potash deficiency and there may also be some yellowing between the leaf veins.

Sometimes other nutrients are needed but there is no need to waste your money unless a deficiency becomes apparent.

Magnesium

Magnesium deficiency can occur on sandy soils, after heavy rain or if the plant has been overfed with potash. Orange tints appear on the leaves, with yellowing between the veins on the older leaves. These leaves fall early and the fruits are small and woody. The solution: apply Epsom salts at petal fall at 1 oz/sq yd (33 g/sq m) or use a foliar feed containing magnesium, which works much quicker.

The Hatton fruit gardens

Iron

Some plants find it tricky to get iron out of alkaline soils. Acidifying the soil with an acid organic mulch such as pulverized bark or bracken helps. If using bracken, wear a face mask and gloves because the spores are thought to be carcinogenic. Raspberries are especially prone to iron deficiency on alkaline soils. Their shoots are stunted and the leaves become yellow or bleached. A foliar feed of iron (especially if mixed with liquid seaweed) does wonders.

If your fruit looks a bit peaky and you do not know what it wants, play safe and spray with liquid seaweed. It is an excellent plant tonic, containing potassium and nitrogen as well as an impressive array of other minerals, trace elements, vitamins, amino acids, plant hormones and carbohydrates. Trials indicate that plants grown with seaweed show increased resistance to red spider mite, aphids, and fungal infections.

FORMATIVE PRUNING OF APPLES AND PEARS

When you have a one-year-old fruit tree in front of you, think hard before you get out the secateurs. As well as being its mother and doctor you are also the architect. The pruning you do in the early years is formative and by making a cut here and a cut there you can make the tree any shape you like. At the Hatton Fruit Gardens, now part of Horticulture Research International, East Malling , the fruit architects had a field day and created trees of all sizes and shapes including standards, bushes, cordons, espaliers and even trees shaped like a table-top, a champagne glass and a boat! The gardens were formerly the kitchen gardens of Bradbourne House and were inspired by Louis XIV's kitchen garden at Versailles.

General rules

Carry out winter pruning between November and March, except with the stone fruits such as plums and peaches which are susceptible to fungal infection at this time. You should avoid pruning in frosty weather, always use sharp secateurs, and generally prune to outward-facing buds. Make cuts just above the bud and sloping away from it so that the water runs off the branch and does not carry possible disease spores into the bud. The weaker the branch the harder you can cut it back, and cutting a branch will stimulate the buds beneath the cut to burst into growth the following spring.

The dwarf bush

A dwarf bush is one of the most suitable tree shapes for the small garden. The aim over the first four years is to cut the tree back quite hard to get it to grow vigorously. The branches will grow from the buds that you have cut back to, and in the direction that that bud is pointing.

The dwarf pyramid

Another shape suited to the small garden is the dwarf pyramid: a pyramid-shaped tree about 7 ft high (2 m)and 3 ft across (1 m).

Formative pruning to produce a dwarf bush

(a) Winter, Year 1: Plant and stake the feathered maiden (a one-year-old tree with side shoots) and cut the main stem back to a bud or lateral at about 2 ft (0.6 m) above ground level.

(b) Winter, Year 2: Choose 4 branches that have formed wide angles to the stem. These primary branches will form the framework of the tree and the wider the angle the stronger the tree. Cut back vigorous branches by half and less vigorous by two-thirds. Unwanted branches can be cut out.

(c) Winter, Year 3: Prune back the current season's growth on the primary branches by half. The primary branches will also have grown some laterals. Some of these can be selected as secondary branches. Prune back the current season's growth on these selected laterals by half as well. Cut back the remainder to 5 or 6 buds to form spurs, or harder if crowding the centre.

Winter in subsequent years. You now have your framework. You need not prune the leaders any more unless growth is weak. Leave laterals on the outside of the tree alone (though where they become overlong or crowded they can be shortened or removed) and prune those on the inside to 4in (10cm).

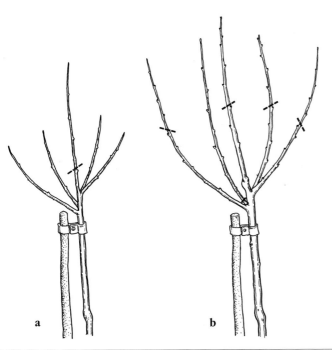

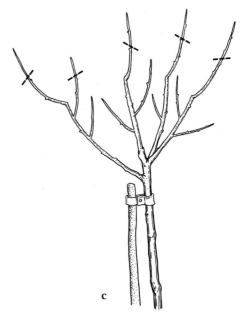

a   b   c

In the first winter treat as a dwarf bush. In the second winter cut back the tallest branch (the central leader) to 9 in (23 cm) of new growth and cut back to a bud facing in the opposite direction to the one you cut it back to the first time, so that the branch grows vertically. Choose four evenly spaced side branches and cut them back to 8 in (20 cm) of the current season's growth, to a downward-facing bud to keep them as horizontal as possible. Remove any other branches.

In the late summer select five branch leaders, one vertical and four horizontal. These form the framework of your pyramid shaped tree. Cut back all the other laterals to three leaves and sub-laterals to one leaf beyond the basal cluster. Shorten the new growth on the side branches to six leaves.

Repeat the process of winter and summer pruning each year until the tree reaches the desired height. After this just keep it in the pyramidal shape by cutting back the leader to its origin each May, removing any other vigorous vertical shoots completely and occasionally shortening side branches, always cutting back to a downward facing bud to keep them horizontal.

The pyramid and bush are not the only shapes you can get. For others, such as the spindle, standard and half-standard, refer to a specialist pruning manual. Fruit trees and bushes can also be pruned and trained to grow along a fence to fit into a small garden as shown in Chapter 8, pages 154-57.

Regulatory pruning

Trees need regulatory pruning to maintain a good overall shape. Every few years stand back and take a look at your tree. Is it looking a bit congested? The aim is to keep the centre of the tree open to let sunlight in and allow good air movement to prevent build-up of disease. To do this, remove dead, diseased and damaged wood and cut out crowded or crossing branches. Aim for both branches and laterals to be 18 in (45 cm) apart.

PRUNING FOR FRUIT

Looking good isn't all there is to it. One tree can give one piece of fruit and another hundreds. The trouble with explaining the pruning of a mature tree is that the tree never reads the book. The best policy is to understand why you are pruning it and what you are hoping to achieve, in this instance fruit.

Spur pruning
Most apple and pear trees are spur bearers. They

Spur pruning of a spur bearing apple tree
This is a simple, common method of pruning trees for fruit. Apply the following to outward-pointing branches that have room to grow.

(a) Year 1. Cut new side shoots back to 4–6 buds in the winter. The buds near the base will develop into fruit buds and the ones near the tip will throw out fresh growth.

(b) Year 2. Cut the extension growth back to 6 buds.

(c) Again fruit buds will develop at the base and the end bud will throw out new growth.

(d) Year 3. Continue taking back the growths produced in the previous year to 6 buds. Cut weak shoots back harder than strong shoots.

For those branches that are pointing inwards or any others where there is no room to extend:
(e) Cut them back as the ones above in the first year and after that cut back the laterals to the topmost flower bud. These will then develop into a spur system.

After a few years the spurs will need to be thinned. To do this, reduce the length of the spur system, cut away the weakest buds and cut away the spurs on the underside of branches.

Renewal Pruning

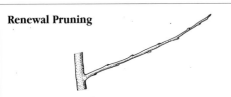

(a) Year 1. An extension shoot grows from the main stem.

(b) Year 2. This shoot ages and forms flower buds at the base.

(c) Year 3. The shoot fruits. After fruiting the shoot is cut out to a 1 in (2.5 cm) stump in the dormant season.

(d) Year 4/Year 1. A new extension shoot grows up from the 1 in (2.5cm) stump.

produce fruit buds on two-year-old wood and on older wood as stumpy growths called spurs.

Renewal pruning

Some experienced pruners use renewal pruning. The method consists of pruning fruiting shoots that grow up from the main framework in a 3-year cycle.

By having shoots on the tree at all stages in the cycle, a third of them will be cropping each year. When the system is set up it is very simple. Each winter cut out those shoots that have fruited. To use this method it is convenient to train the tree as an open-centred bush with a permanent framework at a convenient height. This will enable you to reach all the branches and leave enough headroom to mow underneath.

However, if your tree fails to produce on the re-newal system go back to the spur method. Remember, you are in control.

Tip-bearers

Rules always have exceptions, and here is one of them: the tip bearers. Some fruit trees are tip-bearers and they produce their fruit at the tips of the previous year's growth. If you prune them like spur bearers you get no one-year-old tips and no fruit.

The shoots of tip-bearers tend to be thinner and the tree leaner, but the easiest way is to know what variety you have. Examples include: Irish Peach (apple), Worcester Pearmain (apple), and Josephine de Malines (pear). Pruning true tip-bearers is very easy. Keep the centre open by removing overcrowded and crossing branches and any dead, diseased or damaged wood. Leave maiden shoots less than 9 in (23 cm) long unpruned, as they will form fruit at their tips in the next year, and prune shoots over 9 in (23 cm) long to four or five buds. This will give more short shoots next year to treat as those above. Finally prune the leaders: this encourages more tip-bearing laterals and extension growth. Vigorous tip-bearers such as Golden Noble can be pruned on the renewal system.

Just when you thought you were getting the hang of this... there are also partial tip-bearers, such as Discovery and Bramley's Seedling, which produce spurs on the older wood as well as fruit buds at their tips. Don't worry, treat these like spur bearers.

An open centre tree with a permanent framework.

Trouble-shooting

If your tree is looking puny and tired, it could be because it is hungry. Remove weeds and grass from the base and mulch with well-rotted manure. To rejuvenate it, thin the spurs and cut back new growth by two-thirds every winter for a couple of years. Also, remove most of the fruitlets in the first spring to let the tree put energy back into growth. Once it is on the road to recovery, keep it healthy with regular pruning, feeding and attention to pests and diseases.

If the tree is over-vigorous, grass it down and do not give it any nitrogen fertilizer. Cut out broken, diseased and congested branches but make haste slowly over two or three years. If you attempt all the pruning in one year the tree will get even more vigorous. Cut back limbs to their point of origin or to a large replacement limb. If the limbs to be cut are large, undercut first so that they will not tear off. Prune limbs of apples and pears in winter and stone fruits, e.g. plums and damsons, in July to August to minimize the risk of silver leaf disease. In late summer cut back some of the young laterals that are over 12 in (30 cm) long to five leaves. Generally horizontal shoots are more fruitful. Cut out some vertical shoots and tie some others down to encourage fruiting spurs.

PESTS AND DISEASES

After planting, feeding and performing surgery your tree should hopefully reward you with fruit, but your role as doctor is not over yet. Fruit can have many problems with pests and diseases. The best way to keep them at bay is to keep the plant healthy and in good shape so that it is more resistant in the first place.

Resistance is better than cure

Many varieties of fruits have been bred that show some resistance to pests and diseases, and gardeners are now reaping the rewards. The pests and diseases do, however, fight back. The black currant Ben Lomond, once resistant to American gooseberry mildew, has now been attacked by a new strain.

Cultivar	Some resistance to/ less susceptible to
Apple (dessert)	
Brownlee's Russet	Mildew
Court Pendu Plat	Scab/mildew
D'Arcy Spice	Mildew
Discovery	Scab/mildew
Ellison's Orange	Scab
Golden Reinette	Scab/mildew
Greensleeves	Scab/mildew
Jupiter	Scab/mildew
Kidd's Orange	Scab
Laxton's Superb	Canker
Redsleeves	Scab/mildew
Sunset	Scab (very susceptible to mildew)
Tydeman's Late Orange	Scab
Worcester Pearmain	Mildew
Apples (cookers)	
Arthur Turner	Scab/mildew
Bramley's Seedling	Scab
Crawley Beauty	Scab/mildew
Early Victoria	Scab/mildew/canker
Golden Noble	Scab/mildew
Grenadier	Scab/mildew
King Edward VII	Scab/mildew
Lord Derby	Scab/mildew
Newton Wonder	Canker
Rev. W. Wilks	Mildew
Pear	
Jargonelle	Scab
Hessle	Scab
Catillac	Scab
Plum	
Czar	Bacterial canker/rust
Denniston's Superb	Rust
Edwards	Rust
Jefferson	Rust
Marjorie's Seedling	Bacterial canker/rust
Myrobalan	Bacterial canker/rust
Opal	Bacterial canker/rust
Oullin's Golden Gage	Bacterial canker/rust
River's Early Prolific	Rust
Warwickshire Drooper	Rust
Cherry	
Merchant/Mermat	Bacterial canker

For details of soft fruits with resistance to pest and disease, refer to Chapter 4, Soft Touch.

Common apple and pear pests

Aphids

Aphids suck plant sap, distorting leaves and fruits. The rosy apple aphid causes apple foliage to distort and go red; its effect on young trees can be fatal. Aphids also spread virus disease in their spit and black mould grows on their droppings (honeydew). To control them, spray with soft soap or derris.

Sawfly

The sawfly lays eggs on apple fruitlets in April or May. The larvae tunnel in, eat the pips, then come out to find another fruitlet. Totally stuffed, they fall to the soil in June and pupate to emerge as adults the next year. Many of the infected fruitlets fall as well. Sawflies, unlike codling moths, cause a ribbon-like scar on the surface of the fruit. To control, spray with derris and soft soap at petal fall and clear up and burn infected fruitlets.

Codling moth

This is what causes the maggot in the apple and sometimes the pear. The plum fruit moth causes similar damage to plums. The codling moth lays eggs on the fruit in June and the caterpillars tunnel down into the fruits. When they have eaten their fill, they come out and pupate in the bark or under tree ties. Trap with a codling moth pheremone trap, and ten days after the first moths are caught, which will be in about mid to late June, spray the tree with derris to kill the moths before they tunnel inside. Cardboard collars or sacking tied round the tree will also catch pupating larvae, which can then be destroyed.

Caterpillars

Winter moth caterpillars eat the young leaves, flowers and even young fruitlets, wreaking havoc in early spring. Control by placing grease bands around the tree in October and spray caterpillars as they appear, with *Bacillus thuringiensis*. This is a biological con-

trol that affects only the caterpillars of moths and butterflies. Destroyed in sunlight, there is no chance of it spreading and harming other caterpillars.

Red spider mite

Whole crops have been ruined by epidemics of this pest. The mites hatch on the tree in May and proceed to breed. The leaves turn a reddish bronze and fall early. To control, attract natural predators by not removing the moss or natural lichens on trees.

Tortrix caterpillar

This caterpillar curls the leaves into silken tents; often the leaf is spun on to the fruit itself and the tortrix feeds unseen beneath, clever little beast. The fruit surface becomes scarred and distorted. Pick off and spray with *Bacillus thuringiensis*.

Pear slugworm

These look as if someone has thrown tadpoles over the tree. They are quite revolting and can skeletonize the leaf surface. Spray with derris or soft soap.

Capsid bug

Capsids cause brownish red spots on the leaves that develop into tattered holes and corky bumps on the fruits. Treat with derris or soft soap.

Pear midge

The midge grubs eat the centre of the developing fruits, and cause the fruitlets to turn black and fall off. Collect and destroy infected fruits to prevent re-infection and run poultry in the orchard until harvest time.

Common apple and pear diseases

Mildew

A white powdery mould appears on the extremities in spring. Infected flowers do not set fruit; infected leaves and shoots are stunted. It is worse in dry weather. Prune out infected shoots and burn. Sulphur sprays applied pre-bloom help to control mildew. Some varieties are sulphur shy; if you are unsure spray one branch and if the leaves fall or scorch

Virus-free

Virus-free apple trees can be raised in a hot box. One-year-old trees (whips) are grown on fast in a propagator, and the tip grows faster than the virus. Cut off the top few inches and hey presto, virus-free scion material, though easier said than done.

Dr Tony Adams from East Malling Research Station came up with an even more ingenious method, tissue culture. Strawberry plants are brought on in a type of hot box and the tiny virus-free tips (apical meristems) are removed in sterile conditions under a microscope. These are transferred to sterile agar containing a specific cocktail of plant nutrients and growth hormones and grow into tiny strawberry plantlets, which are then planted out into sterile compost. Tens of thousands of the plants can be produced in this way every year, and the plants you buy are the runners from these virus- and fungi-free mother plants.

within twenty-four hours don't spray any more. With all diseases, clean your secateurs before going on to another tree to prevent spreading the disease.

Scab

This airborne fungus causes corky brown cracked areas on the surface of fruits, blisters on the shoots and dark green/black spots on the leaves, which fall early. It is worse in wet conditions.

Control by removing the fallen leaves, as these will spread the disease, or by mowing the fallen leaves so that worms, which eat and destroy scabby leaves, can take them into their burrows. As a preventative, spray with sulphur before the buds break into blossom, avoiding sulphur-shy varieties.

Canker

Canker, another fungus, is also worse in wet weather. It encircles branches and causes dieback. Sometimes red fruiting bodies of the fungus can be seen on the dying branches. In apples dieback on the branches is a mixture of scab and canker. The canker spores get in due to the lesions caused by scab. Prune out any branches with canker and burn.

Brown rot

A fungal disease that causes whole fruit to turn brown with concentric white rings. Remove and burn affected fruits.

Fireblight

With fireblight, the leaves scorch and shrivel but do not fall and the tree also develops exuding lesions. This bacterial disease is spread at blossom time by the bees, needs warm weather and humid conditions, and affects pears more than apples. It is also more of a problem on late-flowering pears. With apples, the tree seals the damaged area off, but with pears the infection spreads rapidly into the whole tree. There is no cure except to cut off the affected branch, back into healthy wood.

Disorders

Sometimes it's not a bug but the weather or the food which is causing the problem.

Bitterpit

Sunken areas appear on the surface of the fruits and small brown areas in the flesh beneath. This is caused by lack of water and calcium. It is easily cured by correct watering and feeding with calcium chloride.

Russeting

This roughening of the skin is caused by cold weather early in the year. The flaw does not affect the taste.

Details of other ailments relating to specific fruits are given in the appropriate chapters, and there is a year-plan of pest and disease control in Chapter 5.

Keeping out virulent viruses

Viruses stunt plants and reduce cropping. All they are is a piece of DNA in a protein coat. They cannot breed on their own and have to get into living plant or animal cells in order to replicate, just as in the film

Alien! They move by surfing along in the plant's sap system and spread by hitching a ride with sap-sucking pests who stick their syringe-like mouth parts into infected plants and then pass the virus on to the next plant. So keeping the pests off will keep the viruses away. Always buy virus-free plants if you can.

Say it with flowers

One way to keep viruses and pests at bay is to grow specific flowers that will attract predators to the garden to eat the aphids. No winter washes or other chemicals are used in the organic garden because these kill the predators as well as the pests.

Predators for fruit pests

(a) Adult lacewing

(b) Ichneumon

(c) Hoverfly

(d) Ladybird and larvae

(e) Anthocorid bug

Predator	How to attract it
Ladybird and larvae	Nettles are the food plant of a nettle-specific early greenfly. This boosts the ladybird army early in the year so that they are ready to move on to eat the aphids.
Lacewing larvae	Lacewing adults drink nectar from flowers in the daisy family. Their larvae eat aphids and other pests. Lacewings can also be overwintered in a home-made hotel! Remove the base of a plastic bottle and insert some rolled up corrugated cardboard. Hang in the fruit trees to accommo date your hibernating lacewings. The next spring their young will be ready on site for an all-out aphid attack.
Parasitic wasps (e.g Ichneumon)	The adults drink the nectar of flowers in the carrot family (such as fennel) before laying eggs inside the insect pest. In this case the pest is eaten from the inside.
Hoverfly larvae	The hoverfly is attracted by open yellow flowers such as nasturtiums. The mother lays her eggs in aphid colonies. The larvae, which look like bird droppings, eat aphids.

Other useful predators include the black-kneed capsid and the anthocorid bug, which eat vast quantities of aphids in orchards.

There is, however, one problem with the predator equation: the ant. Ants farm aphids and milk them for their honeydew – plant sap which comes out of the back end of the aphid (almost as readily as it goes in the front). Like dairy herdsmen, they do not take kindly to poachers. Ants gang up on the aphid preda-

Pilophorus perplexus (left) and the ant

tors and literally kick them out. The bouncers of the plant world!

Once again, Horticulture Research International, East Malling, may have the answer. They have been studying an ant mimic, *Pilophorus perplexus*. This native predator eats aphids but does not get attacked by ants. Why? Because they think it is an ant!

Growers are now moving into integrated pest control where nature and new technology work together hand in hand. In the orchards predators work alongside laptop computers. Growers can now forecast outbreaks of codling moth, the summer fruit tortrix moth and the pear psyllid with computer

programmes and act upon it. Pheromone traps and selective sprays are then used when and only when needed. This saves money, reduces pesticide usage and results in a healthy fruit tree.

FRUIT TO KEEP YOU FIT

We are told to eat at least 1 lb (500 g) of fresh fruit and vegetables every day, but figures show the average person only manages to average one-eighth of that. Fresh fruits, as well as tasting good, are important to health. They contain a cocktail of goodies, from ones that reduce heart disease to ones that help prevent certain cancers. One of the things many fruits contain are antioxidants which protect the body from free radicals – unpleasant chemicals that cause ageing and trigger cancers.

The antioxidant brigade

Vitamin C is a strong antioxidant, and as your body cannot store it you need regular top-ups. The recommended daily intake of Vitamin C is 50–100 mg for the average person and the amount you get depends on which fruits you eat.

Fruit	mg Vitamin C per 100 g
Kiwi	105
Oranges/ lemons	50
Grapefruit	40
Strawberries	60
Black currants	210
Guava	300
West Indian cherry	1300

With apples, the amount of Vitamin C depends upon the variety you eat!

Apple variety	mg Vitamin C per 100 g
Ribston Pippin	30.6
Sturmer Pippin	29.0
Golden Noble	25.1
Orlean's Reinette	22.4
Bramley's Seedling	16.0
Beauty of Bath	14.0
Peasgood Nonsuch	13.2
Blenheim Orange	13.2
Cox's Orange Pippin	10.5
Worcester Pearmain	8.2
Golden Delicious	8.2
Court Pendu Plat	7.5
Allington Pippin	7.3
James Grieve	6.8
Rome Beauty	3.8

The Vitamin C content also depends upon when you pick or buy the fruit: the longer it is stored at room temperature the more Vitamin C it loses.

Vitamin E is also an antioxidant. Traces of this anti-ageing vitamin are found in many fruits, especially black currants, apples, avocados and bananas.

Finally comes betacarotene. This antioxidant and other orange pigments (carotenoids) are highly protective against blindness. This chemical can come only from fresh fruit or vegetables, not from a pill.

Orange-coloured fruit such as apricots, mangoes and peaches all score high in the betacarotene stakes.

Fibre and folic acid

Dietary fibre is important for a healthy digestive system. Go for citrus fruit, apples, soft fruit, pineapples and pears. Folic acid is also found in many fruits, including bananas and oranges. This is an important chemical, especially for women planning to have a baby, because it can help prevent birth defects like spina bifida.

An apple a day keeps the doctor away?

In medieval times the sour native British apples were

Healthy fruit – if you are good to your fruit it will be good to you

Favours from foreign fruits

Mango, papaya and pineapple juice are good for sore throats. They all contain digestive and healing enzymes. Papain, the enzyme in papaya, has been used for years by boxers, not for their throats but to get rid of bruises.

The Mediterranean nations believe a diet containing lots of red wine and fresh fruit helps prevent heart disease.

Scientists have found that pomegranates contain high levels of oestrogens, which are hormones usually found in humans. They may have many effects, from protecting against prostate cancer to lowering sperm counts!

Bananas provide slow-release energy, which is why they are held in high regard by sporting stars. Tennis players keep bananas as well as tennis balls in their bags. Bananas also contain lots of potash, which helps prevent cramp. After eating the banana, bury the skin under one of your soft fruit bushes. Potash helps fruits to grow too.

thought to be bad for you. Children and wet nurses were banned from eating them and they were always the first suspect when someone had a fever. It was different for the monks. During Lent they were pre-scribed ten apples a day to keep their bowels open!

As time progressed the apple went from being a medieval laxative to a cure all. By the seventeenth century it was used as a cough cure, an antidepres-sant, a poultice for swellings, a cure for gonorrhoea, and even a hand lotion for chapped skin. Before the days of readily available citrus fruits, Whitby harbour used to load late-keeping apple varieties such as Hunthouse and Alfriston on to whaling ships to keep the sailors full of Vitamin C and scurvy-free on their long sea voyages.

Today an apple a day does keep the doctor away.

Research has shown that apple-eaters pay a third fewer calls to the doctor than non-apple-lovers and generally have fewer colds and less sickness and ten-sion. Apples are also good to eat if you are diabetic because they regulate blood sugar levels.

According to health expert Michael van Straten, two apples a day keep the heart attack at bay because pectins combined with other natural chemicals in apples, such as soluble fibres, reduce cholesterol levels by 5 per cent.

Apples contain flavonoids, antioxidants which help prevent furring up of the arteries (*Lancet*, 1993).

Apples are good for the digestion if eaten after a meal, and if eaten fifteen minutes before a meal may act as a dietary aid because cellulose in the fruit takes away hunger pangs.

An apple a day may now keep the vet at bay too! Deer and hares love apples. To keep these animals free from intestinal parasites, apples are injected with an antiparasite medicine and put out in the forests for them to eat.

The curative cranberry
(*Vaccinium macrocarpum*)

Research from the Brigham and Women's Hospital, Boston, USA has shown that drinking cranberry juice treats urinary tract infections. The juice reduces lev-els of bacteria and pus in the urine. A unique muci-

Small is beautiful

Homeopathic remedies sometimes use fruits. Lemon oil is used for circulatory problems, respiratory ailments and sore throats. Homeopathic prepara-tions of cherry plum are said to encourage mental calm and are used to treat a fear of losing control of the mind or body, while preparations of crab-apple are said to have a cleansing and detoxifying effect and are used by people who feel they have low self-esteem.

laginous chemical in the cranberry lines the wall of the bladder so that the bacteria can't stick to it. This is the first large-scale study to show that drinks can have an effect on bacteria levels, and may be very good news for cystitis sufferers.

Talk about getting conditions right to grow healthy plants! To grow cranberries you need soil conditions that would make most other plants nearly curl up and die – waterlogged and acidic, with a pH as low as 3.5. In the States cranberries are very popular, especially as a sauce with the Thanksgiving turkey. Huge artificial bogs are constructed in order to grow them. In the garden, you can prepare a bog by lining a trench with black plastic, filling it with acidic compost and soaking it with rainwater. Always buy container-grown plants and never let the roots dry out. Plant out 12 in (30 cm) apart and peg down trailing stems to encourage rooting. Cranberries can be grown in large pots filled with acidic compost. Don't forget to water them!

They need very little care and attention. Every spring, trim wispy growth and aerial roots with shears, and if growth is poor feed with sulphate of ammonia.

On as well as in

Fruit can be good for you on the outside too. Apples make a good face mask because they are rich in fruit acids, which help get rid of dead skin cells. This is not a new discovery: a sixteenth-century recipe suggests mixing apple pulp, swine grease and rosewater to use as a facewash to prevent skin roughness. Peaches, apricots and melons can also be used in moisturizers because they contain Vitamin A, for smooth healthy skin, while citrus fruits are rich in Vitamin C, essential for skin tissue to repair and maintain itself. Diluted fresh citrus juice can be used on the skin as a toner. And if you have trouble with spots, try pineapple, which contains an enzyme that destroys the bacteria that cause them.

Mashed avocado mixed with lemon juice is a real fruity treat for chemically damaged hair, while mashed banana mixed with grapeseed oil will untangle dry or frizzy hair. With either treatment, apply before shampooing, cover with clingfilm for thirty minutes, then wash as normal.

Avocados

Avocados may contain an anti-cancer sugar. Research from Oxford University found that this naturally occurring chemical inhibited growth of tumour cells and did not affect healthy cells. In the future it may be possible to do clinical trials involving giving cancer patients a drink of avocado extract which would be far less harrowing than radio-therapy or chemotherapy. If it works, the avocado could provide a breakthrough in the treatment of cancer. Here's hoping. Eating other fruits is thought to lower the risk of mouth and throat cancer: many dark-coloured fruits such as plums and cherries contain anti-cancer agents called isothiocyanates.

YOU ARE WHAT YOU EAT

Throughout this book Patricia Hegarty provides some mouth-watering fruity recipes. Fruit is good for you however you eat it. To maximize its health-giving properties, either cook it lightly as soon as it is picked or eat it raw to keep as much of the Vitamin C as possible.

Red Currant and Yoghurt Ribbon Pudding
(with Black Currant Sauce)

This pudding has everything – sparkling red currant juice and yoghurt to satisfy the demands of healthy eating, strong contrasting colours, visual drama with ribands of brilliant red and white – and is beguilingly simple to make.

Red currant bushes are prolific bearers and yield baskets of the juiciest fruit. Fill a casserole with the scarlet skeins and a splash of water and put it, covered, into a low oven, 275°F (140°C, Gas 1) for as long as it takes to draw the juices. Strain through a jelly bag or piece of muslin.

Currants freeze well, and this pudding can be made throughout the year.

Serves 8-10

7 leaves gelatine
¾ pint (450 ml) red currant juice
6 oz (175 g) granulated sugar
¾ pint (450 ml) thick live yoghurt
½ lb (225 g) black currants

Half fill 2 flat containers with cold water. Soak 4 leaves of gelatine in one and 3 in the other. Warm the red currant juice and sweeten with the sugar. Dissolve the 4 leaves of gelatine in this. The sharp fruit juice will need more gelatine than the yoghurt to set. Gently warm a little of the yoghurt – you do not want it to separate or lose its setting quality – and dissolve the 3 leaves of gelatine in it. The rest of the yoghurt can then be stirred in.

Line a 1½ pint (900 ml) horseshoe mould or oblong tin or dish with clingfilm and cover the bottom with a layer of red currant mixture. Put this to set in the fridge and follow with a layer of yoghurt. As each section sets, add an alternating layer.

Turn out on to a board, cut into slices and serve with a black currant sauce. This is a purée of black currants, softened quickly with 5 fl oz (150 ml) water in a saucepan, sieved and sugared to taste. The glossy playing-card colours – red, black and white – always look spectacular.

Gooseberry and Elderflower Cream

Gooseberries are special, as one of the first fruits of the year, traditionally making their first appearance at Whitsun, married with the delicate white lace and haunting perfume of elderflowers. The word 'cream' in the recipe is misleading, since no cream is involved in making it. Egg yolks and a little butter are used to produce a smooth purée the consistency and richness of cream. When elderflowers are not available, orange flower water makes a very appealing substitute.

Serves 6

2 lb (900 g) fresh gooseberries
1 elderflower head or 1 tablespoon orange-flower water
4 oz (100 g) unrefined golden granulated sugar, or to taste
3 egg yolks
4 oz (100 g) unsalted butter
tiny elderflowers to decorate
thick fresh Jersey cream and thin almond biscuits to serve

Tip the gooseberries into a saucepan with the elderflower and 2 tablespoons of water and cook over a very low heat until they soften, about 20-30 minutes. If orange-flower water is used, add it to the purée after the butter. Remove the elderflower and rub the gooseberries through a sieve very thoroughly. Discard the seeds and skins and sweeten the gooseberry purée with the sugar.

Return the gooseberry purée to the saucepan over a very low heat and beat in the egg yolks and the butter, bit by bit. When the purée is nice and thick, cool or chill until ready to serve. Decorate the light green 'cream' with thick, yellow Jersey cream and some tiny, lacy elderflowers. Serve with almond biscuits.

Whole Orange Ice-Cream

Use organically grown oranges for this, as the whole of the peel is eaten. Apart from avoiding chemical sprays, the skin is not hardened with preservatives and wax and is more delicate. The flesh of a fresh orange has a special sparkle and simply melts away in the mouth, while the pith is not bitter at all.

Serves 10–12

6 oranges
6 egg yolks
5 oz (150 g) sugar
½ pint (300 ml) milk
1 pint (600 ml) double cream

Peel the oranges and whiz the peel and white pith quite finely in a processor. Make a custard with the remaining ingredients by whipping the egg yolks and sugar, pouring on the heated milk and returning to the pan, whisking all the while, until the custard thickens. Take off the heat and cool.

Whisk the cream and amalgamate into the custard with the orange peel. Set in the freezer or an ice-cream machine.

Serve the ice-cream with a compote made from the flesh of the oranges. Segment them and steep them in a syrup made by boiling 3 oz (75 g) sugar in 5 fl oz (150 ml) water until syrupy.

This ice-cream has a lovely strong taste on its own, as the whole orange has been used, but is also delicious served with hot or cold fruit puddings and tarts.

Rose-hip Cordial

Wild rose-hips abound with Vitamin C, and just to look at the colour of this cordial makes the heart lift. If you are lucky enough to have some wild roses growing near you, an autumn walk will turn into an additional pleasure if you gather some hips to take home with you and make this heart-warming drink to brighten up the long cold days of winter. It is also a lovely syrup to serve with ice-cream or hot steamed puddings.

Just a note – sometimes the hips can irritate the skin, and it may be advisable to wear gloves to process them. I also find it more successful to use proprietary bottling jars. The cordial can always be decanted into prettier bottles for use.

2 lb (900 g) wild rose-hips
3 pints 1.8 litres) water
10 oz (275 g) sugar to each 1 pint (600 ml) juice
squeeze of lemon juice to taste

To maximize the Vitamin C it is best to bottle the rose-hips as soon as possible after picking. Put them into a processor and chop them up roughly. Boil the water in a large saucepan and put in the rose-hip mash. Bring to the boil again and simmer for 15 minutes.

Strain the juice through a jelly bag or muslin. Measure the juice and add the appropriate amount of sugar and lemon juice. Heat together until the sugar has just dissolved.

Fill up the clean, warmed bottling jars with hot syrup, lay on the glass discs and rubber rings, and stand them in a shallow tray in an oven at 300°F (150°C, Gas 2). Bring to simmering point and then allow a further 20–30 minutes more cooking, depending on the size of the jars.

Lift the jars on to an insulated surface such as a wooden board and quickly screw up the bands. Leave to cool. Before storing, make sure the lids are sealed and there is a vacuum by lifting up the jar by the glass seal. Keep in a dark place and serve diluted.

Cucumber and Apple Mint Salad

An especially cooling salad with a double crunch factor. Try to use a dessert apple with a rosy skin like Scarlet Pimpernel, which looks very pretty amongst the green and white.

Serves 6

1 cucumber
3 oz (75 g) hazelnuts, toasted and skinned
3–4 dessert apples
2 tablespoons chopped fresh apple mint
lemon juice (optional)

Dressing
5 teaspoons hazelnut oil
1 teaspoon cider vinegar
fresh apple mint sprigs and flowers to garnish

Peel the cucumber, scoop out any seeds, and chop into 1/2 in (1 cm) dice. Cut the hazelnuts in half vertically. Slice and core the apples – do not peel them – and cut into matching cubes.

Mix the oil and vinegar together and dress the salad immediately to prevent the apples browning, incorporating the chopped mint. Otherwise, sprinkle the cut apples with a little lemon juice and dress later. This salad will stay crisp longer than a lettuce-based salad, which wilts very quickly after being dressed. Decorate with mint sprigs and flowers.

2
NUTS AND ALIENS

It's easy to get hold of pineapples, oranges, peaches and other exotica: just pop into the local shops. Nowadays we can have fruit all year round, from the four corners of the globe. Hundreds of years ago things were very different. Exotic fruits were for the wealthy: both at the table and in the garden, growing fruit that needed heat was surrounded by kudos. The first conservatory, Orange Court, built at Burghley in Northamptonshire by the Queen's Secretary of State in 1562, contained oranges, lemons, and pomegranates. In the 1700s things really came on when the arts of the blacksmith, the glazier and the architect brought us the glasshouse, and with it protected cropping. Gardeners started with oranges and lemons and then went on to pineapples. The end came in the 1830s, when the invention of the speedy clipper brought fresh fruits speeding in from the West Indies. Now exotica was there for all – far too common, and the landed gentry turned their attention to orchids instead! Today a few gardeners still grow exotic fruits, and like their ancestors, they do it not for necessity or to save money but for a challenge and just for the hell of it. But are they as tricky to grow as everyone makes out? Maybe not!

THE PINEAPPLE PERFECTIONISTS

Back in 1990 Tim Smit and John Nelson embarked upon a project that was to change their lives. They met for a drink with John Willis, who had inherited the Heligan gardens near Mevagissey in Cornwall.

Back in the seventeenth and eighteenth centuries the gardens had been a collecting ground for exotic plants brought back by plant hunters, and also had walled gardens brimming with tasty vegetables and exotic fruits. During the First World War the house was taken over by the War Department and the 57 acres (23 ha) of gardens were closed up and left to their own devices.

Eighty years later, John Willis took his friends for a walk in his new jungle. Among the brambles and sycamore trees they discovered huge walled gardens and a giant vine weaving its way in and out of broken panes of glass. They were enchanted, and decided there and then to resurrect the gardens from their slumbers. Now, only a few years on, the rhododendrons are blooming, the tree ferns are unfurling, the walled gardens are burgeoning with produce and the exotic fruits are back.

One of their most absorbing projects involved the pineapple. In the ruins they had discovered the remains of a pineapple pit dating back to the late 1700s. Using old plans and books, they managed to reconstruct this marvel of eighteenth-century engineering and the pit is now up and running. It uses decomposing manure, which gets up to 120°F (49°C), as a heat source for growing the pineapples. The heat passes from manure trenches on each side of the pit through pigeon-hole brickwork into the pit itself. A slate screen on the inside walls acts as a buffer, preventing the heat from scorching the pineapple leaves. The potted-up pineapples are plunged

A Victorian glasshouse at Heligan

in a deep layer of decomposing tan bark which sits on a bed of slate in the pit. Water evaporation channels under the bed of slate supply the necessary humidity through copper pipes. The whole structure is covered by English lights (glass cold-frame lids) and each piece of glass is hand-crafted in a 'beavertail' pattern, designed to lead rainwater away from the supporting wooden framework and prevent rotting. The pit is also divided into sections so that the pineapples can be grown successionally. Pure genius!

One initial setback in the project was getting hold of some pineapples: the varieties that Tim Smit wanted to grow were no longer available in the western hemisphere. Luckily, good fortune prevailed. The Director of Pineapple Research from the University of Durban just happened to be visiting Heligan. Tim explained his plight, and a week later over 100

The popular pineapple

The pineapple, *Ananas comosus,* originated in South America, where 'ananas' means pine-like. In the late 1700s the pineapple was king, the status symbol of the country house's kitchen garden. They were all home-grown, of course, and a head gardener's skill was measured on his ability to produce them: could he get one ready for the table on Christmas Day? Pineapples also became very popular in architecture and stone ones began to pop up on gateposts, bridges and columns. They are a reminder of the seventeenth century, when sailors marked a safe return from a voyage in the tropics by hanging a pineapple on their front door. The 4th Earl of Dunmore went completely over the top with his hothouse constructed in 1761. His amazing folly on the Dunmore Estate in Stirlingshire has a roof shaped like a pineapple.

Bananaman

Bananas do not grow on trees. After fruiting, the huge plant dies after sending up offshoots from the base. Mr Watts is passionate about bananas and, as a young man, was in charge of the banana corridor of the Watney's Estate in Gloucestershire. This was lined with banana trees planted in beer barrels containing a large percentage of horse manure. The bananas took a year to set fruit and the corridor was kept at 80°F (27°C) night and day from October to March, by burning a ton of anthracite a day. The bananas had to be ready for the shooting parties that visited the estate. When the pheasants went up they used to say, 'Up goes a quid, bang goes a penny, down comes five bob.' However, no one dared work out how much it cost to produce the bananas!

Queen and Cayenne pineapple plants arrived at Gatwick from the other side of the world.

If you haven't inherited an estate and don't fancy constructing a pineapple pit, don't give up, you can still grow them. Although they look very exotic they are easy to grow, which is perhaps why the Victorians were so keen on them. The pineapple can cope with sudden temperature changes without ill-effects and is simple to propagate. Screw out, rather than cut off, the top of a ripe pineapple and pull off a few of the bottom leaves to reveal the little roots beneath. Plant up in a mixture of peat and sand and, as it grows, pot on into a bigger pot with richer compost. It will grow quite happily on a sunny windowsill or in a warm greenhouse. The minimum temperature for winter must be 65°F (18°C) and ideally, but not essentially, 90°F (32°C). The plant will grow up to 3 ft (1m) and will hopefully fruit after three years. Never pick a pineapple before it is ripe: unlike many other fruits it will not ripen off the plant. After fruiting the old plant is discarded, but first repot the babies, offsets that appear at the base, ready for your next crop.

The pineapple pit at Heligan

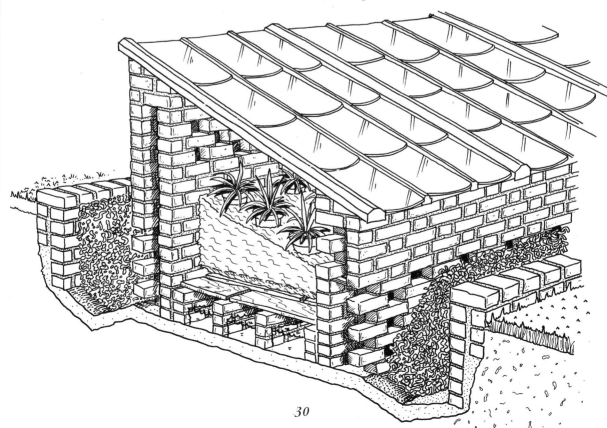

GROW YOUR OWN ORANGES AND LEMONS

Mr and Mrs Colledge grow all sorts of hardy fruits in their garden and make jams, chutneys and wines. Like most keen gardeners they love to propagate, and when they ate some delicious oranges on a Greek holiday they decided to save and sow the pips when they got back home. Two pips germinated and one actually made it to a tree, but that seemed to be it. However, after ten years the tree finally blossomed and fruited and now they make several pounds of marmalade from the fruits each year. Although Mrs Colledge had success with a pip, she was lucky: people have been known to wait for thirty years before the first blossom appears, although some seedlings will fruit within five years . You just can't tell: if you want fruit it is far more reliable to buy a named variety grown on a rootstock. If you do plant a pip don't be surprised when it germinates, as each pip will send up two seedlings.

If you buy a citrus there are lots of varieties to choose from:

Orange marmalade

Marmalade was once a preserve made from honey, quinces, spices and wine, and it was not until the sixteenth century that it was made from fruits, berries and sugar.

Use equal quantities of oranges and sugar and boil the oranges first to soften their skins. Slice the fruit and put in a preserving pan, with the pips (in a muslin bag) to provide the pectin and 1½ pints of water per pound of oranges (1.8 litres per kilogram). Simmer until tender, then add the sugar. When it has dissolved, boil with a jam thermometer until setting point is reached (about 250°F/120°C). To prevent scum forming, add a knob of butter to the mixture while it is boiling. Cool the marmalade slightly before bottling in sterile jars, to prevent the peel rising.

Pomanders and love charms

Oranges were thought to be the only real preventative to the plague, and people were advised to carry them at all times. The use of pomanders (oranges full of cloves) may have stemmed from this.

The orange tree has been in Britain since the eighteenth century and has long been regarded as a fertility symbol. Orange blossom is often included in wedding wreaths to encourage fertility and a large family.

One Norfolk tradition said that if a man was after a particular woman he should take an orange, prick it all over with a pin in the pits of its skin, and sleep with it under his armpit. The next day he was to give it to the girl: if she ate it in front of him then love was in the air.

Moro blood orange
Large fruits with red flesh, excellent sweet flavour.

Jaffa orange
Sweet orange. An old variety which came over from Palestine in 1883. Large, excellent-flavoured fruits. Juicy and easy to peel.

Valencia late orange
Sweet orange. Large, thin-skinned, well-flavoured fruits. Vigorous tree, heavy cropper. Crops stay on tree for a long time.

Satsuma
Produces a good crop of thin-skinned small fruits on compact weeping bushes. Grown in Japan for 400 years. Hardy.

Meyer's lemon
The perfect lemon. Discovered in China in the early

Mr and Mrs Colledge proudly present their orange tree.
1900s. Hardy on a south wall in the south. Good cropper, good flavour, flowers continuously.

Tahiti lime
A large, seedless, sweet lime. Compact plant. Heavy cropper.

Grapefruit
These can take as long as 17 months to mature but are good croppers.

If you want to grow something completely different, try the fingered citron or Buddha's hand. This strongly scented citrus has fruits shaped like yellow rubber gloves, with each segment having a skin of its own. Used in China for perfuming rooms and clothes.

The easiest way to grow a citrus tree is in a pot, in a heated greenhouse. Plant in the spring, in John Innes No. 2 compost. The trees require good light (but need shading in midsummer), good ventilation even in winter to keep the air on the dry side, and dislike sudden changes in temperature and humidity. The minimum temperature for Meyer's lemon is 45°F (7°C), and for lime, grapefruit, oranges and variegated lemons 50–55°F (10–13°C).

Keep the plants moist during the growing season and feed with a general liquid feed, containing trace elements, every week in the summer and once a month in the winter. Every spring put some fresh compost in the top of the pot after scraping off 1 in (2.5 cm) of the old compost: when it outgrows its pot, repot it. Very little pruning is required. In the first few years cut out vertical side shoots that get too long and cut back shoots near the base to allow the plant to grow as a single-stemmed tree. When the plant is well established, just trim back excessive growth to achieve a rounded head.

Most of the few greenhouse pests that attack citrus such as mealy bugs, aphids and scale, can be treated with predatory and parasitic insects available from specialist suppliers. Often citrus leaves turn yellow – this is usually attributed to magnesium or iron deficiency but may also be due to long-term overwatering.

Citrus trees can flower at any time of year. Because fruits can take over a year to ripen, flowers and fruits are seen on the trees at the same time. To let the plant get well established, allow only up to four fruits in the first few years.

AND NOW FOR SOMETHING COMPLETELY DIFFERENT

It's fun to grow your own pineapples and lemons, but if you run out you can easily pop out to the shops to get some. Not so with cactus fruit. Mr Haines in Cornwall grows and breeds Epiphyllum hybrids, a type of rainforest cacti, for their exquisite flowers. To get new flowers he cross-pollinates them and sows the seeds. One in a thousand may come up trumps, so it is a long and painstaking process. After reading that the succulent purple fruits surrounding the seeds were edible, he took the plunge and sunk the teeth in. They were delicious, tasting like a cross between a lychee and a strawberry. Whereas most people would have one or two of these unusual houseplants, Mr Haines had 4,000 and an awful lot of fruits, so decided to make jam. It was so successful he now makes it every year. If you fancy trying it, find someone with an Epiphyllum hybrid cactus and take a cutting. Just break off a section, leave it to dry off and callus over for a few months, then pot it up. Treat it like a normal houseplant, watering and feeding in the summer, and you may get a fruit after a couple of years; you also get some beautiful flowers.

If you want to grow exotic fruits and don't have a greenhouse, don't despair – many alien fruits can be grown outside.

The exotic cacti fruit

The Fig
(Ficus carica)

Fig trees get very big and unwieldy. They can cover half the garden and still not produce any fruit. Harry Baker grows at least six varieties of fig in his garden and manages to accommodate all the plants on a small patio. The secret: he grows them in pots! Figs produce more fruit if they have a restricted root run because the plant tries to produce offspring to find a better home – the result is luscious figs!

Use a 12–14 in (30–35 cm) pot filled with John Innes No. 3 compost. When the figs become rootbound, knock them out of the pot in early spring, tease off the old compost, prune the roots and repot in fresh compost in the same pot.

The trees can be planted in the ground but need restricting. Find a sunny spot with well-drained soil that is not too rich. Dig out a hole 3 x 3 ft (1 m x 1 m) and 2.5 ft (0.75 m) deep and line it with solid walls: paving slabs are ideal. Leave the bottom open for drainage but put some rubble in it to prevent tap roots forming.

Figs can be trained as fans or bushes. Fruits are produced on short-jointed young shoots which can be encouraged by pruning existing side shoots back to five leaves in early summer. Figs can give two crops a year, but only one usually ripens unless the plant is grown in a greenhouse. The figs you need to nurture are the pea-sized fruits formed in late summer near the tips of the shoots. These develop and ripen in September the next year. Fruits produced in the spring on new shoots do not usually get time to ripen in this country and should be removed in autumn to concentrate the tree's energy into the embryo figs.

In April figs need tidying up. Cut out dead and diseased shoots and shorten alternate side shoots back to one bud to induce shoots to form from the base. With neglected trees cut one third of the old branches back to a young branch or to their point of origin. Because figs are susceptible to coral spot disease, paint the cuts with pruning wound paint.

Figs are not frost-hardy. Potted figs can be brought in over winter, even into a dark garage, because they don't have leaves then so don't need the light. Pack hessian or bracken around figs planted outside.

In spring feed with a balanced fertilizer and water well in dry weather, otherwise the developing figs you worked so hard for may fall off.

Figs can be propagated by hardwood cuttings or layering. Peg a branch down into the soil in spring and it will have rooted by the autumn.

Figgy facts

In 1905 Worthing was the centre of British fig culture.

The tree where Thomas à Beckett's murderers threw their coats was probably a fig.

Greek athletes ate lots of figs: they believed it would make them run faster.

The fig variety aptly named Adam has a leaf that is large enough to cover all.

When figs ripen in August and September the fruits droop down, begin to split and change colour. Gardeners used to tell if figs were ripe by looking for a drop of nectar at the base of the fruit, called 'the tear in the eye of the fig'.

The word sycophant means 'one revealing a fig', and was the name given to the informers who revealed the fig smugglers.

Common figs develop without being fertilized and are the swollen bases of flowers. In effect they are a flower turned inside out.

Different stages in the development of a fig in August

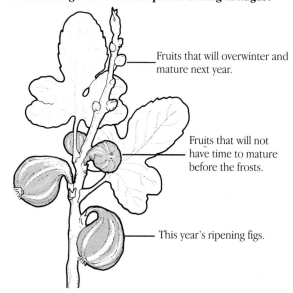

Fruits that will overwinter and mature next year.

Fruits that will not have time to mature before the frosts.

This year's ripening figs.

There are a wide range of different figs, including:

St John's
Early fruiting, good variety for a pot.

Brown Turkey
Mid-season, a reliable cultivar.

White Ischia
Mid-season, good flavour, small fruits, good for pots.

Black Ischia
Small, round dark-purple-skinned figs with red flesh and good flavour.

Rouge de Bordeaux
Mid-season, needs warmth, good for pots.

Bourjasotte Grise
Late, needs warmth, good flavour, good for pots. Violet colour.

Panachee
Very attractive with striped wood and striped sweet figs. They look like little hot air balloons.

THE KIWI
(Actinidia deliciosa)

Another tasty but rampant fruit is the kiwi, a sprawling, deciduous woody climber with heart-shaped leaves and creamcoloured flowers. Heligan gardens boast one of the first kiwis to come to Britain, introduced by the great plant hunter E. H. 'Chinese' Wilson after the turn of the century. Still going strong, the plant has to be pruned five times a year because it grows over 2 in (5 cm) a day in the growing season! Most kiwis bear male and female flowers on different plants – this one was male and so was given a mate. As soon as she was planted he started to grow rapidly in the other direction: he obviously didn't fancy her.

Kiwi names

The kiwi, originally called the Chinese gooseberry or monkey peach, comes from southern China, and has been used there for centuries for wine and for inks, dyes and glues as well as for eating raw. The name monkey peach is very apt. The National Collection of kiwis in Britain is at Bristol Zoo. The fruits are served in the restaurant and when there is a glut they are fed to the primates, who love them.

The New Zealanders made the fruit famous when they marketed the Chinese gooseberry as the 'kiwi'. It made all the difference in the world, and the fruit is now sold world-wide. Its attributes are its incredible bright green flesh, its delicate taste of gooseberries crossed with strawberries and its Vitamin C content, one of the highest of any fruits, 105 mg per 10 g of edible flesh.

Kiwis need a long growing season to ripen the fruit and are susceptible to early frosts. If you live in the south and can grow dessert grapes outside then you can grow a kiwi, preferably on a south-facing wall, sheltered from north and east winds. Plant in well-drained fertile soil and mulch to conserve moisture. The Hayward female cultivar is a good choice, with the Tomuri cultivar as a pollinator in the same planting hole. The plant should fruit within four years on the one-year-old wood. Allow fruiting laterals to form at about 20 in (50 cm) intervals off a few framework branches, and after fruiting cut back the fruited laterals to a point above the last bud that bore fruit. Pick the fruits in October and store for one to three months in a cool frost-free place before use. To hasten ripening, place some in a polythene bag with an apple. There is a mini kiwi called Issai, which is self-fertile and produces large crops of sweet, hairless fruits with edible skins.

If your garden is a little cool for kiwis, try its northern relation, the Siberian actinidia, with smooth skin and fruits the size of grapes which are sweeter and contain as much Vitamin C as their relatives. Although the plant can tolerate hard winters, it becomes vulnerable as soon as it comes into growth in the spring and can be hard hit by late frost. Like the kiwi, it needs a partner, although some hermaphrodite varieties are available.

EDIBLE FLOWERS

You can eat the fruits and the flowers of the subtropical shrub *Feijoa selloiana*. With its attractive silvery grey foliage and red-centred, fuchsia-like flowers, the plant is hardy enough to grow outdoors in Britain. You eat only the petals and leave the reproductive structures to develop into fruit, getting two bites of the cherry or, in this case, of the feijoa. Once, in New Zealand, birds eating the flowers were shot to save the fruits. But the fruits did not appear: the birds had been pollinating them by eating the petals. In the garden you will need two plants for cross-pollination. To guarantee fruits it is safer to grow them indoors in pots over the winter and spring.

THE PERFECT PEACH

The peach (*Prunus persica*) is far more controlled than the fig or the kiwi. It can be grown outside in a warm spot and is well worth the effort, as nothing beats the sweet, juicy taste of a fresh peach straight off the tree. You can easily grow one from a seed (stone) and get results much quicker than with an orange. The seed needs to be stratified: it has to go through a cold period before it will grow. Bury it in a pot of compost for the winter before bringing it into the warm the following year. If you want to be sure of success buy a maiden, or for a little more money a ready fan-trained tree.

Good varieties include:

Peregrine
Crops early August, good flavour.

Rochester
Crops early August.

Duke of York
Crops mid-July, good flavour.

Grow peaches, and especially nectarines (bald peaches!), in a sheltered site, ideally as a fan against a south- or west-facing wall (which needs to be at least 6 ft (1.8 m) high). Plant 6–9 in (15–22 cm) away from the wall, with the stem sloping towards it.

Peaches shaped like doughnuts

When Harry Baker was in a market in Minorca he spotted some strange-looking peaches. They looked dreadful, but were more expensive than the good-looking round ones, and they were also covered in honey bees. Looks are only skin deep, and when he bought some he found they tasted wonderful. This was his first brush with the flat or China peach. The plant originated in Java and travelled along the trade routes to the Mediterranean. Harry grafted some scionwood he got from fellow enthusiast Fred Roach, and now has a small tree covered in peaches. The fruits are shaped like a doughnut.

Another oddity is the compact peach, e.g. Bonanza, ideal for growing in a pot. It is a short bush with a mop head of leaves at the top. It flowers early and needs protection from frost. Because it is a genetic dwarf it often grows true from a peach stone.

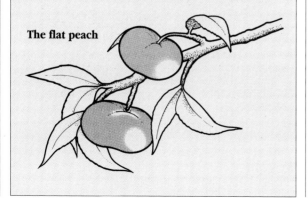

The flat peach

Peaches like slightly acid (pH 6.5–7.0), deep well-drained loamy soil that is moisture-retentive. When preparing the site, break up any impervious subsoil and incorporate generous amounts of well-rotted manure to hold the moisture. When the tree is in bud, protect from frost by covering with hessian at night. Peaches are self-fertile but the flowers need to be hand-pollinated, because pollinating insects are not around when they are in blossom. It is essential to use something very soft such as a rabbit's tail, because if they are brushed too hard the delicate parts will be damaged.

Pruning peaches
There is no getting away from it, peaches are tricky to prune. The first rule is not to panic, but sit down and work out what you are aiming to do. Peaches fruit on the young wood produced in the previous year, and the first thing to do is to lay down a structure to carry the fruiting branches. Carry out the winter pruning in the early spring and the summer pruning in the summer (strangely enough), because pruning in the dormant season increases the risk of infection from bacterial canker.

Pruning a peach for shape
You can either buy a fan-trained tree or do it yourself. Fix horizontal wires to the wall 6 in (15 cm) apart. Plant a feathered maiden (a one-year-old tree with side shoots) in the dormant season and cut back to a strong side shoot about 2 ft (60 cm) above ground level. All the other laterals can be cut back to one bud. This pruning will stimulate growth in the following growing season (see diagram opposite).

Pruning for fruit
Once you have the shape you can start thinking peaches. The one-year-old shoots carry two sorts of buds: fruit buds (fat ones) which will flower and fruit in the same year, and wood buds (pointed ones) which will grow into next year's laterals and then produce fruit the following year. These buds may be triple (two flowers and one wood bud), double (one

Stages in fan training a peach

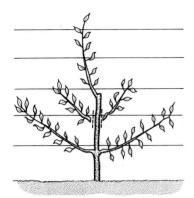
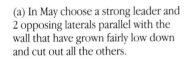
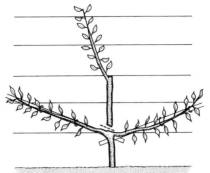
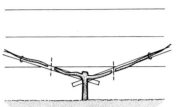

(a) In May choose a strong leader and 2 opposing laterals parallel with the wall that have grown fairly low down and cut out all the others.

(b) In the summer cut out the leader as well and tie the laterals in at a 45° angle. These are called ribs and form the basis of the fan.

(c) In the second winter cut back the 2 ribs to about 12 in (30 cm), to the nearest upward-facing bud, to stimulate new growth in the next growing season.

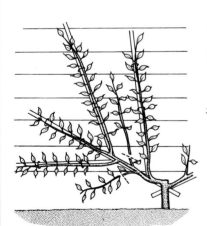
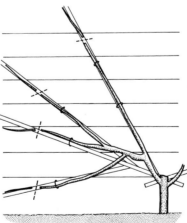
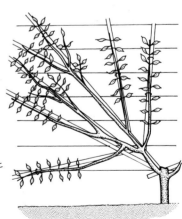

(d) In the summer train in the growing shoots by tying in the ones at the tips of the ribs to extend the stem, selecting and tying in 2 strong shoots on the upper side of each rib, and selecting 1 strong shoot on the lower side and tying in. Cut back all other side shoots to 1 leaf.

(e) The following winter shorten the main stems of the fan by half to downward facing wood buds. This again stimulates growth.

(f) The following summer train more shoots into place to form the framework of the fan, and thin the side shoots to about 6 in (15 cm) apart. Remove shoots growing towards or away from the wall.

Pruning a peach for fruit

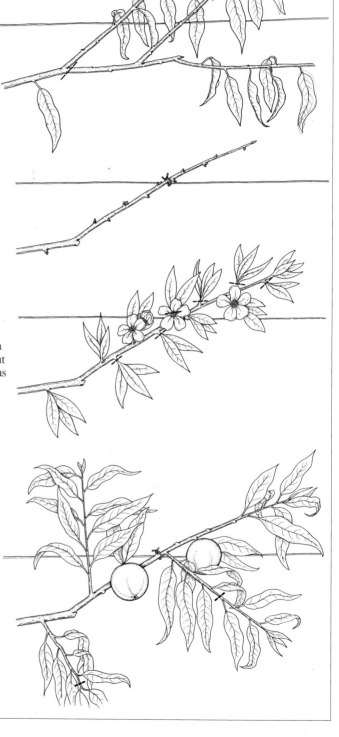

(a) Peach branch in August that has been harvested

(b) Replacement shoot tied in. After the peaches have been harvested in August, cut the fruited laterals back to a replacement shoot and tie it in for next year.

(c) Replacement lateral in the spring. This replacement lateral will carry fruit and new shoots in the following year. Leave shoots with flowers at their base, 2 leaves to feed the fruit. Find the wood buds that have sprouted on the 1-year-old laterals. Thin these new shoots to leave 1 at the base (a replacement for next year), 1 in the middle (as reserve replacement) and the terminal one at the end. Pinch back all the others to 1 leaf.

(d) Replacement shoot that has formed fruit. When the three selected new shoots are 18 in (45 cm) long, pinch out the tips, also pinch out any secondary shoots to 1 leaf. When the peaches form, thin them. They should be thinned to 4 in (10 cm) apart when they are the size of hazelnuts and to 8 in (20 cm) apart when they are the size of walnuts.

flower and one wood bud) or single (a flower if fat and a wood bud if thin). It is safer to cut to a triple or double. The aim of pruning is to think a year ahead and select new shoots which will fruit the following year. These young shoots should be spaced about 6–8 inches (15–18 cm) apart along the ribs of the fan (see diagram opposite).

The busy person's peach tree

If this all seems a bit much, grow the peach (on a dwarfing rootstock) in a pot. Move the pot indoors from February until the frosts have finished. After harvesting the peaches, cut back all the laterals that have fruited to a point where a new shoot has arisen.

Early each spring feed the tree with a general fertilizer and mulch to conserve moisture. From flowering to just before fruit-ripening give a liquid potash feed every two weeks.

Aphids, glasshouse red spider mite and brown scale can be controlled with biological controls or soft soap. The main problem with peaches is peach leaf curl, a fungal infection which causes the leaves to curl and fall. Covering the peaches with a plastic or glass structure from December to May stops peach leaf curl completely. This keeps off the airborne spores and is a very successful control method.

APRICOTS AND ALMONDS

The apricot (*Prunus armeniaca*)flowers earlier than peaches and so needs more protection. It is best grown under glass, though in the South and Midlands it can be grown as fans on walls. It likes a soil full of humus with a bit of lime, so if you live on well-composted chalky soil the apricot is for you. Apricots fruit on spurs on the older wood as well as on one-year-old shoots, so fan-trained apricots can be pruned more like plums (see Chapter 7, Old and Wild) and as stone fruits should still be pruned in the spring and summer.

The almond (*Prunus dulcis dulcis* and *Prunus amygdalus*) is one of the earliest trees to bloom after winter and is grown for its blossom as well as its nuts. A nut is a one-seeded fruit with a hard, woody wall. The almond makes a good small tree, and can be grown just like a peach. If you want the nuts don't buy the ornamental flowering almond, as its nuts may contain too much hydrocyanic acid and be poisonous. Almonds have long symbolized fruitfulness and were considered to be the sacred trees of life by the Phrygians of Asia Minor around 1000 BC. They have been grown in Britain since the sixteenth century. If you can't decide between a peach and an almond, have both. As they are so closely related you can buy them grafted on to the same tree, a real fruit and nut tree.

Nuts about you

Nuts, like other fruits, have always had strong associations with love.

In Devon, the bride used to be met by an old woman as she came out of the church and presented with a bag of hazelnuts to promote childbearing.

In many counties, a good nut harvest was said to signify a lot of births in the coming year.

'Going a-nutting' once meant going off to make love.
When a girl wanted to test her lover's faithfulness, she would put two nuts side by side on the edge of the fire. If they burned together, their love would be true. If they flew apart or didn't burn, that was it, off to the dating agency.

But if you want true love, find a nut with two kernels and divide it with the partner of your dreams: good luck, and let's hope he or she likes nuts.

Plats from the past

In the eighteenth century beans, turnips and hoeing crops were planted between the trees for 'upon the constant stirring of the ground does the vigour of the tree principally depend'. The trees themselves, being fairly shade-tolerant, were sometimes planted beneath larger apple and plum trees.

THE WALNUT

Another foreign nut tree which grows well in Britain is the English walnut, which comes from China and Iran. Like the apricot it needs limy, compost-rich soil. Buy a three-year-old grafted tree of a named variety and plant it where you have a lot of room: in time it can get up to 70 ft (21 m). Choose a late-flowering variety so it doesn't get hit by the frost. Walnuts are easy to grow and don't need much pruning apart from the removal of dead or awkwardly placed branches. Prune in the summer, as walnuts bleed if pruned in the spring or winter.

Good varieties include:

Mayette
Late-flowering with large, round tapering nuts that ripen in November.

Cornet du Perigord
Late-flowering, with medium to large nuts with good flavour that ripen in November.

Franquette
Late-flowering, with large, oval nuts with a sweet flavour. Crops better if cross-pollinated.

There is an old (dreadful) saying: ' Your dog, your wife and your walnut tree, the more you beat them

Pruning hazelnuts in the Silverhill nut plantation with Fred Bromley

Pruning cobnuts

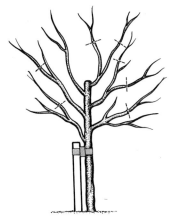

(a) Regular pruning consists of shortening the ends of the branches and side branches in February to make them produce short young growths on which the flowers and nuts are carried. Also suckers are twisted and pulled out from the base. Some growers use sheep to do the lower pruning: Southdowns are a good breed because they are short and cannot damage the higher branches.

(b) In late summer new strong growths are broken by half and left to hang to encourage the branch below the break to form fruiting buds. Locals call this brutting. These brutted laterals are cut to 4 buds in the winter.

the better they be.' In a garden in Worcestershire there was an old walnut tree that never produced many nuts. After it was struck by lightning, however, it started to crop regularly. So get out there and start beating your walnuts.

• Walnuts contain over 60 per cent oil and can be used as a furniture polish.

• Plants were once used to cure ailments they resembled, and this was known as the 'doctrine of signatures'. Walnuts were used to cure headaches, as they looked like brains.

• Walnuts were used as a base for some oil paints, as a lamp fuel, and as a clothes and hair dye.

• An infusion prepared from the husks was once used to kill worms on lawns.

• Wear gloves when handling fresh nuts or foliage as they contain an indelible brown dye.

• While you are waiting for your tree to bear nuts you can use the leaves, which smell like Golden Delicious apples, to make a tasty wine.

THE COBNUT

At the beginning of the century there were over 7,000 acres (2,800 ha) of Kentish cobnuts. Now there are 250 acres (100 ha). Fortunately, however, the tide seems to be turning. With help from grants, new nut orchards, or plats as they are known, are being planted to give an increase in the acreage of 10 per cent a year, especially on the Kentish ragstone soils extending 15 miles (24 km) north-east and 15 miles

There is always someone who does things differently. In the nineteenth century a Mr Webb, from Reading, bred many varieties of cobnuts. He did not seem to believe in pruning. He had a forty-eight-year-old nut tree 30 ft (10m) high and 50 ft (15 m) across. One year six pickers gathered 110 lb (50 kg) of nuts from it. He was very proud of his nuts and guarded them well. His 14 acre (6 ha) walled garden was protected from humans by half a dozen mastiffs and from vermin by some sixty cats.

(24 km) south-west of Maidstone. In the early 1990s Britain was producing 300 tonnes a year and importing about 8,000 tonnes, mainly from Turkey. If the old plats were replanted, the Kentish Cobnut Association believe that we could supply the UK market with home-grown nuts within ten years. Production costs for cobnuts are far less than for other fruits because they have a very low pesticide input and a plat's cropping life usually exceeds 100 years.

Varieties

Cobnuts are relatives of hazels (*Corylus avellana*) and filberts (*Corylus maxima*). Our native hazel was one of the first trees to colonize the land after the end of the Ice Age, while the filbert comes from south-eastern Europe. Hazelnuts have a short husk and filberts a long husk. The name filbert has been around since the 1500s . Harvesting begins on about 22 August, St Philbert's day, and the nuts are called *noix de Philbert* in Norman patois. Others believe the name to have come from 'full beard', referring to the long calyx (husk) that in filberts protrudes well beyond the nut.

Cobnuts have been grown commercially in Britain since the eighteenth century, and since then many new varieties have come on to the market. One of the best by far is the Kentish Cob (alias Lambert's Filbert), developed by Mr Lambert of Goudhurst, Kent, in the 1800s. Others include the cobnuts Cosford and Nottingham Cob, both of which are good pollinators and produce heavy crops of well-flavoured nuts, and the Purple, Red and White Filberts, attractive ornamental trees with excellent-flavoured nuts.

For something completely different, try *Corylus* x *colurnoides*, the trazel. This vigorous tree is a cross between the common hazel and Turkish hazel, and produces a heavy crop.

Planting

Cobnuts do best under cultivated conditions, with a little well-rotted organic manure added each winter. After planting a new young tree, cut it back to

What's in a name?

A plat is the name given to a cobnut orchard.

In the fifteenth century cultivated hazelnuts were called cobill nuts, as they were like a cobble or round stone. The term cob is also applied to a rounded loaf, a round lump of coal and even a type of (rounded?) horse.

In the sixteenth century cobnuts were used to play an equivalent of conkers (long before horse chestnuts were used). Cobnuts were also used for other games. Four nuts were piled in a pyramid shape and a larger nut called the cob was thrown at them. All the nuts knocked down were the property of the pitcher.

Cob also means to throw gently or lightly.
'Ud' refers to the calyx-like spiky green covering that encloses the nut. The 'slip-ud stage' refers to the time when the nut ripens sufficiently for the nut to fall out of its covering. The seasonal inquiry 'do um slip-ud' was used to inquire whether the nutting season had begun. Ud or Hud is probably a derivation of the word hood meaning cap or hat.

Kipsies are the wicker baskets that were once used to gather nuts.

Spawning is when nut trees throw up shoots from the roots. These are usually removed to prevent the tree forming a thicket!

The name Corylus may come from the Greek *korys*, hood or helmet, referring to the husk.

The name hazel may similarly come from the Anglo-Saxon *haesil*, a headdress.

18 in (45 cm) from the ground to encourage the development of side shoots.

Pruning

Native hazels are often cut back to the base (coppiced) to stimulate new shoots. These were used to make baskets and hurdles. The Kentish cobnut is grown for its nuts, not its shoots, so needs a different, stricter type of pruning. If left unpruned the nuts would be found on the extremities of the trees because they tend to grow on the young wood.

When pruning, the aim is to produce a bowl-shaped tree, 5–6 ft (1.5–1.8 m) high with about six branches radiating from a central stem. To achieve this, leaders are cut back to half the current season's growth each winter for about six years.

To renovate a neglected tree, the whole thing is cut to ground level, and six to eight new shoots are allowed to grow up to form the new framework. Alternatively, four or five well-placed branches are selected to form the framework of the tree, and these are pruned to 4 ft (1.2 m), removing any other branches at ground level. The following year two or three of the new shoots on each branch are selected to form the cropping units, and cut back to encourage side shoots to develop.

Pollination

If you see a group of happy people with yellow faces wandering down a country road in Kent in early spring, carrying saws and secateurs, do not fear. It is not some strange ritual, nor do they have a contagious disease – the pruners have merely caught a bit of pollen as they worked, happy in the knowledge that their nuts will be growing this year. Hazels are wind-pollinated, and have prominent catkins loaded with pollen waiting for the wind to carry them to their female partners, often referred to as 'red ladies'. They need to be pollinated by another type of cobnut or by wild hazels in the hedgerows. Cobnuts are often pruned at pollination time, the movement dispersing large clouds of pollen. The right weather is crucial for pollination: a warm winter puts things out of phase because the female flowers come out before the males and a wet spring means the pollen cannot blow about.

Pests and diseases of cobnuts

A little circular hole in a cobnut shows that the nut weevil has been at work. Adult weevils feed on young leaves and nuts from April to July, and the eggs are laid in the developing nuts in June. Most growers put up with losing a few nuts and rely on natural predators and cold winter weather to kill off the pupae. Chickens can help, as they eat the grubs which pupate in the soil.

Harvesting the nuts

Cobnuts can yield up to 40 lb (18 kg) of nuts a tree. They can be picked in August when green and eaten fresh or fully ripened in September when the husks are brown and the nuts have a sweeter flavour. An entrepreneur in Oregon is using helicopters to harvest ripe nuts. The rotor downwash shakes the trees and knocks the nuts to the ground, where they can be harvested.

To store ripe nuts of any sort, spread them out in a warm place to dry. Pack dehusked cobnuts in earthenware jars with alternate layers of salt, or simply hang them up, husks and all, in a dry place free from frosts and vermin. Walnuts can be packed in alternate layers of salt and dry peat and sweet chestnuts packed in layers of sand. These will all keep for six months or more. Nuts will keep for several months if kept in an open polythene bag in the refrigerator with a little salt.

Nutty uses and remedies

Cobnut kernels contain 12 per cent protein by dry weight and 10 per cent fibre. They are rich in Vitamin E (21 mg/100 g dry weight) and provide 0.4 mg and 0.55 mg of Vitamins B1 and B6 per 100 g dry weight. A bowl of nuts, a Cox or a Russet apple and a glass of port make a marvellous end to a meal.

The Greeks prescribed ground filberts mixed with bear grease as a cure for baldness.

Pliny said that nuts cured coughs, yellow jaundice and also piles!

In the wars the husks provided dye for khaki and the ground shells were added to gunpowder.

It is now thought to be a shortage of hazelnuts that is reducing numbers of red squirrels, rather than illness or attacks by greys. Outgraded cobnuts from commercial plats are sent to Cumbria and the Isle of Wight to feed red squirrels.

Cobnuts form part of the vital food source for the declining dormouse. Nut plats are a good habitat for these creatures, especially where branches of neighbouring trees interlink and other food sources are present such as honeysuckle, hawthorn and oak trees (for the aphids and caterpillars).

Walnut and Parsley Pesto with Pasta

Pesto with basil, garlic and pine-nuts seems to have entered the national consciousness, and I often use this English version. It is lovely as a crunchy dressing for pasta or used as a grilled crust on chicken or fish.
There are no hard and fast rules about amounts – just go on until it looks and tastes attractive for your purpose.

Serves 6 approximately

2–4 cloves garlic
sea salt
as good an olive oil as you can afford
bunch fresh parsley, chopped
approximately 2 handfuls walnut pieces
freshly ground black pepper
lemon juice

Using a pestle and mortar, crush the peeled garlic cloves and salt until pulpy. Add a tablespoon of olive oil, mix it in, then add some parsley to make a green sludge. Add more oil, some walnuts and more parsley and carry on adding and crushing until you have the consistency of a rugged dressing – fairly loose for pasta, thicker for a grilled crust. Add more seasoning if you wish, and lemon juice to taste. This can be made well in advance of serving.

Opposite: Walnut and Parsley Pesto with Pasta

Figs Stuffed with Yoghurt

Serve these sweetmeats with coffee after a special meal or as an alternative to a formal pudding.

Serves 6

½ pint (300 ml) thick goat's yoghurt
18 dried or fresh figs

Drain the yoghurt in a muslin bag for several hours or overnight.

Cut a slit in each fig and fill the body of the fruit with the firm yoghurt, rounding out the skin to make a good shape. Chill for at least 2 hours before serving.

Stuffed Peaches or Nectarines

Nothing can compare with a really ripe peach or nectarine plucked warm from the tree. In good years with long hot summers, the peaches grown against the old brick wall are a succulent treat to look forward to. The nectarine Pineapple in the greenhouse always has some delectably sweet fruit just before the outdoor crop.

Serves 6

6 ripe peaches
2 oz (50 g) sugar
2 egg yolks
1 oz (25 g) unsalted butter, softened
6 oz (175 g) macaroon crumbs

Skin – easy if the fruit is ripe – and halve the peaches. If you have time, crack open the stones and crush some kernels to add to the filling. They have a delicious almond taste.

Mix all the ingredients together and stuff the peach halves. Bake them in an ovenproof dish for about 30 minutes at 350°F (180°C, Gas 4) until the top has browned and cracked a little. Best served hot with cream or some rich custard.

Carrot and Hazelnut Terrine

Make this in the autumn with fresh hazelnuts and serve with Cucumber and Apple Mint Salad (page 27).

6 oz (175 g) hazelnuts
1½ lb (675 g) carrots, peeled, diced and cooked
3 eggs, beaten
chopped fresh thyme
sea salt
freshly ground black pepper

Toast the hazelnuts on a tray – a round pizza tray gives the most even results – at 400°F (200°C, Gas 6) for 15 minutes or until the nuts turn colour and give off a lovely aroma. It should now be easy to rub off most of the skins. Process the nuts into rough, chunky crumbs and remove.

Put the cooked carrots into the same processor and whiz until they are mushy but with one or two small pieces of carrot remaining to give some character to the terrine. Briefly whiz in the chopped thyme, beaten eggs and seasoning.

Turn the mixture into a 1½ pint (900 ml) terrine tin lined with Bakewell paper and bake at 350°F (180°C, Gas 4) in a roasting tray half full of warm water for 1½ hours, when the terrine will have risen and become firm.

This can be served warm as a vegetarian dish, or cold as a starter with salad or for a light lunch.

3
FRUIT RULES

From the day you plant it to the day you eat it, fruit is governed by rules.

First come the rules of thumb in the garden: how fruits are identified, how to choose the right trees, and how to get one of the right size for your plot. Once your fruit is in and growing, it's all plain sailing. Well, almost. A few more legal issues can crop up when you least expect it and for the commercial grower rules abound, from fruit registration to quality control. But don't worry, stick to the rules and you will soon be home and dry.

FRUIT IDENTIFICATION

Fruit experts have devised many helpful rules when it comes to working out which fruit is which, from examining the shape and colour to analysing the smell.

Identification of apples by the fruit

On Apple Day, 21 October, people hold shows and stage demonstrations to celebrate our favourite fruit, the apple. One of the most popular events of the day is apple identification. Most shows have their own expert, who has the onerous task of dealing with queues of people laden with their unknown apples from dawn to dusk. How do they do it? Each one of the hundreds of apples that exist in cultivation has distinct characteristics which can be used to help identify it. These include:

• Where it was found growing, because any rare varieties are locally common.
• The season of ripening.
• Whether it is dessert, culinary or cider.
• The colour of the skin.
• The overall size and shape of the fruit.
• The shape of the eye and the basin that surrounds it.
• The size and shape of the stalk and the stalk cavity.
• The taste, texture and colour of the flesh.

To complicate matters, the appearance of a single variety can vary. Trees grown in poor, hungry soil produce highly coloured fruits, and a cold spring can lead to skin russeting. Young trees produce bigger,

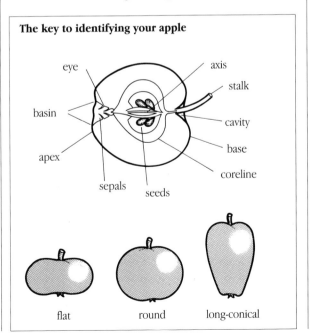

The key to identifying your apple

eye · axis · stalk · basin · cavity · base · apex · coreline · sepals · seeds

flat · round · long-conical

fewer fruits and on mature trees apples in the centre of a cluster tend to be larger. And to make the identification even more tricky, apples grown in the north are sometimes longer!

Give-away blossom

Nurseries often stress the ornamental values of apple trees with their beautiful spring blossom. As well as being very attractive, however, fruit blossoms can give a glimpse of things to come – not only quantity but variety too. Many fruit varieties such as apples can be identified by their blossom.

Apple variety	Blossom
Bess Pool	Deep cerise flowers.
Brownlee's Russet	Dark pink blossom.
Golden Pippin	Rich, deep pink blossom.
Lord Suffield	Huge, pale pink flowers.
Upton Pine	Large pink blooms.
Worcester Pearmain	Delicate, silvery white blossom with faint pink veins; salmon pink and yellow on the underside.
Warner's King	White blossom.

Smelly raspberries

Raspberries and hybrid berries at the Scottish Crop Research Institute are identified by their smell as well as from their mugshots. They are subjected to an electronic nose, which gives each cultivar its own olfactory profile like a fingerprint.

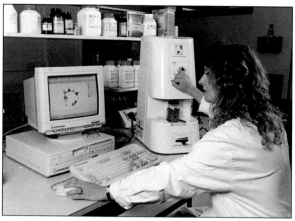

The machine with a nose for raspberries.

Perry pear identification in winter

Ray Williams can identify perry pear trees from 100 yards in midwinter using a technique similar to plane-spotting: identification by silhouettes.

There are about eighty varieties of perry pear, the pear equivalent of the cider apple, mainly restricted to Gloucestershire, Herefordshire and Worcestershire. A rule of thumb states that a good perry pear can only be grown within sight of Yarleton Hill (now renamed May Hill) in the Severn Vale. Ray Williams was brought up on a farm in the Vale and made perry from an early age. His grandfather was responsible for naming the perry pear Billy Williams. One cold winter's day Ray identified the following perry pear varieties in a matter of seconds.

Moorcroft
(syn. Malvern Hills) Large semi-spreading limbs.

High Pear
Branches sweep out, then up, then out again.

Thorn
A small upright, stiff and compact tree.

White Moorcroft
(syn. Newbridge) A tall tree with a limited number of upright limbs. The small, sparse, brittle branches are often littered around the base of the tree. Unlike other pears this pear has fragrant pink blossom.

What is a fruit?

A fruit is a protective structure around a fertilized seed. Many wild fruits taste good because they want an animal to eat them and take the seeds off to grow elsewhere, an effective dispersal mechanism. Man has manipulated fruits for centuries, making them bigger and tastier for their own ends. There are now thousands of varieties to fill the garden and tempt the palate.

Butt

A small, heavy-looking tree with a prominent, clustered spur system.

The fall and rise of the perry pear

Whatever the name, the poor old perry pear, which has been with us since Norman times, is in decline. There are still a few orchards and old individual trees around which are amazingly long-lived. At Holm Lacey, on the banks of the river Wye, stand the remnants of a 300-year-old tree which once covered ¾ acre (0.3 ha) and carried 7 tons of fruit a year. This tree had layered itself and become a small woodland. There is even a picture of it in the *Herefordshire Pomona*, published 150 years ago.

There are still a few perry-makers in the area and in the last fifteen years small producers have begun to plant again, so the perry industry may be on the return. A perry pear collection has recently been planted at the Three Counties show ground in Malvern, Worcestershire, so if they do make a comeback all the varieties will be there waiting.

Perry and cider are made very differently. Cider is made from a blend of varieties while perry is usually produced from a single variety: mixtures of varieties tend to make a cloudy perry. The harvesting time of perry pears is far more precise than with cider apples, and the perry-makers therefore had to be very skilled and know when to press the fruit from individual trees. Perry is a delightful drink, regarded by some as a good alternative to champagne. As with many other fruits, the same variety of pear grown in different soils produces a very different tasting perry.

Perry pear silhouettes in winter

Firm favourites

You will be pleased to hear that apple varieties usually fall into one of the following eight groups. Here are the distinguishing features of a few old favourites, one from each group. Do you recognize any?

Cultivar	Skin colour	Size and shape	Basin and eye
Lord Derby group. Smooth, culinary green apples, e.g.			
Lord Derby	Green turning yellow.	Large round/conical .	Medium width and ribbed with a partially closed eye
Granny Smith group. Green, sweetly flavoured apples, e.g.			
Sturmer Pippin	Greenish, yellow with a brown flush	Medium size, with an oblong, conical, ribbed shape.	Broad, deep basin with a slightly open eye
Lane's Prince Albert group. Sour green apples with striped red flush, e.g.			
Lane's Prince Albert	Green flushed with red stripes	Large, round and conical	Broad, ribbed basin with a closed or slightly open eye
Peasgood Nonsuch group. Striped, smooth and sweet. Mainly dessert, some dual purpose varieties, e			
James Grieve	Pale green, yellow skin with a red flush	Medium size, with a round conical shape	Medium width deep basin with a large closed eye
The Golden Noble group. Golden and flushed with pink, with no stripes, e.g.			
Golden Delicious	Green to yellow with russet dots	Medium size, with a round, conical to oblong shape	Medium width deep basin with a slightly open eye
Worcester Pearmain group. Red-skinned with shiny or rough finish, e.g.			
Worcester Pearmain	Bright red flush on a greenish yellow background.	Medium size, with a round conical shape	A narrow, shallow basin with small closed eyes
The Cox group Some russet, with red flush and stripes			
Cox	Yellow, green to yellow. Flushed with red. Some patches of russet	Medium size, with a round, conical shape	Shallow, wide basin with a small, half-open eye
Russets. Russeted over a gold, green background. Usually sweet, dessert types, e.g.			
Ashmead's Kernel	Yellow/green with red flush and a little russetting	Medium size, with a flattened, rounded shape. Slightly flat-sided and ribbed	A shallow russetted basin with a half-closed eye and medium to long downy sepals

Cavity	Flesh	Notes
Shallow and broad, with a short thick stalk	White	Best used soon after picking Strong and sharp taste
Broad, deep and russeted with a long thick stalk	White, pale cream	A popular Victorian variety with a sweet, crisp, juicy taste
Wide and deep cavity with a short, thin stalk	Greenish, white	Culinary, with an acidic watery taste and firm, juicy flesh
Broad and deep with a long thin stalk	Pale cream	A juicy, crispy savoury apple that becomes less acid as it matures
Narrow and deep with a long thin stalk	Deep cream	Juicy, crisp flesh that is honeyed rather than tangy
Medium width, deep, and russeted with a short, thick stalk	White.	Juicy, firm flesh with a sweet strawberry flavour
Wide, medium-size lipped cavity	White	Sweet, aromatic, spicy, honeyed, nutty and pear-like
Russeted cavity with a thick, short stalk	White	A juicy russet, with the flavour of pear drops. Slightly sweet, slightly acid with a tight texture

RULES IN THE GARDEN

When it comes down to choosing the fruit for the garden, adhere to a few simple rules and success should follow.

CHOOSING A TREE

When buying a fruit tree, the cheapest and often the best option is to purchase a bare-rooted maiden. You can examine the roots before you buy it, you can prune it as you want straight from the word go, and as a young plant it should settle in quicker. Many trees are sold in containers. Although these can be obtained at any time of year, they are best bought and planted in the winter.

Look out for:

A good general shape, ideally with well-feathered, well-positioned branches to give a good framework later on.

The branch angle. Wide branch angles are desirable. Narrow-angled branches can create a weak point, and the branch can rip especially when the tree is laden with fruit.

Labels. Some trees, described as EMLA, are certified virus-free.

Inspecting apple varieties at the RHS Autumn Show

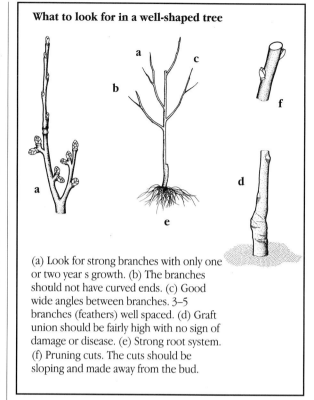

What to look for in a well-shaped tree

(a) Look for strong branches with only one or two years growth. (b) The branches should not have curved ends. (c) Good wide angles between branches. 3–5 branches (feathers) well spaced. (d) Graft union should be fairly high with no sign of damage or disease. (e) Strong root system. (f) Pruning cuts. The cuts should be sloping and made away from the bud.

The age of the tree. Many containerized specimens which are not sold one year are cut back and put back out the following year. Count the number of years' growth on one branch. Some can be up to 7 years old, and are effectively bonsaied from the stress of being in a small pot in old compost. As these trees are older you may even be expected to pay more for them, though they are inferior!

The height of the graft union. It should be high worked to ensure that the scion (top part) does not come close enough to the soil to grow roots. If this happens the tree could get really big (see Rootstocks, below). Check for dead tissue around the graft; if it has canker now, the tree will not live long.

Pest and disease. Curled round young shoots are a tell-tale sign of rosy apple aphid damage.

Every name tells a tale

The perry pear has been with us for a long time and has acquired some interesting names and some interesting stories, especially in connection with the perry it produces.

Flaky bark This perry pear can be identified from its piebald white and grey bark, which flakes like a plane tree. If you eat the fruit your mouth flakes too. High in tannin, the pear shrivels your gums and causes the skin on the inside of your cheeks to flake off.

Blakeney Red This perry pear, from Blakeney, was called Port by the locals because Blakeney was a port used to ship out cider mill stones. Blakeney Red was a very popular variety in the Second World War. It provided 'drink and food for your belly and clothes for your back' in the form of perry, jam and dye for the khaki jackets.

Holmer The perry made from the Holmer pears was strongly diuretic, especially if the fruits were overripe, and the pear soon acquired a new title: the 'Piss and Piddle' pear. During a survey of Gloucestershire's perries a local was asked if he had any 'Piss' pears. He replied that as a polite country man he would not use that name, in case a lady heard him. He then announced that their local name for the pear was 'Startle Cock'!

Other perry pears also acquired diuretic nicknames, such as Jug Rumbles and Circus Pear (alias Blakeney Red). The latter was named after a circus act 'one more round and out again'. On the same theme another pear was nicknamed 'Steal Your Balls' because of the perry's acid and bitter taste, which according to those that drank it really made you shiver. On investigation it was found that this was a derivation of the original name, Steelyard Balls, as the pear resembled the shape of the weights on the arm of weighing machines at the steelyard. These perry drinkers must have one track minds!

Perry certainly put the drinkers in a party mood, hence the local name of 'Merry Legs', and gave a few problems the morning after, hence the name 'Dead Boy'. As for the names 'Stinking Bishop' and 'Bloody Bastard', least said soonest mended!

ROOTSTOCKS

When you buy a tree you are buying more than one. The top of the tree, or scion, gives you the variety, the bottom or rootstock determines the eventual size of the tree. These are grafted together to give you the tree of your dreams. Apples have been grafted on to rootstocks for hundreds of years, as often they do not do as well on their own roots. It is also a good way of propagating a plant that does not root well from cuttings.

Rules for rootstocks

The rootstock you choose does not depend only on the size of tree you want. In a poor soil you need a more vigorous rootstock to get a stronger tree; if your scion variety is naturally vigorous, such as Bramley, you will need a dwarfing rootstock; and if you want to train the tree as a cordon you will also be better off with a dwarfing rootstock. Tops and bottoms are mixed and matched by the nurseries, and some offer a 'graft while you wait' service. Most nurseries will tell you what you will need for your situation, and the table below should help too.

Which rootstock do you need?

Every rootstock has a name, but there are no sensible rules here. The numbers are not in a logical order, and are denoted by the order in which the rootstocks were discovered rather than what size of tree they produce.

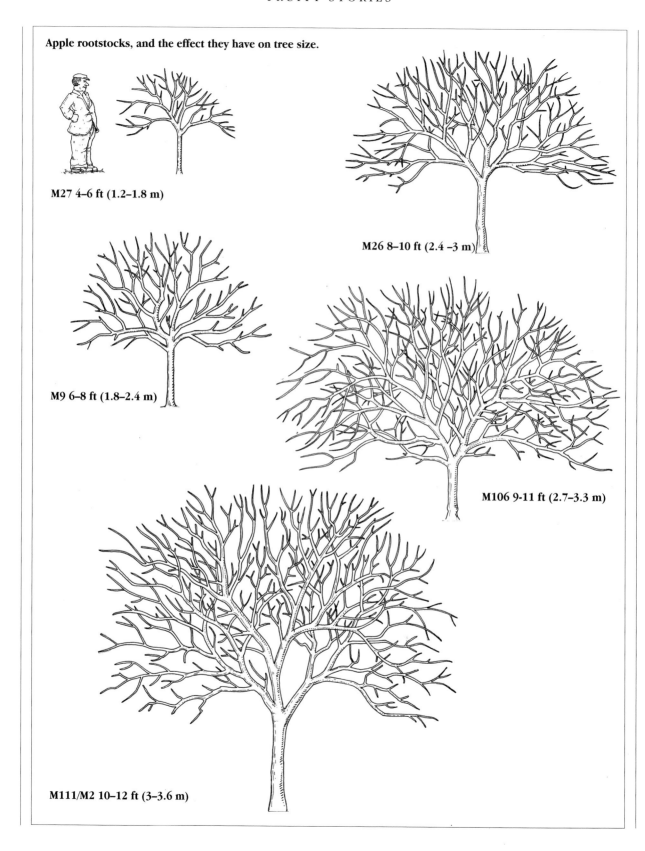

Apple rootstocks, and the effect they have on tree size.

M27 4–6 ft (1.2–1.8 m)

M26 8–10 ft (2.4 –3 m)

M9 6–8 ft (1.8–2.4 m)

M106 9-11 ft (2.7–3.3 m)

M111/M2 10–12 ft (3–3.6 m)

Apple Rootstocks

M27: Extremely Dwarfing

The tree on this rootstock will need very good soil and staking throughout its life.

Good for grafting with vigorous cultivars. Also used for restricted forms of trees such as cordons.

Plant trees 6 ft (1.8 m) apart. A dwarf bush makes a tree with a 4–6 ft (1.2–1.8 m) height and spread.

Trees crop within 2–3 years. Mature free-standing trees will yield 10–15 lb (4.5–6.8 kg) of fruit.

M9: Very Dwarfing

Needs good soil and support. Often used for trees trained as cordons, dwarf bushes, spindlebushes, and dwarf pyramids.

Plant 10 ft (3 m) apart. A dwarf bush makes a tree with a 6–8 ft (1.8–2.4 m) height and spread.

Trees crop within 3 years and when mature yield 30–50 lb (13.5–22.5 kg) from a free-standing tree, and about 8 lb (3.5 kg) from a cordon.

M26: Dwarfing

Needs average soils. Suitable for bush trees, dwarf pyramids, spindlebushes and cordons.

Plant 12 ft (3.6 m) apart to give a tree with an 8–10 ft (2.4 to 3m) height and spread.

Trees crop within 4 years and when mature yield 30–50 lb (13.5–22.5 kg) on a free-standing tree, about 8 lb (3.5 kg) from a cordon.

MM106 and M7: Semi-dwarfing

Good on most soils. Used for bush trees, spindlebushes, cordons, espaliers and fans.

Plant 12–15 ft (3.6–4.5 m) apart to give a tree with a 9–11 ft (2.7–3.3 m) height and spread.

Crops within 4 years and when mature yields 50–100 lb (22.5–45.5 kg) on a free-standing tree, and about 40 lb (18 kg) from a 3-tiered espalier.

MM111 AND M2: Vigorous

Large trees on good soils, medium trees on poor soils.

Plant 15–20 feet (4.5–6 m) apart to give a tree with a 10–12 ft (3–3.6 m) height and spread.

Yields 100–400 lb a tree (45.5–180 kg).

M25: Very Vigorous

Suitable for a grassed orchard, and to grow as a full standard.

Plant 20 ft (6 m) apart. Makes a tree with a 15 ft height (4.5 m) and spread, possibly more.

Yields 200–400 lb a tree (90–180 kg).

It's not just apples – other fruit trees are grafted too:

Pear Rootstocks

Quince C Moderately dwarfing.

Quince A Semi-vigorous.

Plum Rootstocks

Pixy A dwarfing rootstock, suitable for bush trees planted 8–10 feet (2.4–3 m) apart.

Not as dwarfing as some of the apple rootstocks.

St Julien A

A semi-vigorous rootstock suitable for bush and half-standards planted 12–15 ft (3.6–4.5 m) apart. Also suited to peaches, nectarines and apricots. Peaches and nectarines are sometimes grafted on to Mussel, but beware: it can sucker badly.

Brompton or Myrobalan B

Suitable for half-standards planted 18–22 ft (5.5–6.5 m) apart. Brompton is also suited to peaches, nectarines and apricots.

Cherry Rootstocks

Colt Semi-vigorous, plant 15–18 ft (4.5–5.5 m) apart.

Malling F12/1 Vigorous, plant 18–24 ft (5.5–7.3m) apart.

Medlars

These are often grafted on to quince and hawthorn rootstocks!

Rootstock rumours

Dwarfing rootstocks are not just a product of the 1990s and the needs of a small garden. Medieval gardens grew the Paradise apple tree, a naturally small tree with sweet, yellow apples. These became very popular and were used as rootstocks for other varieties. Renaissance princes were keen on orchards of these tiny trees. The Stuarts set the dwarf trees in pots around parterres and the Edwardians trained them into arches and tunnels.

Apple varieties have been grafted on to rootstocks of the Siberian crab-apple so that they can grow in colder climates.

By the early 1900s there was a great deal of confusion about the names of the ever-increasing number of dwarfing rootstocks which had come from both Paradise trees and wild crabs. The newly formed research stations sorted them out and selected the best. The rootstocks selected at East Malling were prefixed with an M, and those developed at the John Innes Institute at Merton with MM. The MM series were bred for resistance to root aphid as well as for the size they conferred on the scion.

Stages in grafting top fruit.

(a) Cut the scion into a 4-in (10 cm) length and make a sloping cut on it with the tongue pointing down.

(b) Make a similar cut in the rootstock with the tongue pointing up

(c) Slip the two together like a jigsaw puzzle.

Bind with raffia or polythene tape and cover any exposed part with grafting wax to exclude the air.

GRAFTING

Whip and tongue

Grafting takes a little practice but is easier than some people think – have a go!

First get your top and bottom. The top, or scion, is a twig from the variety of your choice. Cut it off the parent in the dormant season and store it over the winter by putting two-thirds of its length in a box

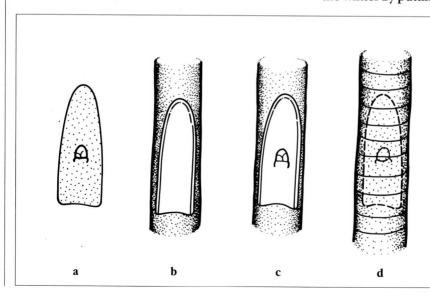

Stages in the budding of top fruit.

(a) Cut off a slice of bud and bark from the parent of the scion.

(b) Cut a similar sliver off the rootstock, leaving a little lip at the base to slot the scion into.

(c) and (d) Slip the two together and bind.

If all goes well, a bud on the scion will grow into a shoot and you will have the tree of your choice.

a   b   c   d

Grafting isn't a new technique – Virgil (70–19 BC) had a thing or two to say about it:

The arts of budding and grafting differ.
In the former, where the buds push out of the bark
And burst their delicate sheaths, just in the knot,
A narrow slit is made. In this an eye
From an alien tree is set and taught to merge
Into the sappy rind.
In the latter, knotless trunks are trimmed, and there
Wedges are driven deep into the wood,
Then fertile slips inserted. Presently
Up shoots a lofty tree with flourishing boughs,
Marvelling at its unfamiliar leaves
And fruits unlike its own.

The Georgics, Book II

Apple blossom, the inside story

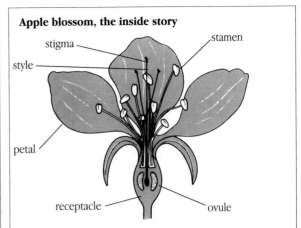

Pollination is the transfer of pollen from the stamens (the boy's bits) to the stigma (the girl's bits). When the pollen has fertilized the female eggs it swells into a fruit containing the seeds, the next generation.

of sand, making sure to get it the right way up! Rootstocks, the bottoms, can be obtained from specialist nurseries or as cuttings from someone who has rootstocks. Graft in March and April when the sap is starting to move, because the aim is to join the cambium (the sap vessels just under the bark), on the rootstock and the scion.

Budding

If your graft didn't work or it is the wrong time of year, try budding in July and August.

Crown grafting

To save space you can always make a family tree by grafting varieties of trees you want on to a similar type of tree you already have. Using this method, two to four scions can be placed on every branch. The more scions per branch the quicker the branch heals over, as each scion draws sap to the part of the crown in which it is growing.

As with whip and tongue, the scion has to be dormant and the sap of the tree you are grafting it on to has to be just starting to rise.

POLLINATION AND POLLINATORS

The next rule is to find the right partner for your fruit tree. To produce good fruit, blossom needs pollinating, or fertilizing. Some fruits are loners and pollinate themselves, others need a mate, and like most of us they are rather fussy about that and will only be pollinated by a specific partner. Some are even all take and no give; these are the male sterile types which do not produce much pollen. So when you buy a tree take its love life into account and ask the nursery whether it has a preference.

If the tree does need a partner, make sure you get one that flowers at the same time. The nursery will help here, because the fruit trees will have been put in numbered pollination groups. Some apple trees, called triploids, are quite fertile on the female side but don't produce much pollen. They need two partners to pollinate them and each other. Pears are fussy too, needing partners that flower at the same time in order to get a good set: Conference will set fruit on its own but it will be a funny shape because it does not have any seeds inside. Many cherries, even though they flower at the same time as each other, are incompatible and will not accept each other's pollen. To be safe go for the self-fertile varieties such as Stella, Sunburst and Cherokee.

It's not all hard graft

Grafting is a way of conserving many of the fruit varieties grown by our ancestors thousands of years ago.

There are some expert grafters around, and so there should be – grafting may have been practised since the third millennium BC. They use the same methods today as they did then!

Most fruit trees in this country have been grafted. The graft mark is usually clearly visible on the trunk.

When a farmer's daughter married a farmer she would take her scionwood to her new husband's orchard, where it was grafted. Traditionally the orchard then became her domain.

If you spot a field of men and women bent earthwards wearing grass skirts, do not be alarmed. This is raffia, tape they use for grafting, tied around their waists. These days polythene is more usually used for grafting.

The inhabitants of the Caucasus and Turkestan cleared wild forests of fruit trees for the cultivation of cereals. They took grafts of the best trees and introduced them on to wild seedling rootstocks in their orchards.

Some types of pears are not compatible (they will not grow on a chosen rootstock). These varieties are often double-worked, with a different variety grafted between the chosen rootstock and scion which is compatible with both.

In Somerset grafts were protected from the elements by 'cat', a paste made from clay and horse dung. Now most grafters use grafting wax and/or grafting tape.

Fruit trees have been known to graft on their own if two branches rub together.

With all these rules, imagine what a fruity newspaper dating agency would look like.

• Cox's Orange Pippin seeks compatible mate, pollination group 3 preferred but will accept candidates from groups 2 or 4 at a push. Kidd's Orange Red and Holstein need not apply, bad past experiences.

• Bramley's Seedling hunting two partners to enable them to start a family. Pollination group 3 types preferred.

• I'm Stella, a sweet cherry, and I don't need anybody but I'm willing to come over to pollinate the other sweet cherries Van and Merchant, who are fussy about their partners.

• Conference pear successfully managing alone would like to meet partner in pollination group B for the occasional day out to improve fruit shape.

• Peach blossom requires rabbit's tail for a bit of slap and tickle.

The go-between

Many fruit blossoms use bees as go-betweens to transfer their pollen. Trees need to be closer than 50 ft (15 m) for good pollination, although bees can fly for up to a quarter of a mile (400 m). Bees tend to go for one type of flower and unfortunately prefer dandelions to apple blossom. To keep the bees on course, growers mow any flowers off the grass in spring when the trees are in blossom. Oil seed rape can also cause a major problem as bees seem to be addicted to it. They go AWOL, flying straight past the orchard to the sickly-smelling yellow flowers. The beekeepers get just as upset as the owner of the fruit trees – rape honey is hard and gritty.

In effect a fruit is a pregnant flower. We usually eat the fruit and that is the end of it. But if you plant the pip you may have a new variety! The fruit's offspring, like our own, are always different from the parent.

BE A GOOD SPORT

Occasionally a fruit branch mutates, producing fruits and possibly growths that are atypical of the rest of the tree. These are sports. Many apple and pear sports have redder fruits, for example Queen Cox and the red sport of William's pear. A sport of a very different kind arose in British Columbia, Canada, when a mutated branch growing straight up with no side shoots was discovered on a Macintosh Red apple tree. When grafted on to a rootstock, the branch grew like a natural cordon with one difference: it did not need pruning. It was named Wijcik after the owner of the orchard. When the apples were bred some passed the characteristic on and soon many varieties of the columnar tree were found on the market. The 'Ballerina trees' as they became known, were very popular, a tree to save space and work. However, they do have a few drawbacks. Some tend to crop every other year and some are more vigorous than originally thought.

RULES FOR THE HARVEST

Growers have to be able to predict apple harvest dates to the day so that they can get pickers in. For commercial cold storage, Cox's on M9 rootstocks are usually ready on 10 September, while on a more vigorous rootstock the picking date for Cox's is around 22 and 23 September. The weather can change the harvest dates by two to three weeks. In the commercial orchard the Agricultural Development and Advisory Service (ADAS) comes to the rescue and works out last-minute harvest dates by testing the starch/sugar content in a sample of apples.

In the garden you can tell when your apples are ready when they taste of sugar and when they come away from the branch easily, too late for the commercial growers to store but just right to sink the teeth into! Another way is just to stand quietly and listen. In an orchard full of ripe Cox's, the apples make a spitting, tapping sound as the ripe pips come away from the centre of the core and hit the side of the cavity.

There are a few rules of thumb during the harvest:

• Fruit from the centre of a tree is often more poorly flavoured than fruit from the outside edges. Pruning helps to minimize this effect, opening the tree up so that light can reach all its parts.

• If there is a light crop, the apples mature early.

• If there is a heavy crop, the apples mature later.

• Leaves make sugar, much of which moves to the fruits. The more leaves per fruit, the fewer days it will take to reach maturity. With apples at least thirty leaves are required per fruit. Too many leaves and the fruit can be too large, too few and the fruit can be too small. For a good crop, follow the rules and thin fruits to about 4 in (10 cm) apart along the branch when they are about ½ in (1 cm) in diameter. Don't leave it too late; the later you thin the less effect it will have.

REGISTRATION

You can get a dog licence, you can get a gun licence, but did you know that you can also get a fruit licence? If you breed a new variety of fruit you can apply for Plant Breeders' Rights. This gives you the exclusive right to sell or propagate material of the protected variety and to authorize others to do so. Holders of rights can claim royalties on sales of protected varieties. Most Plant Breeders' Rights are held by commercial concerns, because there are costs involved with making an application and there is an annual renewal fee once rights are granted.

Testing a new variety takes at least two years and new varieties are compared against the nearest known varieties. Every new variety has to be DUS, that is D=distinct from any other variety, U=uniform, in that all offspring must be the same, and S=stable,

Apple blossom

in that it must remain true to type for several generations when propagated vegetatively. A tall order! When granted, Plant Breeders' Rights last from twenty to thirty years depending on the species. Lots of fruits have rights on them, including many garden favourites such as:

The apples Falstaff, Greensleeves, and Jupiter.

The blackcurrants Ben Alder, Ben Connan, Ben Lomond, and Ben Sarek.

The gooseberries Greenfinch and Invicta.

The raspberries Autumn Bliss, Delight, Glen Clova, Glen Lyon, Glen Moy, Glen Prosen and Leo.

The blackberries Fantasia and Loch Ness.

Many strawberry varieties.

And as for the rules…

The application for Plant Breeder's Rights must be made by the person who bred or discovered the variety, or by his successor in title. It is an offence for a person, knowingly or recklessly, falsely to represent that he is entitled to exercise Plant Breeder's Rights. The fine for so doing is up to £1,000.

The variety must not have been sold to anyone prior to the application.

The new variety's name must be sufficiently distinct from other names, must not deceive or cause confusion as to the characteristic of the plant, and must not be liable to give offence or be otherwise objectionable. The apples 'Lemoen' and 'Irish Peach' and the 'Piss and Piddle' pear are not on the registered list. Just as well.

Gardeners and growers are not allowed to propagate for sale plants which have Plant Breeders' Rights on them unless they have been authorized to do so by the holder of rights. There is no problem if plants are propagated for your own use.

You can do it too

Several private individuals have had success at breeding a new variety and have the Plant Breeding Rights.

Dr Derek Jennings used to breed raspberries and other hybrid berries at the Scottish Crop Research Institute. The tayberry, named after the river Tay, and the blackberry Loch Ness are his doing. Now retired in Kent, he is continuing his work as a private individual. These days he names his fruits after the ladies in his life, and they include Joan Squire, a day neutral autumn raspberry named after his wife; Terry Louise, a day neutral raspberry named after his granddaughter, and Adrienne, a blackberry named after another of his granddaughters. He is also breeding strawberries: one of his young granddaughters Claire Maree is hopeful because she has always wanted to be a strawberry!

GARDEN RIGHTS

Once you have planted up your garden, fruit rules can still affect you. There are a few civil laws even in the back garden, especially where the neighbours are concerned.

If a neighbour's branch overhangs your garden you are well within your rights to cut it off, but you must give it back to them. If it has fruit on it, that is theirs as well, but if the fruit naturally drops off on your side you can keep it. In the law's eyes the neighbour has abandoned it.

You also have a right to light in your garden. If you have enjoyed a certain amount of light to a structure, a window or a glasshouse for twenty years or more, you are entitled to keep a reasonable level of light for normal purposes (within certain guidelines). This stipulation does not cover the garden itself, so if your garden has been cast into shade you cannot complain. If a neighbour erects a building which obstructs that light you are within your rights to tell them to take it down, but if the shade is cast by a neighbour's tree or bush there is nothing you can do, as this is deemed a natural obstruction. So when you plant up your greenhouse with peaches, grapes and early strawberries, check whether your neighbour is thinking of putting up an extension first!

One serious legal case concerned a huge mulberry tree whose roots had spread into a neighbouring garden and caused subsidence of their house. The house owners took the tree owners to court. As both parties knew there was a clay soil and the owners of the tree knew the tree was taking a lot of moisture out of the soil, causing cracking, the judge ruled that the tree owners were responsible for paying a large part of the damages to their neighbours. Let this be a stern warning: check your tree roots! If the top of the tree is getting large then so is the bottom. You may have to root prune (see Chapter 5, Seasons of Fruitfulness) before it is too late! If you are on the receiving end and a neighbour's tree has invaded your garden, be careful. If you poison it deliberately you are liable and will have to pay damages. You are entitled to cut off the tree's roots or branches at the point where they cross the boundary but you must ask the neighbour if they want them back. If the tree has a preservation order on it you are not allowed to touch it. Also, if you live in a conservation area you must tell the council before you cut. They then have six weeks to decide whether to put a tree preservation order on the tree.

TPOs

Local authorities have powers to protect trees by putting tree preservation orders (TPOs) on them. It is an offence to cut down or carry out work on a tree protected by a TPO without the consent of the local authority. If you break the rules the magistrates' court can impose a fine of up to £20,000.

When it comes to fruit trees the law becomes as clear as mud. The consent of the local authority is not always required where the tree concerned is 'a fruit tree cultivated for fruit production, growing or standing on land comprising an orchard or garden'. So if you see someone chopping down an old, rare fruit tree there may be nothing you can do. Fortunately, in some cases, TPOs can be, and are, made in respect of fruit trees, and in this case the local authority's consent would be required. If in doubt, contact your local authority.

RULES FROM TREE TO TABLE

In your own garden you can eat any fruit you like, large or small, with bumps, lumps and all. But if you buy fruit from the shop or supermarket it has to look good and needs to conform to many rules and regulations.

Any fruit that enters the marketing chain must conform to EU quality standards to ensure it is of good quality. It must be sound, clean, of marketable quality, and clearly marked with its quality class, its country of origin and, in some cases, the variety of the produce.

Some of the rules which apply to apples are as follows. Fruit must be:

• Whole and undamaged.

• Free from rotting or deterioration.

• Clean and free from pests and diseases.

• Not so excessively misshapen as to prevent identification of variety.

• Not excessively russeted for the variety.

• Capable of ripening to the appropriate degree of maturity.

Russeting is natural in some varieties and becomes a blemish only when it occurs in excess and disfig-ures the fruit. This is usually due to adverse weather conditions during blossom time or at the fruitlet stage.

EU standards apply to all points in the marketing chain, but many retailers apply their own product specifications over and above the EU minimum quality standards.

Class 1 apples and pears
These must be of good quality, and must have the characteristics typical of the variety. However, the following may be allowed:

• A slight defect in shape.

• A slight defect in development.

• A slight defect in colouring.

• The stem may be slightly damaged.

The flesh must be perfectly sound. Skin defects not liable to impair the general appearance and keeping qualities are, however, allowed for each fruit within the following limits:

• Defects of elongated shape must not exceed 2 cm in length.

• In the case of other defects, the total area affected must not exceed 1 cm^2, with the exception of speckles, which must not extend over more than 0.25cm^2 in area.

• Pears must not be gritty.

Class 2 apples and pears
This class includes fruits which do not qualify for inclusion in higher classes but satisfy the minimum requirements. Defects in shape, development and colouring are allowed provided that the fruit preserves its characteristics. The stem may be missing

provided that the skin is not damaged.

The flesh must be free from major defects. Skin defects are, however, allowed for each fruit within the following limits:

Defects of elongated shape; maximum length 4 cm.

In the case of other defects, the total area affected shall be limited to $2.5cm^2$ with the exception of speckles, which must not extend over more than 1 cm^2 in area.

So the fruits you see in the shops have been through a lot and have all definitely passed their entrance exams.

RIGHT RECIPE, RIGHT FRUIT

Britain is the only country that distinguishes between culinary and dessert apples. All of the hundreds of varieties, be they cookers or eaters, have their own flavours and textures and are suited to certain recipes. Even with raw apples in the fruit bowl, people have their own personal preferences. One gardener will only accept Orlean's Reinette with his cheese and biscuits, because it tastes of walnuts; another prefers Pitmaston Pine Apple, sharp, rich, nutty, honeyed and sweet all at the same time, with a touch of pineapple flavour.

The same applies when the fruit arrives in the kitchen. Many fruit cooks, Patricia Hegarty being no exception, use particular fruit varieties in particular recipes. For example, King's Acre Pippin and Grenadier apples in the salad, May Queen apples in the apple tansy, and grilled honeyed pears with William's or Baron de Mello. The list is endless: here are a few of her favourites.

Patricia's rules

When Patricia grows and picks her own fruit she applies the rules of the three Rs: Regionality, Ripeness and Rapidity.

Regionality Grow the fruits that suit your locality and soil the best, then you will get the true flavour.

Ripeness Pick the fruit just at the peak of ripeness, so that the garden dictates the recipes rather than the kitchen.

Rapidness of pick This applies particularly to soft fruit and stone fruit. Use the fruit as soon as you have picked it to maximize the flavour and nutritional value. Apples and pears are slightly different. The early varieties are best picked and used straight from the tree, but the later varieties should be left and only harvested in October and November. They are then stored in a cool dry place and selected for use, dessert or cooking, as they ripen over an extended season.

To appreciate the fruit at its best, keep the recipes simple. Patricia often uses the raw, perishable soft fruits as a richly-tasting instant sauce, grills her pears at the moment of perfection and cooks a crumble with whole plums fresh from the tree. These quick recipes retain the intensity and strong identity of the fruit.

Demerara Meringues

Using unrefined sugar makes for a richer-flavoured meringue. I dry the demerara sugar in the oven at 200°F (100°C, Gas ¼) for an hour or two, then whiz in the blender. I try always to keep a storage jar of this fine sugar handy.

Makes approximately 32 meringues

8 fl oz (225 ml) egg white
1 lb (500 g) unrefined fine demerara sugar
light, tasteless oil to grease trays

Whisk the egg whites until stiff, using an electric mixer on the highest setting. Spoon in two-thirds of the sugar with the motor still on high. Reduce the speed of the machine and add the remaining sugar.

Preheat the oven to 200°F (100°C, Gas ¼). Oil 2 baking sheets and set out about 16 spoonfuls of meringue on each. Unless you can fit the baking sheets side by side on the same shelf in the oven, put one baking sheet in the centre of the oven for 30 minutes. Then move this down to a lower position and put in the second. It will not harm the second tray of meringues to wait. After another 30 minutes lower the heat as far as possible and continue cooking for at least another 2 hours. Change the baking sheets around to even up the cooking if necessary. When the meringues will slide off the trays with a rustle they are ready to eat or store in a perfectly airtight tin.

Serve sandwiched with fresh thick Jersey cream, surrounded by a strong fruit sauce made from puréed loganberries, raspberries, black currants or strawberries.

Variations
1 Marble the whipped cream with a little of the fruit sauce for a fetching effect and spoon a swag of darker sauce over each meringue half.

2 Fill the meringues with a thick chocolate and chestnut purée, and a dollop of thick whipped cream. Decorate with crumbled marrons glacés.

Grilled Honeyed Pears

Serves 6

6 ripe dessert pears, such as William's or Baron de Mello
juice of 1 lemon
2 oz (50 g) unsalted butter, melted
3 tablespoons honey
ginger ice-cream to serve

Peel the pears, halve and scoop out the core with a teaspoon. Brush all over with lemon juice and lay, cut-side down, on a grill rack – line the tray with aluminium foil. Brush thoroughly with some of the melted butter.

Grill under a medium heat for 10 minutes or so, until the pears begin to brown. Turn the pears over, brush with the remaining butter and drop some honey into each hollow. Grill the pears again until the honey bubbles and the pears are lightly browned. Serve hot with ginger ice-cream.

These pears are also delicious served cold, but they do not keep well for more than an hour or two.

Opposite: Grilled Honeyed Pears

Durondeau Pears Poached in Perry

Perry is a delicious drink made in the south-west of the country from small, hard little perry pears. Usually they are too unpalatable to eat straight off the tree, but after a long hot summer a variety such as Barland can be sweet and juicy, though with that characteristic drying of the tongue lurking underneath, and could be used in this recipe too. Durondeau is a charming little early pear, shiny chestnut red and yellow when ripe, and bottles well.

Serves 6

1½ lb (675 g) Durondeau or small dessert pears
¾ pint (450 ml) perry
4 oz (100 g) sugar
juice of ½ lemon
cinnamon stick (optional)
2 strips orange peel (optional)

Peel and halve the pears, leaving the stalk on one half. Then core them – a melon baller does the job very neatly. Put the pears in a casserole. Warm the perry, dissolve the sugar in it, add the lemon juice and pour over the pears. If you feel the pears lack fragrance, add the cinnamon and/or orange peel. Put the lid on the casserole and bake at 300°F (150°C, Gas 2) for about 30 minutes or until the pears just yield to a fork, depending on how ripe they were in the first place. Concentrate the juice by boiling it down on its own if you wish.

Serve either warm or chilled, with custard or clotted cream.

Apple Snow Cap

I think this recipe makes the traditional baked apple a little more fun. A crisp dessert or multi-purpose apple such as James Grieve or Cox's Orange Pippin is ideal for baking, as it holds its shape and does not burst into a soft flurry.

Serves 6

8 medium-sized apples
4 oz (100 g) dates, chopped lightly
3 tablespoons Calvados
ground cinnamon
2 egg whites
4 oz (100 g) whizzed demerara sugar

Slice off the tops of 6 of the apples and core. Add these off-cuts to the other 2 apples, which have been roughly chopped up whole. Cook these with a splash of water until soft, then purée and sieve.

Stuff the remaining apples with dates and sprinkle on some Calvados and cinnamon. Bake at 400°F (200°C, Gas 6) for about 20 minutes.

Whip the egg whites until stiff, whisk in the sugar, then fold in the apple purée. Pile the apple meringue on the semi-cooked apples and bake for a further 10 minutes or until the meringue has set and browned a little.

Serve hot with traditional English custard or perhaps some cinnamon ice-cream for a special occasion.

Apple and Horseradish Stuffing (for fish)

A lovely stuffing for oily or smoked fish like mackerel and haddock can be made with apple and fresh horseradish. You will need a really sharp apple such as Bramley for this. If you cannot get fresh horseradish, try a couple of teaspoons of English mustard instead.

Serves 6 as a starter

2 Bramley apples, to yield about 8 oz (225 g)
  prepared apple
2 oz (50 g) organic porridge oats
rind and juice of ½ a lemon
about 2 tablespoons grated fresh horseradish root
2 oz (50 g) butter, melted
sea salt
freshly ground black pepper

Peel and core the apples and cut into chunks roughly ½ in (3 cm) square. Cook for about 7 minutes in 3 tablespoons of water. Take off the heat (there should be very little liquid left but the apple should still be fairly firm) and stir in the porridge oats, lemon juice and horseradish and most of the melted butter and seasoning.

Stuff the cavity of the fish with this, or spread it over a fillet and grill or bake.

As an alternative, cut diagonal thin strips of skinned smoked haddock 1½ in (4 cm) long (2 medium-sized haddock fillets should be enough), fold round to make a ring, pin with a cocktail stick and fill lightly with the apple stuffing mixture. Brush with the remaining melted butter and bake in the oven at 425°F (200°C, Gas 7) for 15 minutes, until the stuffing has browned a little. The apple stuffing is quite moist and the fish does not need another sauce. Dress with parsley butter and a sprinkling of paprika.

4
SOFT TOUCH

'Soft' is not the first word that springs to mind when you get attacked by thorns while picking the gooseberries and caught up in the blackberries simply by walking past them. But the rewards make it all worth while: versatile, sumptuous fruits that are delicious eaten straight from the plant or cooked in a pie.

The soft fruits crop for only a few weeks of the year so, delicious or not, why do people bother to grow them? Is it for rivalry or edibility, business or pleasure, or do they hold even more secrets?.

BLACK CURRANTS

Before the eighteenth century the poor black currant was very unpopular. The herbalist Gerard describes the fruit as being 'of a stinking and somewhat loathing savour'. However, when their medicinal properties were discovered they got a reprieve. A sweetened cooked juice from the fruits called 'rob' was taken to cure sore throats, and soon the curative black currant was nicknamed the 'quinsy berry'. During the Second World War there was a big push to pick blackcurrants in order to provide a source of Vitamin C that would keep everyone healthy and this led on to the commercial production of the well-known black currant drink! Black currants are still popular today, but due to their tart taste they are still preferred cooked.

Which variety?
The choice is endless, with different sizes of berries and bushes, disease-resistant varieties and plants that crop from early to late July. One exception is Malling Jet, which produces its small berries on large bushes in late August.

Variety	Season	Comments
Ben Lomond	Mid season	Compact, heavy cropper. Some resistance to frost and gooseberry mildew.
Ben Sarek	Mid season	Very compact bush with frost- and mildew-resistance. Heavy cropper, so needs support so that the branches do not break.
Ben Connan	Mid to late	Very high yields of large fruit on compact plants. Good resistance to mildew and leaf-curling aphid.
Baldwin	Late	Highest Vitamin C content. Compact, suited to small gardens. Needs fertile, well-drained soil. The Hilltop strain is best.

A big-bud-resistant black currant is in the pipeline and hopefully will soon be released.

Cultivation tips
To get a good crop, plant black currants in a sunny position in well-drained, fertile soil with a fairly neutral pH. They fruit best on one-year-old growth, so pruning, as well as generous feeding, aims to produce new growth each year. When you first plant the bush, take drastic action and cut back all the

branches to three buds. This will really get the new shoots going!

When the bush is established, after about five years, cut out about one-third of the old wood each year, after fruiting or in the dormant season to stimulate new growth. Nitrogen is needed to produce these strong new growths, but be careful not to overdo it. Too much nitrogen gives rise to sappy growth which is susceptible to disease. One old wives' tale suggests burying an old leather boot under your black currant bush. This is not as daft as it sounds: leather provides slow-release nitrogen which feeds the plant slowly over several years. If your boots are not ready for the bin yet, feathers or hoof and horn will have the same effect. Alternatively, apply a slow-release fertilizer in early February followed by a mulch of well-rotted compost or manure.

Pest and disease control

Birds Net bushes against bud-biting bullfinches in the winter and fruit-filching blackbirds and thrushes in the summer.

Frost Cover with hessian or fleece on frosty nights if the bushes are in flower.

Sawfly/magpie moth If you go down one morning and your bushes have been stripped, literally, then it is probably the work of caterpillars. The easiest solution is to pick them off or, in the case of the magpie moth, spray with *Bacillus thuringiensis*. This biological control is specific to caterpillars of moths and butterflies.

Currant aphids These suck plant sap and can spread viral diseases. Treat with soft soap and derris.

Big bud mites These mites cause buds on black currants to swell. They also spread reversion disease, which reduces cropping. Once you've got this the bush has had it, so you need to nip this problem in the bud, literally. Cut off and burn big buds as soon as you see them. The jostaberry is resistant.

Leaf spot This fungal disease shows as spots on leaves, which fall early. Treat with a copper fungicide such as Burgundy mixture.

Gooseberry mildew Black currants get this too: grow resistant varieties and refer to gooseberries for cure!

Gooseberries are packed in special boxes for the show

The gooseberry clubs

In the past gooseberries were always more popular than blackcurrants. Initially they were used in the kitchen and to cure ailments: gooseberry juice was used to reduce inflammations, and as early as the sixteenth century they were recommended to plague victims, to help those troubled with 'hot, burning ague'.

In the seventeenth century many new types were selected from seedlings: greens, reds and even a 'blew', which looked more like a small damson. Nearly every garden in the land had a gooseberry bush, and England became known as the gooseberry capital of the world. Two of the earliest varieties to be named, Hedge-hog and Early Green Hairy, still exist today.

By the eighteenth century growing and breeding gooseberries had become a popular and competitive garden hobby along with pigeon-racing and giant leek cultivation. In 1740 the handloom weavers and other workers in Lancashire started the annual gooseberry shows, competing to grow the heaviest berry, and in 1786 the Gooseberry Growers register was set up, listing the weights and names of the best and biggest fruits. The gooseberry competitions soon spread to other counties and are still going on today! Competitors have devised their own formulas to get some huge fruits. They select the best varieties, use secret compost recipes, severely prune the bushes, and pick off most of the fruits so that only three or four are left to grow to an immense size. The plants are treated like kings and fiercely protected from pests, diseases and bad weather.

In Goostrey, Cheshire, tension runs high the night before the show. The chosen gooseberries are sealed in special boxes and competitors wait in anticipation for the big day. When one of the growers was asked if he ate his berries, he replied, 'Certainly not, that's murder, it would be like eating your children!'

The record for the largest gooseberry is 39 penny-weight and 19 grains (about 2¼ oz/65 g). The winning berry was a Montrose, grown by Kelvin Archer for the Marton Show in Cheshire in 1993. The variety was originally raised by Frank Carter from Cheshire in 1971.

As with the wassailers, the gooseberry growers have their own song:

Come all ye jovial gardeners, and listen unto me,
Whilst I relate the different sorts of winning gooseberries,
This famous institution was founded long ago,
That men might meet, and drink, and have a gooseberry show.

So come all jovial gardeners, let's merry be:
We'll sing and dance, we've all a chance, but the London is for me.

There's Dan's Mistake and Catherina, Magenta and Careless too,
Clayton, Drill and Telegraph, Antagonist and Peru;
Mount Pleasant, Plunder, King of Trumps, Australia and Railway,
Ploughboy, High Sheriff and Gretna Green; but the Bobby wins the day.

And so on… The song is just like a national gooseberry register set to music.

GOOSEBERRIES

Gooseberries herald the start of the fruit season and bring the first taste of summer. The gooseberry features in many well-known sayings and there are many ideas as to why it was so named, so take your pick:

The berries were once used to make a sauce to go with goose.

The thorns on gooseberries resemble a goose's foot.

Gooseberries are prickly, and the name may have derived from gorseberry.

In Cheshire, Lancashire and Yorkshire they were called 'Feaberrie', in Norfolk 'Feabes' and in Scotland 'Grozer'.

The sayings 'to be a gooseberry' and 'found under the gooseberry bush' may have come from the French for gooseberry: *groseille à maquereau*. *Maquereau* is French for pimp! *Une femme grosse* is the term given to a pregnant woman in France – charming! This may have led to the saying that babies come from under the 'gooseberry bush'.

Some say *groseille à maquereau* indicates that gooseberries were used in a sauce with mackerel.

The National Collections

Thanks to the gooseberry shows, about 3,000 named gooseberries have been recorded over the years. Many of these were synonyms and others have been lost. Today three National Collections of gooseberries exist: at Granada Arboretum, Jodrell Bank, with 200 cultivars; Mr Harbutt's nursery at Roughham Hall, with 140 cultivars; and, last but by no means least, at Brogdale Horticulture Trust in Faversham, which holds many of the National Fruit Collections, including 155 cultivars of gooseberry.

It is vital to conserve all these fruit varieties not only for our heritage but for their hidden virtues.

They may contain genes that can be used in future breeding programmes for pest- and disease-resistance and ability to grow in different conditions. The aim of the fruit collections is therefore to create a gene bank which breeders can draw on in the future. The gooseberry shows, by having a bit of fun, have helped to build on this important genetic resource.

Varieties

Variety	Season	Comment
The Greens		
Keepsake	Early July	Almost white when ripe, best picked young and green in late May for the first fruit tarts of the season.
Careless	Mid-July	Popular but susceptible to mildew.
Invicta	Late July	Vigorous and thorny, but a heavy cropper with good flavour and mildew resistance.
Greenfinch	Late July	Cooker, some resistance to mildew.
Lancer	Early August	Big, vigorous and tasty.
The Reds		
May Duke	Early July	Vigorous. Picked green for cooking.
Whinham's Industry	Late July	Good in poor soils and shade. Susceptible to mildew.
Lancashire Lad	Late July	Needs good soil.
Lord Derby	Early August	Small bush, very dark fruits.
Captivator	Early August	Sweet, red fruits. Almost thornless.
The Whites		
Whitesmith	Late July	Vigorous and tasty.
Langley Gage	Late July	Very scrummy.
The Yellows *This group contains some of the richest flavours, and the wine made from the berries tastes almost like champagne.*		
Golden Drop	Mid-July	Small bush, when ripe, as good as any grape.
Leveller	Late July	Large tasty fruits.

Grow your own

Gooseberry bushes were traditionally grown in orchards between the trees and used to produce jam and also pectin for other purposes. These days, the consumer seems to have gone off gooseberry jam and the commercial gooseberry is in decline. So the best way to get a good gooseberry is to grow your own. They are well worth the effort and can be used for a wide range of culinary delights, from pies to freshly squeezed gooseberry juice, a refreshing and very underrated drink.

Planting and training

Plant gooseberries in a sheltered spot, 5 ft (1.5 m) apart, in a well-drained, slightly acid soil. After planting, remove branches less than 6 in (15 cm) above the old soil mark because gooseberries like to grow on a short stem or leg. This increases air movement around the plant, reducing the risk of disease, and of course enables you to put the baby under it! Remove any suckers that grow up from the base.

Gooseberries can be trained like a miniature dwarf bush apple tree (See Chapter 1, page 13). The aim is to produce a goblet-shaped framework. Cut back to outward-facing buds if your bush tends to grow upright and vice versa if the bush has a drooping habit. Plants can also be grown as cordons (See Chapter 8, page 155).

When the bush is established, prune for fruit. Gooseberries fruit on spurs on the older wood and at the base of the previous summer's lateral growth. If the bush has been neglected, remove dead, diseased and crossing-over branches and growth that crowds out the centre.

Pests, diseases and problems

Birds and frost See blackcurrants.

Gooseberry sawflies/magpie moths See black currants. An old market gardener in Bath used to call cuckoos to his bushes to eat the caterpillars, and swore by this method. Cuckoos can eat their own weight in insects a day! If you have no cuckoos and

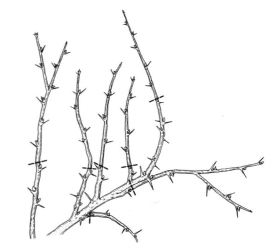

Winter pruning of gooseberries
In the winter, cut back leaders by half and cut back the laterals to two buds. This will encourage fruiting spurs on the old wood.

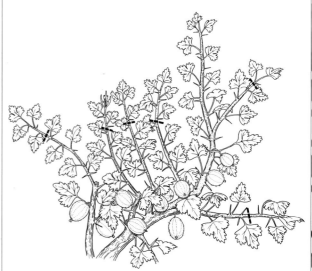

Summer pruning of gooseberries
In early July, prune all the laterals (but not the leaders) produced that season to five leaves. This removes aphids and opens up the bush.

do not have time to pick the caterpillars off, a last resort is to spray with derris or pyrethrum as soon as the small larvae are found.

Aphids See black currants.

Capsid bugs These suck sap and cover the leaf with small holes. Treat as for aphids.

American gooseberry mildew This debilitating disease can rapidly reduce the fruit to brown fuzzy balls after starting as innocent-looking white powdery patches on new shoots. Prevention is better than cure. Choose mildew-resistant varieties, avoid planting in damp, shady or overcrowded spots, and keep the bushes open and airy with suitable pruning. Avoid overfeeding with nitrogen.

As a cure, if it is not too late, spray with sulphur except on sulphur shy varieties such as Leveller, Lord Derby, Early Sulphur, Careless and Roaring Lion. If in doubt, spray one shoot, and if the leaves go brown or drop off forget it. Some gardeners use bicarbonate of soda, at ½ oz per gallon (5 g/l) as a preventative spray and 2 oz per gallon (20 g/l) as a curative spray. This practice cannot be recommended here because the 'Control of Pesticides Regulations 1986' requires that any substance used as a pesticide must be tested and approved by the Ministry of Agriculture for safety and efficacy. Some home-made sprays may be safe but others could be toxic. If you do try bicarbonate of soda it is at your own risk.

Leaf spot See black currants.

Grey mould Causes the branches to die back. Prune out and keep the bush goblet-shaped to let in air.

THE JOSTABERRY AND THE WORCESTERBERRY

The jostaberry is a cross between a black currant and a gooseberry and looks like a small black gooseberry. Like many hybrids it exhibits vigour and is strong and fruitful. But how do you prune it? The fruits are borne on the base of the one-year-old shoots and on the older wood, so the plant can be grown and trained like black currants or standard gooseberries. One major benefit is that you can prune it without gloves, because it is thornless like its black currant parent. It is also resistant to gall mite, mildew and leaf spot.

The worcesterberry is a small, purple, very thorny gooseberry, and is resistant to gooseberry mildew.

RED AND WHITE CURRANTS

Red currants have been around as long as gooseberries and have been eaten raw, used in savoury and sweet dishes, and made into vinegar and wine. Gardeners even devised ways of extending the growing season, by planting them under glass against a south wall to get an early spring crop, and planting against a north wall to get crops as late as the autumn. In the days before freezers, they were stored by filling clean bottles with dry, just ripened berries, corking them and stacking them upside down in sand.

Pick of the crop
The red currant season goes from early July to mid August. They are well worth planting even as ornamentals, with fruits like red jewels.

Variety	Season	Comment
The Reds		
Jonkheer van Tets	Early	Heavy cropper with good flavour. Makes a good cordon.
Laxton's No 1	Early	Heavy cropper with good flavour. Flowers late, so slightly frost-resistant.
Red Lake	Mid-season	Heavy cropper with good flavour, easy to pick.
Stanza	Late	Heavy cropper, large berries, good flavour. Resistant to leaf spot.
Redstart	Late	Heavy cropper, tart flavour.
The Whites (a sport of the red)		
White Grape	Early	Moderate cropper with very good flavour.
White Versailles	Early	Good cropper with good flavour. Can be eaten raw.

Looking after your currants
If you can cope with a gooseberry bush, then you can cope with a red or white currant. They are planted,

spaced and trained in much the same way. When they go red, leave them on the plant for a few days before picking so that they develop a full flavour. Don't forget to net them, because the birds won't wait. The pests and diseases are similar to those for black currants and gooseberries. In addition watch out for:

Currant red blister aphid Treat as for other aphids.

Coral spot Cut out and burn any branches affected by this fungus.

RASPBERRIES: TIPS FROM THE HIGHLANDS

Up beyond Hadrian's Wall the raspberry is the pick of the fruit, but it deserves a place in any garden wherever you live. It doesn't take up that much room, crops soon after planting, and treated right can give heavy yields for twelve years or more.

The Scottish connection
Wild raspberries have always been associated with Scotland, pips having been found in glacial deposits in Edinburgh and the Scottish Lowlands. The name raspberry comes from their old name 'raspis', referring to the scratchy thorns. The real link between raspberries and Scotland goes back to the end of the First World War, when local Scottish landowners gave 10 acre (4 ha) parcels of land to each returning soldier to get them reinstated. Most of them grew raspberries, which enjoyed the cool, moist climate, and this started a thriving industry in the area. Scottish raspberries are renowned for their flavour, possibly due to the slow ripening this far north. The cold winds in Scotland also reduced risk of infection from virus diseases, because the aphids that transmit viruses simply don't like the wind up them. In the late 'fifties raspberries were taken from Scotland to Covent Garden on the steam train, the Raspberry Special. The area still produces more raspberries than anywhere else in the world, and within 30 miles

The Raspberry Special on the move

(48 km) of Dundee there are now 140 raspberry growers with 6,200 acres (2,500 ha) of raspberries. Today over 90 per cent of them go for processing.

> In the nineteenth century many soft fruits were grown in the market gardens around Isleworth and Brentford, in Middlesex. Raspberries for processing were bumped up in carts to London, where they were transformed into brandy, vinegar, sweets and pastries. The fruits bruise very easily, and those to be sold in the London markets for dessert needed a more gentle mode of transport. Women were paid 3s 6d to carry the fruit 10 miles (16 km). Each managed to carry a 12 gallon (55 litre) load in a basket, on their heads, and cover the journey in two hours.

Where do they all come from?
The first raspberry varieties were accidental seedlings. Then the nurserymen started to breed them and finally the Research Stations, East Malling and the Scottish Crop Research Institute, moved in. They have produced the majority of the well-known and disease-resistant types prefixed with the name 'Malling' or 'Glen'. SCRI have a huge germplasm collection of over 3,000 raspberries and hybrid species from all over the world from which to choose the parents. So far only ten have been used in breed-

ing: what potential for the future!

You can easily have a go at breeding your own. The raspberry blossom has both male and female parts, so the first step is to decide on a good mother and emasculate the flower, that is castrate it, by removing the male parts. Then pollinate her with pollen from the chosen father and put a bag over her head to prevent other suitors getting in. Several weeks later you can remove, dry and sow the seeds from the fruit, and three years down the road you will know if you have found a winner.

SCRI do this on a big scale, and Ronnie McNicol has the job of tasting all the fruits from potential new varieties. Each summer he samples over 5,000 plants, amounting to over 11 lb (5 kg) of raspberries a week. Apparently it has a far greater effect on his digestion than muesli! His latest children are Glen Magna, Glen Ample, Glen Rosa and Glen Shee, known as the MARS series, so nicknamed because they are 'out of this world'. Glen Magna, a dark red, extremely large-fruited late cultivar, is proving popular in the garden already.

Ronnie often compares raspberry breeding to the car industry. When cars were first invented there were vast improvements in a short time, from the cartwheels to the tyre, to the introduction of brakes and suspension. Now there are minor changes, different colours and different shapes. The same goes for the raspberry and hybrids: the changes nowadays are minor but the consumer always wants the new model. Everyone has their favourites: some like to eat them fresh, some like to make jams, juices and wines. Others like to pick raspberries for as long a season as possible.

Choice raspberries

Summer fruiters

Glen Moy	Early to late July	Vigorous, no spines, good yields, some aphid and virus resistance. No good on heavy, wet clays
Glen Garryn	Early to late July	Large , firm pale fruits of good flavour.
Malling Jewel	Early to late July	Excellent flavour, yields not brilliant. Compact and not easily affected by virus.
Glen Prosen	Mid-July to mid-August	Spine-free. Resistant to virus and aphids. Good cropper if on good soil.
Malling Admiral	Mid-July to mid-August	Excellent. Spine-free, disease-resistant, good flavour, high yields.
Joy	Mid-July to late August	High yields, good flavour, aphid resistant, spiny!
Leo	Late July to late August	Aphid- and botrytis-resistant. Good flavour, low yields.

Autumn fruiting

Autumn Bliss	Mid-August to September	Good flavour and yields. Sturdy and needs little support. There is a yellow sport called Allgold.
Ruby	Mid-August to October	High quality berries with good flavour.

The basics

Despite the connection with the cool north, it is best to plant raspberry canes in a sheltered site, protected from the wind in sun or semi-shade, although autumn raspberries need full sun. The soil needs to be well-drained but moisture-retentive and slightly acidic (pH 6.5–6.7). To get the right soil conditions dig a trench 18 in (45 cm) deep and 3 ft (1 m) wide and fork a 3 in (7.5 cm) layer of well-rotted manure into the bottom. To give the canes a bit more of a boost, mix some general fertilizer with the topsoil when you put it back in.

Plant the canes 2–3 in (5–7.5 cm) deep, and spread out the roots along the trench to encourage new canes (spawn). Plant about 15 in (38 cm) apart in rows 6 ft (1.8 m) apart. Then cut the canes to a bud at 12 in (30 cm).

As the plants grow, control annual weeds by mulching with organic matter; don't lay it on too thickly because the new canes need to be able to grow up through each year. Feed with potash in late winter for fruit and with nitrogen in spring for cane growth.

In a dry year water is as important as food. Water when the fruits start to change colour, to help the fruits swell and promote the growth of the new canes for the next season. Try to avoid splashing water on the canes because this can lead to fungal diseases.

Support your local raspberry

Like all of us at one time or another, raspberries need a bit of support. There are two well-tried and trusted methods. With the post and wire system, canes are tied to horizontal wires with soft string. This is suited to summer raspberries. The double fence system, suited to both summer and autumn raspberries, consists of growing the canes up between 2 sets of wires. (See diagram below.)

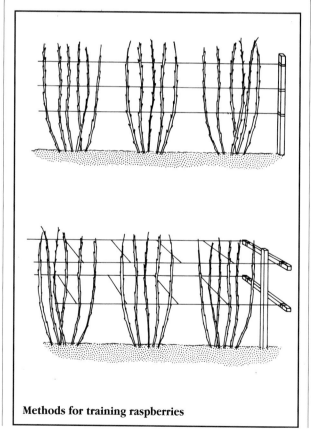

Methods for training raspberries

Pruning

Summer raspberry canes grow one year, bear fruit in the second and then die; new canes take their place. After picking simply cut out the old fruited canes and tie in the new canes which will fruit the following year. In February cut the tips back to 6 in (15 cm) above the top wire to encourage the production of fruit along the length of the cane.

Autumn raspberries fruit on the current season's growth in late summer. Pruning these could not be easier. All the canes are simply cut to ground level in February.

Trouble shooting

Raspberry beetle You don't want these appearing on top of your raspberries and cream. Eggs laid in the blossoms develop into grubs which feed on the fruit. Young fruitlets can be sprayed with derris at petal fall, but this should be done after dusk to minimize damage to bees. Fork very carefully around the canes in the dormant season to expose overwintering adults and pupae to birds.

Aphids Grow resistant varieties. Spray with soft soap or derris.

Raspberry moths Look out for the withering shoots in which the moth caterpillars tunnel in March. Cut out and burn.

Leafhoppers These sap suckers cause a white mottling on the leaves. Control as for aphids.

Virus Appears as yellow mottling or blotching of the leaves. Remove and burn canes. Plant on a new site with virus-resistant cultivars.

Spur blight Purple, then silver blotches appear around the nodes on the canes. Spray with Bordeaux mixture when buds are ½ in (1 cm) long. Remove and burn severe cases.

Cane spot All parts show purple spots then elliptical grey areas with purple edges. Treat as for spur blight.

Cane blight General withering of leaves and dieback of shoots. Cut out dead canes and treat as for spur blight.

BLACKBERRIES AND HYBRID BERRIES

Raspberries are fairly controlled, but what about their aggressive, thorny relation the blackberry? Try Loch Ness, a blackberry that acts like a raspberry. The stout, thornless stems are semi-erect, requiring little or no support. There are also many blackberry/ raspberry crosses around. The original cross, the loganberry, was made by J. H. Logan of Santa Cruz, California, in 1881. SCRI now have a better choice of parents, and Dr Jennings has come up with some promising results such as the tayberry and the tummelberry.

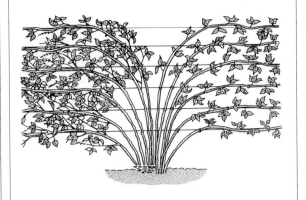

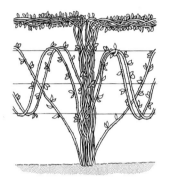

Hybrid discipline, caning and training

Blackberries and hybrids need similar conditions to raspberries. They can put on a lot of growth each year and need discipline from the word go. To increase cropping and to maximize use of space, train them along horizontal wires spaced 12 in (30 cm) apart. Fruit is borne on the canes that were produced the previous year. To save getting in a muddle, train the one-year-old canes one way and the new canes the other way. In the autumn, cut out canes that have fruited. The new canes will become the fruiting canes in the next season. For the more experienced trainer, the canes can be trained in curves or complete circles to check sap flow and stimulate fruiting.

Which one?

Blackberries

Bedford Giant	Late July to August	Early and very vigorous. Large, sweet fruits but no tang.
Ashton Cross	August to September	Heavy cropper. Good flavour. Wiry-stemmed.
Fantasia	Late July to August	Very thorny, very vigorous, very big and very tasty. One plant will provide enough fruit to last until the next year, but you need body armour when you come to prune it.
Loch Ness	Late August and September	Semi erect thornless stems. Good yields.
Oregon Thornless	Late August to late September	Thornless. Decorative leaves.

Hybrids

Tayberry	Mid-July to August	Raspberry x blackberry. The best hybrid berry. There is a virus-free Medana clone. Sweeter than the loganberry. The tayberry is not as hardy as the tummelberry.

Tummelberry	Mid-July to August	Tayberry x Tayberry seedling. This was bred for cold-resistance but in doing so some of the tayberry flavour was lost, and it tastes more like a loganberry. Upright hairy canes.
Loganberry	Mid-July to August	Raspberry x black berry. Good cropper, LY59 is an improvement on the original. The thornless type, L654, is just as tasty. Loganberries win hands down in the jam stakes.
Boysenberry	July and August	Loganberry x black berry x raspberry. Drought-resistant, blackberry taste.
Japanese wineberry	August	*Rubus phoenicolasius* Very decorative but low-yielding bland berries.
Veitchberry	August to September	Raspberry x blackberry. An older hybrid, strong grower, heavy cropper.

The wild ones

There are over 2,000 microspecies of wild blackberry. It's all down to their promiscuous habit of cross-pollinating and to the birds which spread the seeds in their droppings. Keep your eyes open – you may discover a variety in the hedgerow that is worthy of cultivation. The blackberry Fantasia was discovered as a chance seedling on a London allotment. The plants are a haven for wildlife and attract emperor moths, ringlet and gatekeeper butterflies, wasps, flies, spiders and snails. The fruits get a little too attractive to bugs and maggots towards the end of the season. Folklore states that it is unlucky to eat blackberries after 29 September, as the devil is said to have spat on them.

In the past

Herbalists used blackberries and their juices to treat eye and mouth infections. This would really give you a black eye!

Blackberry juice was added to grape wines to sweeten them.

Blackberries were used to protect the superstitious against evil runes.

Desiccated fruits were used as a remedy for dysentery.

In the nineteenth century they were known as bumblekites and scaldheads because children who ate too many were told they would get a disease in their hair.

Rooting tips

Blackberries and their hybrids are unusual in that their tips start to form roots when they bend earthwards. It is a very effective and rapid way of spreading. In New Zealand they say there are only two blackberry plants, one on the South Island and one on the North Island. To propagate them, bury a bent-over tip under 6 in (15 cm) of soil in July. By the following spring it will have rooted and can be severed from the parent and transplanted.

Pests and diseases

As a raspberry relative, blackberries and their hybrids get the same problems: raspberry beetle, aphids, leafhoppers, cane spot, spur blight and virus, so treat as for the raspberry.

PROSTRATE RASPBERRIES, THE EDIBLE GROUND COVER

The Arctic raspberry is perennial, prostrate, has pretty purple flowers and is deciduous with beautiful autumn colour. The fruits are delicious despite being small and fiddly to pick.

They are easy to grow. Plant in a sunny, sheltered spot, in well-drained moisture-retentive soil enriched with well-rotted compost. Good varieties include Anna, Linda, Beata, Sophia, and Valentina, all clones of a type of Arctic raspberry known as the All-fieldberry. Plant more than one type, as they need to cross-pollinate. Although plants only live for five to six years, they can easily be replaced from the rooted tips.

For an edible, evergreen, weed-suppressing, shade-tolerant, wildlife-friendly, non-invasive plant, try *Rubus calycinoides 'Emerald Carpet'*. It has dark, crinkly leaves, grows in partial shade, is attractive to bees and produces fruit like a yellow raspberry.

Rubus illecebrosus has bright red fruits like raspberries, which although boring when raw taste good when cooked. Also the plant serves as a burglar deterrent: it is a vigorous, creeping, herbaceous plant with prickly leaves and stems about 12in (30cm) tall.

THE STRAWBERRY

Fragaria x ananassa

Strawberries are delicious, and can even be grown without a garden, in pots, hanging baskets and window-boxes. Each plant will yield between 8 and 20 oz (225–600g) of strawberries, the best crop coming from well-established two-year-old plants.

The wood strawberry (*Fragaria vesca*) has been with us since before the Iron Age, and comes in red, white, yellow and green. Next came the alpine strawberry (*Fragaria vesca semperflorens*) from Switzerland and the Hautbois (*Fragaria elatior*), with its small, aromatic fruits, from the woods of Central Europe. It was not until the nineteenth century that the larger fruiting varieties arrived.

Love at first sight

Our large strawberry fruits arose from a love affair between a Virginian and a Chilean. The Virginian strawberry (*Fragaria virginiana*) with its small, pointed fruits, was brought to Europe in the seventeenth century. Nearly 100 years later a French naval officer, Captain Frezier, discovered a large fruiting species in Chile (*Fragaria chiloensis*) which he brought back home.

These two strawberry species, which had always been separated by the Equator, were accidentally brought together by a Frenchman, Duchesne, in the eighteenth century. Strawberries cross-pollinate but different species are not always compatible. An unsuspecting insect carried some pollen from a Virginian's flower to a Chilean's flower. It was love at first sight because the strawberries each had the same number of chromosomes and so could breed. Duchesne found that the offspring had beautiful large fruits but did not get any further because he was cut short by the French Revolution.

There is, however, a happy ending. The strawberries finally got together in England in the late eighteenth century, when Thomas Andrew Knight hybridized them, producing varieties such as Elton and Downton. Michael Keen , a market gardener at Isleworth, also raised seeds from the Chilean which had probably once again crossed with the Virginian (can't keep these two apart!). The result: Keen's Imperial and Keen's Seedling, which caused a real sensation and went on to become the parent of many other varieties. So next time you eat some strawberries spare a thought for their great-great-grandparents, the American species that made it all possible.

The Arctic raspberry

What's in a name?

Strawberries were so called long before they were strawed up. In Anglo-Saxon the strawberry was called '*streabariye*', referring to the runners which allowed the plant to stray. The name may also have originated from the old practice of threading these berries on straws of grass. Today, children still pick wild strawberries and collect their straws of berries to take back home.

Varieties

Now there are many strawberry varieties on the market, all with their own virtues. The range gives you a chance to go for a choice of flavours, disease-resistant varieties and continuity.

Summer fruiting, also known as short day varieties

These crop between late May and early July and the large fruits come in a single flush.

Variety	Season	Notes
Honeoye	Late May to mid-June	Large, attractive shiny red fruits. Excellent flavour, good for forcing.
Elvira	Early to mid-June	Heavy yield, large glossy red berries. Good flavour, ideal under glass.
Cambridge Favourite	Mid-June to mid-July	Widely grown, reliable good cropper. Good disease-resistance. Fair-flavoured medium-sized berries.
Elsanta	Mid-June to mid-July	Crops well. Attractive, glossy, large fruits with good flavour. Widely grown commercially but susceptible to disease.
Hapil	Mid-June to early July	Excellent flavour. Crops well on light soils. Tolerates some drought. Susceptible to verticillium wilt.
Redgauntlet	Mid-June to mid-July	Heavy cropper with medium to large fruits of moderate flavour. Good under cloches, often bearing a second crop in the autumn.
Tamella	Early June. Mid- to late June thereafter	High yields; large conical fruits. Fair flavour, in first year good for forcing. Does well in the north.
Rhapsody	End June to end July	Crops well; large bright red fruits of good flavour. Vigorous, with some resistance to soil borne diseases.
Symphony	End June to end July	Heavy cropper. Shiny orange, red berries. Excellent flavour. Good resistance to soil-borne diseases.
Tenira	Early to late July	Medium-sized firm fruits of excellent flavour, ideal for dessert and preserves. Moderate to heavy cropper, good disease-resistance.

Symphony strawberries

Two new ones soon to hit the market are Eros, a disease-resistant form of Elsanta, which the commercial growers should love, and Emily, a new very early variety.

Potatoes have eyes but strawberries can see too!
Strawberries and other plants contain a chemical called phytochrome that tells them whether it is night or day and how long the day is. The early summer-bearing strawberries need short days in order to form flower buds; the day neutral varieties don't!

Perpetuals, (also known as everbearers, day neutrals, autumn fruiting or even remontant)
These strawberries, although maybe not as tasty as the summer fruiters, are useful for extending the season because they crop in flushes from summer into autumn.

Aromel Excellent flavour, but only moderate cropper. Susceptible to mildew.

Rapella Good flavour, heavy cropper. Susceptible to mildew. Earliest of perpetuals.

Mara des Bois Combines flavour of woodland strawberry with size of English summer varieties. Resistant to mildew.

Horticulture Research International, East Malling have just brought out a couple more. Tango, which will be the earliest ever bearer, two weeks ahead of Rapella, and Calypso, also fairly early, with all round disease-resistance and a good flavour. The plants have a compact habit and runner freely.

Alpine strawberries
These smaller strawberries crop from midsummer to late autumn. Although they are sweet-tasting, they are small and not very juicy and only crop well the first year. Plant in the spring, grown from seeds sown in the autumn. After that they will seed themselves and pop up in all kinds of unexpected places. Suitable varieties include Alexandria, Baron Solemacher, Productive, and Yellow Wonder.

Planting

Plant strawberries in late summer to crop the following year. You can also plant in April, but you should remove the flowers in the first year to let the plants get established. Choose a sunny sheltered site with well-drained, fertile, slightly acid soil. Add some well-rotted manure to hungry soils. Avoid planting in frost pockets or land that has grown a lot of potatoes, other strawberries or tomatoes, because all these plants are susceptible to verticillium wilt and eelworms.

Planting strawberries

Start by using plants that are certified virus-free, then you can propagate your own for 3–4 years. When planting, take out a good-sized hole, form a pyramid of soil in the bottom of the hole and spread the roots out over it so that the base of the crown is in contact with the soil (a). Fill the hole with soil and firm well in with your hands to prevent the crown of the plant shaking around in the wind. Water well and keep down the weeds. Black plastic mulches will give earlier strawberries as they warm up the soil, while white mulches will delay cropping. This also smothers weeds.
Plant the strawberries 14 in (35 cm) apart in rows 18 in (45 cm) apart, with every other row 30 in (75 cm) apart (b). If planted too close, competition will lead to smaller fruit, delayed ripening and build up of pests and disease. One way of keeping the plants under control is to plant single rows at the edge of vegetable beds and rotate them. Every year remove runners and start a new edge. After 3 years remove the parent plants, because the fruit tends to become smaller and the plants more susceptible to pest and disease. When the old plants are removed, leave the area free of strawberries for 3 years.

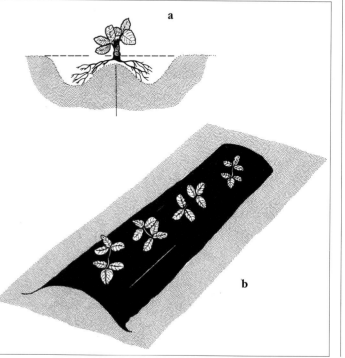

Growing, before and after picking

Feed in spring with a general fertilizer (2 oz per sq yd/50 g per sq m) and give them liquid potash feeds in the summer. As the fruits develop, 'straw up your plants', tucking the straw under the trusses of fruit. Don't do this before the fruits have started to touch the ground, because the straw reduces ground temperature, increasing the risk of frost damage and delaying cropping. If you don't have any straw use bark, old carpets or leaf mould. Wood chips are less useful because they rob the soil of nitrogen and can also taint the fruit.

When they are fruiting, cover the plants with nets to keep off the birds. To get as long a season as possible, choose varieties that crop at different times. Some growers phase the planting of strawberries, such as Elsanta, to extend the season. The plants are cold-stored until needed, then planted out between May and mid-summer. They crop sixty days after planting. One way of getting late strawberries is to cover the plants with straw in January. This keeps the ground cold and keeps the light off the plants. The straw is 'tickled off' in April, because the plants need good light by this time of year. Tips for early crops are given in Chapter 5, Seasons of Fruitfulness.

After fruiting, remove debris and old leaves, cutting 4 in (10 cm) above the crown, which must be kept intact. Also remove runners, leaving a few healthy specimens pegged into pots of compost to form next year's row. Use only the first one on the runner string to propagate new plants.

Pests and diseases

Aphids Control greenfly and strawberry aphid with soft soap sprays.

Spider mites Several mites attack strawberries. With red spider mites the leaves turn pale or bronze, with minute mites on the underside. These can be controlled by the predator *Phytoseiulus persimilis*. The strawberry mite is much more difficult to control and is a far more serious pest. Young leaves turn brown and the older leaves crinkle up. Infected plants should be removed and burnt.

Strawberry seed beetles These ½ in (1 cm) long grey beetles simply love strawberry seeds and mess up the fruit when they eat them. Woodlice and ground beetles, which are usually very useful predators, are also partial to strawberries. Keep the plants weed-free and clear away old leaves and debris to keep the pests at bay. Beetles can be trapped in jam jars sunk up to the neck in the soil and pheromone traps are available to catch woodlice.

Wireworms and leatherjackets These soil-dwelling creatures devour strawberry roots. Running chickens or quails on the ground before planting helps, because they are very partial to a grub or two.

Vine weevils Adult weevils make small notches in the leaves but the larvae eat roots, sometimes all of them! If your plant wilts and when tugged comes away in your hand it is likely that it has either wilt or the dreaded weevil. The persistent soil insecticides once used to control them commercially have been withdrawn for safety reasons. A biological control, containing microscopic nematode worms and bacteria, is now available to both amateurs and professionals. It specifically kills vine weevil but will only work if the soil temperature is above 50°F (10°C).

The new strawberry variety, Symphony, is showing tolerance to the evil weevil. It has shallow, vigorous roots and can also survive with fewer roots than other varieties. Sometimes (you can't have everything) if a pest or disease-resistance is bred in, the flavour or size is bred out. But at the moment Symphony seems to have high yields, good flavour and disease-resistance too. A super strawberry?

Slugs What is worse than finding a slug in your strawberry? Finding half a … no, that's too revolting to mention! Attract predators such as frogs and hedgehogs. Lay traps full of beer, pour salt on them, go out at night and squash them, get some ducks – they love slugs (and strawberries!). And if you are still having problems, try Nemaslug. Yet another biological control, this nematode worm kills slugs. It is very effective, non-toxic to other creatures, but quite expensive. How much do you value your strawberries?

Strawberry tortrix moth This is a serious pest in some areas. Caterpillars make a tent of silken threads around the leaves to keep out predators while they feed. Control by spraying with *Bacillus thuringiensis*.

Strawberry mildew Caused by one or two different fungi, this disease causes grey or red patches on the older leaves. Remove older leaves after fruiting and burn. Some growers actually flame the rows *in situ* to get rid of all the pests and diseases after fruiting.

Red core Once your strawberries have this disease it is time to move the strawberry bed and get in new virus-free stock. There is no cure, hence the importance of soil rotation. The disease is spread by water so grow your plants in well-drained soil, using raised beds if your soil is heavy.

Botrytis The grey mould botrytis starts on the petals and is worse when there is little air movement and it is damp. Prevention is easier than cure. Space plants well and keep them weeded. If you are a real strawberry fan, get out the vacuum and hoover up the petals as soon as they drop! When plants are grown through black plastic there is far less of a problem. If your plants do get it, remove diseased fruits as soon as you see them.

Frost Frost turns the middle of the strawberry flower black and kills the potential fruit. Protect plants when frost is forecast if they are in flower. In the USA on large strawberry farms, helicopters are used to fly just above the fields to keep the air moving and prevent ground frost.

Growing in containers

For the patio, strawberry barrels are very popular. Take any large container, drill holes 2 in (5 cm) in diameter about 12 in (30 cm) apart, and make some drainage holes in the bottom. Before filling, place a watering tube through the centre of the barrel with holes along its length. Plant with a good-flavoured variety such as Elsanta plus a few ever-bearers on top, into a good potting compost with slow-release fertilizer. Water and feed regularly. Many commercial growers use containers even on a very large scale because they prevent the spread of soil-borne disease such as Phythothera wilt and red core and keep the fruits clean up off the ground.

In search of summer's forgotten flavours

Brogdale Horticulture Trust is still hunting for many old favourites to add to its collection and to start new collections.

In 1994 they put out a plea for old strawberry varieties. High on the wanted list were varieties such as Sir Joseph Paxton, Keen's Imperial, King of the Earlies, Black Prince, British Queen, Eleanor, Laxton, Elton and Downton. Many of these old varieties are mentioned in the renowned manual of Robert Hogg, a nineteenth-century authority on fruit. The fruit Sir Joseph Paxton was described as 'a large fruit, roundish, even and regular in outline, bright crimson with seeds prominent. Flesh is salmon coloured, firm, rich and highly flavoured.' This fruit was found as late as the 1950s, but has since disappeared. Plants have poured in from all over the country in response to the plea. Now, David Pennell at Brogdale has the unenviable task of working out what they all are.

Blackberry and Apple Pancakes

Cooked blackberries taste almost nicer than raw ones, which can be rather a matter of luck straight off the bramble bush. I still connect pancakes with springtime and Shrove Tuesday when, in the days before supermarkets, eggs and milk suddenly became more plentiful, but these ingredients make a lovely filling for an autumn pancake. The gin in the pancakes makes them lighter (a tip from Jane Grigson), but Calvados will intensify the appleyness. Blackberries freeze very well, so this pudding can be enjoyed well into the winter if you have picked several baskets from the hedgerow. You need apples that will make a robust, creamy purée – cookers like Golden Noble, Bramley or Sturmer Pippin.

Serves 6

1½lb (675 g) cooking apples
sugar to taste
8 oz (225 g) blackberries

Pancakes (makes about 12 small ones)
2 eggs
4 oz (100 g) 100 per cent wholemeal flour
½ pint (300 ml) milk
1 tablespoon gin or Calvados
unsalted butter for cooking, or a little sunflower oil

Chop the apples roughly, and then cook them with 2 tablespoons of water – you will need a thick purée for the filling – until soft. Press them through a coarse sieve while still warm and sweeten to taste. Lightly fold in the blackberries.

Put all the pancake ingredients into a liquidizer or beat to batter in a basin. Heat a smidgen of butter in a small frying pan (about 5 in (13 cm) across is a good size) and when it is foaming ladle in just enough batter to cover the bottom of the pan. Cook until the batter has set, turn or toss over, and cook for about 30 seconds more. Repeat, stacking up the pancakes as you go to keep them moist and succulent. Finally cover them with foil or clingfilm until ready to serve. They will keep well in the fridge till the next day.

Lay out the pancakes on a buttered baking tray. Either put the apple down the middle and roll up, or fold in half, fill one quarter and fold over to make a triangle. Brush with melted butter and bake at 400°F (200°C, Gas 6) for 10 minutes or until the pancakes are hot and sizzling. Serve with plenty of thick cream or crème fraîche.

NB. If you have spare blackberries cook them lightly, sweeten as necessary, and serve them scattered over the pancakes with a dusting of caster sugar.

Rhubarb and Honey Jelly

This is a very light and pretty coral-pink jelly – the sharpness of the rhubarb is counteracted by honeyed sweetness. Select and pull only the brightest red young rhubarb stalks. The tenderest and pinkest come early from the forcing pots. I find leaf gelatine much easier to use than the powdered sort and it has no hint of taste.

Serves 6

2 lb (900 g) fresh rhubarb
2 tablespoons water
3 tablespoons honey, or to taste
6 leaves gelatine
fresh whipped cream and toasted flaked almonds
to serve

Cut the rhubarb into 1 in (2.5 cm) lengths, discarding the white or green parts of the stalk. Put the rhubarb in a heavy saucepan with the water and cook until very soft and juicy, about 30 minutes. Strain off the juice into a measuring jug – you will need 1½ pints (900 ml). If there is a shortfall, put that amount of water in the pan with the rhubarb pulp and cook for a further 5 minutes. Strain this liquid into the jug containing the rhubarb juice and dissolve the honey in the liquid while it is still warm.

Meanwhile, cover the gelatine with a little cold water and leave to soak in a shallow dish.

When the rhubarb juice has cooled to blood heat, carefully stir in the soaked gelatine pieces one by one. Make sure no lumps of gelatine remain, strain the mixture once more, and pour into a glass bowl or individual wine glasses. Chill in the refrigerator. The jellies should be firm within 4 hours.

To serve, decorate with whipped cream and toasted almond flakes.

Apricot Curd Tart

This is a useful pudding for the spring, as it uses dried apricots from the store cupboard – in a season when really ripe, fresh fruit is still at a premium – combined with curd made from an ever-increasing daily milk supply. Try to find unsulphured, sun-dried apricot pieces which have some edge to their taste. Use sweeter whole apricots on top to provide a pleasing contrast.

Makes 1 x 9-inch (22.5 cm) tart

Oatmeal and Honey Base
3 oz (75 g) rolled organic porridge oats
3 oz (75 g) unsalted butter
1½ oz (40 g) unrefined light muscovado sugar
1½ (40 g) honey

Filling
12 oz (350 g) dried apricot pieces
4 oz (100 g) whole dried apricots
¾ pint (450 ml) fresh apple juice
lemon juice (optional)
2 tablespoons fresh single cream
few drops natural vanilla essence
2 tablespoons finely ground unrefined demerara
sugar
12 oz (350 g) curd cheese
apricot jam or apple jelly to glaze
fresh double cream to serve

First make the base. In a medium-sized saucepan, melt all the ingredients together over a low heat. Remove from the heat and mix well to amalgamate.

Preheat the oven to 400°F (200°C, Gas 6). Turn the oat mixture into a fluted 9 in (23 cm) flan tin with a removable base. Spread the mixture evenly over the base of the tin and bake for about 10–15 minutes, until firm and lightly browned. Set aside to cool.

Make the filling. Soften the apricot pieces and whole apricots separately by simmering them slowly in the apple juice. (The whole apricots may respond to simply soaking overnight.) Process the apricot pieces to a purée, adding lemon juice if it seems appropriate.

Pour the cream into a cup with the vanilla essence and dissolve the sugar in it. Turn the curd cheese into a bowl and lightly fold in the cream mixture. Spread the curd cheese over the base of the tin, pressing it into the fluting. Cover with the apricot purée and set the whole apricots into this. Glaze the tart with a little warmed apricot jam or apple jelly.

When the outer ring of the flan tin is removed, the cheese should mould to a firm fluted pattern which is quite striking.

Serve with extra cream.

Variations
This recipe lends itself to endless adaptations using fresh, dried or frozen fruit. It is best, though, with intensely-flavoured fruits such as black currants and damsons, which cut through the bland creaminess of the curd cheese.

Crushed Tayberry Ice-cream

Tayberries are a newly developed fruit similar to loganberries and likewise bred in Scotland. The deep maroon berries are longer and more polished-looking than loganberries and have, I think, a rather more mellow flavour. It seems a shame to crush them, but when you have a plentiful crop they make a stunning ice-cream surrounded by more fresh fruit and some extra sauce. The whole fruit is included, which makes for a more interesting texture, not to say roughage, and of course these very perishable fruits are preserved in delicious form for several months in the freezer if not gobbled up straight away.

Serves 8-10

½ pint (300 ml) milk
6 egg yolks
4 oz (100 g) demerara sugar (dried and whizzed fine)
½ pint (300 ml) double cream
1 lb (500 g) fresh tayberries

Heat the milk and pour it on to the beaten egg yolks and sugar. Return the mixture to the pan and cook, whisking all the time with a balloon whisk, until the custard has thickened to a creamy consistency. Add the double cream.

Hull the berries and either crush them well with a fork or potato masher or process them very briefly. Mix all the ingredients together. You may like to sweeten the ice-cream a little more, depending on the acidity of the fruit and your own taste, so now is the time to try it and add a little more sugar if necessary.

Freeze in a metal tray until just beginning to firm, then whisk again and refreeze. Alternatively, use an ice-cream churn.

Allow 10–15 minutes for the ice-cream to relax out of the freezer before serving.

This method works beautifully with all strongly flavoured soft fruit.

Loganberry Trifle

The traditional English trifle is a pudding of high summer. Layers of sponge cake, fruit jelly, whole red fruits, custard, cream and nuts are arranged in a glass dish to display their gaudy, fairground colours. Loganberries have a deeper, more intense flavour than raspberries and a trifle makes a sumptuous party dish. All you need is patience to keep building up the layers.

Serves 8

4 oz (100 g) sponge cake or sponge biscuits
5 fl oz (150 ml) medium Amontillado sherry
½ pint (300 ml) lightly sweetened raspberry juice
 or red currant juice
2 leaves gelatine, soaked in cold water
1 lb (500 g) fresh loganberries

Custard
4 egg yolks
2 oz (50 g) demerara sugar
½ pint (300 ml) double cream
vanilla pod or natural essence of vanilla

whipped cream
toasted almond flakes

Cut the sponge cake into small pieces and lay in the bottom of 8 wine glasses or a glass bowl. Sprinkle about a tablespoon of sherry over the cake and let it seep in.

Warm some of the raspberry or red currant juice and dissolve the soaked gelatine in this. Add the rest of the juice and mix well to make quite sure there are no lumps of gelatine left. Pour this over the cake layer, drop some fresh fruit into the jelly and leave to set in the fridge.

Make the custard by beating the egg yolks and sugar together in a china bowl. Heat the cream with the vanilla pod and pour over the egg mixture before returning it all to the pan. Whisk over a very low heat until the mixture thickens. If it starts to curdle, pour it back into the cool bowl. Or, if you would prefer to play safe, stir the custard in a china bowl set in a saucepan of simmering water, which will help control any tendency to curdle. Cool the custard and add a few drops of vanilla essence to taste if not using the pod.

When the jelly has set, add more of the fresh loganberries and cover them with custard.

Put back in the fridge till firm. Finally, decorate with whipped cream, any remaining whole fruits, some toasted flaked almonds and perhaps a dusting of fine sugar.

Opposite:Loganberry Trifle

5
SEASONS OF FRUITFULNESS

Fruit-growing is not just twelve months' labour for one month's reward. True, to get good fruit there is some work to do each month but if you plan carefully you can reap the benefits all year round as well– not only from the store or from preserves, but by carefully planning for continuity, growing the right varieties, and extending the season in both directions.

SPRING

Spring, a time of procreation in the fruit garden. As the sap starts to rise it's time to get out there and feed the fruit trees and bushes ready for their task ahead. One of the first signs that things are warming up are the dangling hazel catkins, waiting for the wind to carry the pollen to the tiny red female flowers. Later, as the pears and apples burst into flower, out come the bees, which as well as pollinating the flowers give us our first produce of the year: honey.

With spring also comes the danger of late frost, ready to destroy blossoms overnight. Pests are on the increase too, and need to be nipped in the bud.

Forced fruits

Honey is not the only reward in spring. Strawberries and raspberries can be picked from May if they are forced under cover.

Strawberries need a cold period to get the flowers to form. Pot up early strawberry varieties into 6 in (15 cm) pots in the autumn and leave the pots outside, on their side, against a north-facing wall. In late February bring them into a warm greenhouse at 65°F (18°C), and water and feed with potash as they start to grow. Pollinate the flowers with a soft paintbrush and by early May it's time for just desserts. If you don't have a greenhouse, cloches placed over outdoor plants in February will also give an early crop in late May.

Ventilate greenhouses and cloches to avoid build-up of fungal disease, to let in vital pollinators, and to prevent overheating on sunny days. If temperatures exceed 77°F (25°C), the flowers and therefore the fruits can become distorted. The optimum temperature at flowering time is between 59°F and 68°F (15°C and 20°C).

The strawberry house

William Ingram, head gardener to the Duke of Rutland, invented the Victorian strawberry house in order to produce early fruits to impress the hunting parties. The house consisted of narrow cold frames stacked up in tiers like a block of flats, designed to catch as much light as possible. It was put up against a south wall and filled with pots of strawberries in the winter.

In the 1940s gardeners devised a novel way of bringing raspberries on early by cutting the canes back to 12 in (30 cm) in February and covering them with cloches. The short side shoots that grew out in the following year gave very early fruits. Another method was to cut the tips off ordinary vertical canes and to tie the whole lot carefully down to wires 12 in (30 cm) off the ground before cloching them.

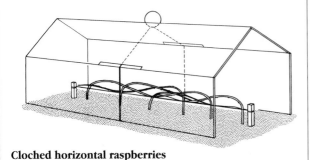

Cloched horizontal raspberries

MARCH

Month planner
• Prune cobnuts when the male catkins are in bloom.
• Mulch bushes and young trees in late March unless the soil is still very cold.
• Feed black currants with nitrogen.
• Graft top fruits.
• Prune blueberries and acid cherries.
• Plant strawberry runners, and sow strawberry seed.
• Train and tie in blackberries and hybrid berries.
• Protect early blossoms against frost.
• Finish winter pruning early this month.

Pest and disease control
• Start weekly inspections of fruit for pest and disease and pick off pests now before they do the damage.
• Remove and burn dead twigs and buds of apples with budrot and disinfect tools to prevent spread.
• Treat rosy apple aphid with soft soap.
• Treat apple mildew by pruning off the affected shoots.
• Spray gooseberries and black currants for mildew just before blossoms open and continue every two weeks.
• Spray canes for cane spot.
• Cut out withered shoots of raspberries that may have raspberry moth caterpillars or cane blight.
• Inspect greasebands and regrease to catch winter and March moths as well as capsids and weevils.
• Treat black currants against big bud mite.
• Sow nasturtiums, poached-egg plants and marigolds now to plant out round fruit trees and bushes in May. These will attract predators to eat the aphids.

Harvest
Fruity choice: from the store, the dessert apple D'Arcy Spice with its spicy, hot, nutmeg-like flavour.

Also from the store: dessert apples such as Tydeman's Late Orange, Idared, Pixie, and Sturmer Pippin. Cooking apples such as Howgate Wonder, Lane's Prince Albert, Bramley's Seedling, Newton Wonder, Dumelow's Seedling, Crawley Beauty, and Annie Elizabeth. Dessert pear: Olivier de Serres and culinary pear: Catillac.

APRIL

Month planner
• Protect blossom from frost.
• Remove blossoms from newly planted strawberries so that their energy goes into new roots.
• Hand-pollinate nectarine and peach flowers with a rabbit's tail.
• At the end of the month untie and prune figs that have been bundled up for the winter.
• Whip and tongue graft top fruits.

Pest and disease control
• Watch out for and control aphids, capsid bugs, winter moth caterpillars and gooseberry sawfly eggs.
• Check and treat apples for mildew and scab.
• Spray gooseberries and black currants for mildew.
• Treat raspberries affected by cane blight.
• To avoid powdery mildew on raspberries, water plants in dry weather.
• Destroy clay-coloured weevils by picking off at night. Avoid mulching raspberries if the weevil is prevalent.
• Watch out for and treat raspberry moth.

The author's children enjoy some forced fruit in May

• Treat magpie moth caterpillars on gooseberries with *Bacillus thuringiensis*.
• Remove greasebands from apples and pears.

Harvest

Fruity choice: the dessert apple Sturmer Pippin lasts well into April, if not beyond. A sweet, crisp, juicy apple which, according to the fruit historian and taste connoisseur, Joan Morgan, has a strong characteristic taste like cold steel.

Other apples from the store are as shown for March except for Pixie. The culinary apples Woolbrook Russet, Edward VII , Encore and Annie Elizabeth may still be going, as will the Catillac pear.

MAY

Month planner

• Remove the blossoms from newly planted trees and newly planted strawberries.
• De-shoot peaches and nectarines.
• Net strawberries against birds.
• Remove first flush of flowers on perpetual strawberries.
• Remove polythene covers from fan-trained peaches by the end of the month.

Pest and disease control

• Watch out for capsid bugs, leaf weevils, apple leaf hoppers, gooseberry sawfly, fruit tree red spider mite,

aphids and clay-coloured weevils and treat when necessary. Always spray after dusk to avoid harming the bees. Never spray when the blossom is fully open.
• Put up codling moth traps.
• Remove leaves affected with leaf blister mite from pears provided there are not too many.
• Pick off cherry slug worm or spray with derris or soft soap if there is a bad infestation.
• Leaf weevils can be caught by placing a greased board beneath apple and pear trees and shaking the tree.
• Treat apple sawfly and gooseberry sawfly with derris or pyrethrum after petal fall and two weeks later.
• Watch out for fireblight and prune out as soon as seen.
• Pick off any strawberries that have botrytis and net the fruit against birds.
• Spray for cane blight, cane spot, and purple blotch on raspberries with Bordeaux mixture.
• Spray gooseberries and black currants against mildew.
• Spray raspberry fruitlets with derris after dusk to destroy raspberry beetle and cane midge.
• Plant out attractant plants sown in March.

Harvest

Fruity choice: the forced strawberry Royal Sovereign, an excellent strawberry as far as taste is concerned.

Also pick forced raspberries and outdoor gooseberry thinnings for the first of the gooseberry pies, regarded as a delicacy by the Victorians. Enjoy your fruits with a spot of honey if the bees have done their work.

The apples Annie Elizabeth and Sturmer Pippin will still be available from the store.

SUMMER

The season of gluts, sunshine and cream teas. There are masses of soft fruits to harvest and masses to do to top and soft fruits, including thinning and summer pruning. Summer pruning restricts vegetative

growth and encourages fruiting. Watch the weather as well as pests – drought can restrict crops as much as an aphid attack.

Blueberries (*Vaccinium corymbosum*)
Blueberries – once sampled, these delicious fruits are never forgotten. Known as the swamp or high-bush blueberry, they come from the eastern United States where they are very popular. Blueberries grow well in our climate but need very acid, moist soil because they are naturally heathland plants. If you haven't got naturally acid soil, grow blueberries in an ericaceous compost in 12–15 in (30–37 cm) pots. Plant in the winter, using two- or three-year-old plants and if in open ground space 5 ft (1.5 m) apart. The bush has an open habit and is very vigorous.

Good varieties include: Earliblue, tasty and early; Bluecrop, early to mid-season; and Ivanhoe and Berkeley, both mid-season varieties.

Feed and mulch blueberries with an acidic compost every spring and weed the plants carefully because their surface feeding roots do not like distur-

The blueberry

bance. Ensure they are well watered (with rainwater) during the growing season and give them a high potash feed every two weeks from flowering until the berries start to ripen. The bushes start cropping in late July, yielding 7–8 lb (3–3.5 kg) of fruit.

Start pruning four years after planting in early March. Fruit is borne on two- to three-year-old wood, so the aim is to stimulate new growth each year. Cut out one quarter of the old wood back to the base or a strong upright shoot annually.

Picking perfection

Fruit grown with care needs to be picked with care. To prevent bruising, strawberries should be picked by the stalk without touching the fruit. Black currants fruit mainly on one-year-old wood and can be picked 'on the rise'. Drooping, fruiting branches are cut off and the currants stripped off with a fork. If the fruit is to be used for jamming or juice straight after picking, a little damage will not hurt.

Glut!!

However well you choose your varieties and plan continuity in the garden, there are times when the raspberries and currants will start coming out of your ears. There are many delicious things that you can do with them but sometimes there isn't the time, not even to preserve them as jams or jellies, so freeze.

Freezing

Freezing soft fruit brings out the flavour because it bursts the cells of the fruit. Raspberry jam has far more flavour as well as memories of summer if you freeze the raspberries first. To freeze, choose only good-quality fruit and remove the stalks first. Only wash if absolutely necessary, as it will dilute flavour.

Dry freezing Spread the fruit in a single layer on a tray and freeze. Then remove, pack into bags and return to the freezer before they thaw.

Sugar freezing Layer the fruit in an airtight container with sprinklings of sugar using 4 oz sugar per lb. (125 g per 500 g) fruit. Freezing reduces the pectin content, so when following a jam recipe use 110 per cent of the fruit stated.

Syrup freezing Make a syrup solution with 1 lb sugar to 1 pint (400 g per 500 ml) of water and then cool it. Put the fruit in an airtight container and pour the syrup over it. Leave about ½ in (1 cm) space below the lid because the mixture will expand when frozen.

Purées Sweetened, puréed cooked fruits freeze well.

Kebabs For the children, try a frozen strawberry kebab. Thread large, firm strawberries on to a lollipop stick and freeze.

Fruit can be stored for up to eight months at –18°C in a freezer. Package carefully to keep out as much air as possible, prevent drying out and prevent tainting from other frozen foodstuffs. If your freezer goes wrong all is not lost. If the fruit has gone into the freezer raw and it is still very cold, you can cook it and refreeze it. Never refreeze anything raw or refreeze thawed-out cooked foodstuffs.

Bottling

If you do not have or do not want to use a freezer, soft fruit can easily be bottled. If done properly the colour and flavour of the fruit will be the same when it comes out the bottles as when it went in. See Patricia Hegarty's bottling recipe (p.107) for instructions on bottling fruit.

Drying

Drying used to be one of the only ways of preserving fruit. Apricots, plums, grapes and peaches dry very well, as do early apples and pears.

First wash and prepare the fruits. Halve and stone the peaches and apricots, leave the plums and grapes whole, and cut apples and pears into rings after peeling and coring. Rinse the pears in salty water before drying to stop them going brown.

Place the fruit on a muslin covered rack and dry at 120°F (50°C) for one hour and then at 150°F (65°C) for a further four to six hours or until dry. Whole plums can take up to two days. The fruits are ready when they feel soft but not brittle and do not give out moisture when squeezed. Cover with a cloth and leave to cool before storing in boxes in waxed paper.

Dried grapes are simply delicious, and you may never learn how long they can keep as they are too tasty to leave hanging around for long. Fruits can also be dried on racks above a boiler or airing cupboard. In the sixteenth century whole apples were cored, strung up and dried up the chimney!

JUNE

Month planner

• Summer prune red and white currants and gooseberries.
• Continue to thin gooseberries.
• Tie in new shoots of raspberries, blackberries and hybrid berries.
• Tie in selected shoots of peaches, and disbud.
• Straw up strawberries to keep the fruit clean.
• Peg down or remove strawberry runners.
• Water trees and bushes if needed.
• Thin apples, pears, plums and peaches.

Pest and disease control

• See May.
• Net fruit against birds.
• Check codling moth traps.
• Pick off and destroy leaves affected with red spider mite, if there are only a few.
• Pick off and destroy caterpillars of the tortrix moth and look for webbed leaves in which they may be hiding.
• Collect apples from June drop and destroy: many of these fruitlets may be harbouring sawfly.
• Remove pear fruitlets affected with pear midge and destroy.

Harvest

Fruity choice: a red currant with a name like a Dutch painter, Jonkheer van Tets has large, glistening berries which make a superb jelly.

Pick early raspberries, black currants, red and white currants, gooseberries and the early cherries, Early Rivers and Mermat. One old apple, Allen's Everlasting, with its strong, sweet, sharp flavour is renowned for lasting in store up until June.

JULY

Month planner

• Thin apples after the June drop.
• Support heavy crops of apples, plums and damsons.
• Train plum and cherry fans.
• Protect stone fruit from birds.
• Train in new canes of blackberries and hybrid berries.
• Tip layer blackberries and hybrid berries.

Pest and disease control

• See June.
• Spray for gooseberry mildew after harvest.
• Second spray for raspberry beetle.
• Cut out any raspberry shoots and fruits affected with grey mould and destroy.
• Put corrugated cardboard bands around the trunk of trees to catch codling moth larvae.
• Clear up old strawberry leaves, mulch and runners after fruiting to prevent the spread of disease.

Harvest

Fruity choice: the raspberry Malling Jewel, true to its name, has a superb flavour though not as large as its northern counterparts.

Pick blueberries, currants, cherries, gooseberries, peaches, raspberries, and strawberries. The culinary plum Early Rivers will be ready now, and the excellent self-fertile cherry Stella.

AUGUST

Month planner

- Summer-prune trained fruits.
- Prune summer-fruiting raspberries.
- Begin pruning over-vigorous trees.
- Cut out fruited laterals of peaches and nectarines.
- Prune plums after fruiting, if necessary, to reduce risk of silver leaf disease.
- Plant out strawberry runners in prepared beds.

Pest and disease control

- See July.
- Watch out for bacterial canker on stone fruits.
- Remove codling moth traps.
- Protect fruit from birds.
- If wasps are a problem, carefully put derris into the nest after dark. If the nest is at ground level, cover with grass mowings. These will suck oxygen out of the air as they rapidly decompose and this suffocates the wasps. Wasps should not be harmed earlier in the year because they are excellent predators and eat many of the fruit pests.

Harry Baker grows a wide range of fruits in his fruit cage

Harvest

Fruity choice: Reeves Seedling, a self-infertile plum with crackly, juicy, aromatic flesh.

This is the good month, with loads of fruits ripe for the picking. The soft fruits: strawberries, blackberries, hybrid berries, blueberries, raspberries, gooseberries, and currants. The early top fruits: peaches, plums, figs and early apples and pears. Ripe plums include the succulent dessert varieties Opal, Oullin's Gage and Denniston's Superb and the culinary plums Early Rivers, Belle de Louvain and Czar. Early dessert apples include Discovery, George Cave, Irish Peach and Redsleeves and for cooking Grenadier and Arthur Turner. One of the first pears to ripen is the scab-resistant Jargonelle, followed later in the month by William's Bon Chrétien.

AUTUMN

As the soft fruits finish it is time to prune them. As one fruit finishes another starts. Autumn raspberries lead us on to the main harvest, first plums then apples and pears to last from September through to the following spring.

Perfect picking

If you want to store your apples, pick them ripe but before they fall. To pick, lift the apple gently and twist slightly with a slight upward movement of the cupped hand – if it is ready it should come off. The ones at the top of the tree ripen first, then those at the sides and finally the ones that have been shaded in the middle. Pears are also picked with the lift and twist method. Firm when picked, pears ripen quickly off the tree. When ready to eat, a pear should give slightly when pressed gently near the stalk. Some say the only place to enjoy a really ripe pear is in the bath!

If you can't reach the high ones get a fruit picker. Many devices using the bag on the pole technique are available. This is not a new idea; the Victorians had some beautiful tools for the job.

Commercial pickers use specially designed bags. These have rigid tops to keep the bag open and are

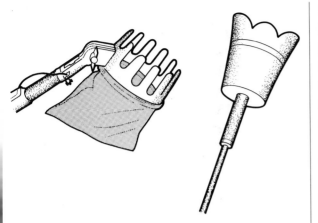

Fruit picking aids, new and old

worn like a baby sling. When the bag is full it is held over a box and two hooks are released which open it from the bottom.

Storage

Early dessert apples can be eaten straight from the tree but others need a period in storage to finish the ripening process. The later-maturing varieties store the best.

Of the culinary apples, both Bramley's Seedling and Dumelow's Seedling will keep until Easter. Of the eating apples, Egremont Russet stores well until Christmas but is not a late keeper, whereas others such as Suntan and Fiesta will keep happily until

February and Sturmer Pippin and D'Arcy Spice until Easter. Many of the late apples such as Sturmer Pippin do not develop their full taste and aroma until they have been stored. Of the dessert pears, Comice does not keep beyond Christmas but Easter Beurre ripens in the New Year to a buttery texture and a musky taste a little like William's.

Refer to the month planner for a list of fruits to enjoy from the store each month.

Store apples and pears in a frost-free shed or room at an equable temperature of –2–5°C. Mice love apples, so keep them out with a trap, a cat, or hang the containerized stored fruit from the ceiling! Store only sound fruit, with no sign of damage or disease, and make sure the stalks are attached, because disease can enter through the point of detachment. Avoid storing onions, paraffin or creosote with the apples because, like milk, fruit is easily tainted. Wrap dessert apples and pears individually in tissue to stop any rot spreading and layer in shallow boxes so they can be examined easily at regular intervals during the winter. You can also store apples in plastic bags. Put 4–5 lb (1.8–2.2 kg) of a single variety in a bag with five to ten pencil-sized holes in it. Culinary apples can simply be laid on straw on the shed floor, mice permitting, and bits of rot cut out before cooking. The store should be well ventilated, checked over regularly and any rotten fruits removed.

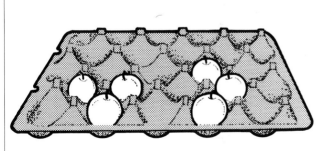

Fruit storage methods

Stories from the store

If only apples and pears could talk they would have a tale or two to tell in the store. They all have fascinating histories and, for many, the fact that they are in the garden at all is pure chance.

Sturmer Pippin

This apple, from the 1800s, has a very distinct flavour: acidic and crisp, with crackling flesh. It is named after Sturmer, a village on the border of Suffolk and Essex where it was first discovered in the garden of a Mr Dillistone.

It grows best in the southern counties and needs long hours of autumn sunshine to develop its full potential flavours. It was a firm favourite with the Victorians, keeping until June. They recommended it to the New Zealanders as an apple suitable to export to the motherland. It survived the long steam journey very well and went on to found the New Zealand commercial apple industry.

Suntan

This apple, raised in 1956, is a cross between Cox and Court Pendu Plat. It stores better than the Cox, lasting until well into February, but has Cox in its flavour. It is sweet and rich with a hint of pineapple. It is a bit tart when picked and the true flavour develops in storage. Court Pendu Plat is a very old variety, known in the sixteenth and seventeenth centuries, and has passed on its excellent keeping qualities to its offspring.

Golden Delicious

This apple tree was discovered in the orchard of a Mr Mullin in West Virginia in 1890 and was originally called, unsurprisingly, Mullin's Yellow Seedling. He sent samples to the Stark Brothers' nursery, with the story that it was a good cropper and keeper. They came to Mr Mullin's place, put a cage round the tree with a built-in burglar alarm to stop anyone else taking grafts from it, and paid for its maintenance. The nursery already had a campaign going for their Red Delicious and so renamed the new apple Golden Delicious. The tree lived until 1958 and was even portrayed on Clay County bank cheques. By the 1930s the tree had been extensively planted in the United States and also in Kent. It did not really take off here because it needs a very warm climate to do well, but we really got to know it when it arrived as a French import in the 1970s. Colonialists arriving back from Algeria settled in France and were encouraged to go into fruit farming in the Loire. Grants were made available and they were recommended to grow Golden Delicious.

Black Worcester

Despite being brick hard and gritty, many people over the generations have had a soft spot for the culinary Black Worcester pear, which has been with us for nine centuries. In 1574 Queen Elizabeth I visited Worcester. She was so impressed that a heavily laden black pear tree she saw had not been plundered by the locals that she ordered the inclusion of three black pears in the city's coat of arms. The local alderman did not dare admit that the tree had been deliberately transplanted to the site the night before in readiness for her visit! The pear may still adorn the badge of Worcester City Council but is thin on the ground and in the last four decades has come close to extinction. To remedy this the council are encouraging landowners to plant the tree, with the stipulation that it must be maintained by the owner and inspected by the council for five years, to ensure it gets off to a good start. At that rate it may end up back in the store yet.

Commercial apple storage was revolutionized in the 1920s when Doctors Kidd and West discovered how to keep apples in a sort of suspended animation. Apples mature and eventually decay due to the production of a simple chemical called ethylene. Kidd and West found that by putting fruits in a sealed cold store and keeping oxygen levels down, the fruits would keep until April. Your polybag is in effect a mini gas store!

Now controlled atmosphere storage is the state of the art. Samples of apples destined for storage are tested to make sure they are up to it. They need to have adequate calcium and phosphate to keep them firm and ensure they survive the long wait. Trees grown in grass rather than bare ground produce apples that store better. Scientists have found that this is due to a little fungi called mycorrhiza, which lives among the grass roots and actually feeds the trees with phosphate.

Sound apples are sent to the store. The air is flushed out with nitrogen, the oxygen level reduced to 5 per cent to slow down the apple's bodily functions, and the temperature is kept at around 38°F (3.5°C). Carbon dioxide given off by the apples has to be removed chemically as it can cause brown marks under the apple skin (scald) and ethylene is removed by a type of platinum scrubber, the apples' equivalent of a catalytic converter.

The Transgenics Department at Horticulture Research International, East Malling, is going one step further. Rather than remove the ethylene from the apple in store they aim to stop the apple producing it in the first place. They have inserted genes into the apple to turn off ethylene production. Who knows, soon we may be eating English apples all year round.

SEPTEMBER

Month planner
• Prune plums, damsons and wall-trained peaches no later than the middle of the month.
• Prune black currants and gooseberries, and take cuttings from healthy plants.
• Prune hybrid berries and blackberries.
• Tie in wall-trained cherries and shorten pinched back shoots.
• Finish summer pruning of apples and pears.

Pest and disease control
• Spray for bacterial canker.
• Cut out canker on apple and pear trees. Burn prunings and disinfect tools.
• Spray currants with Bordeaux mixture against coral spot and leaf spot.

Harvest
Fruity choice: Edward Bunyard was a fruit nurseryman and pomologist *par excellence* in the 1920s and was passionate about apples and taste. For him the apple of the month was the dessert variety Worcester Pearmain: firm, juicy and sweet with the taste of strawberries.

Late strawberries are also ready, as are autumn raspberries, blackberries, blueberries, dessert and culinary plums, peaches, figs, and hazelnuts.

Apples and pears to harvest and eat now include the dessert apples James Grieve, Fortune, St Edmund's Pippin, Ellison's Orange, Merton Knave and Merton Beauty and the culinary apples Rev. W. Wilks, Peasgood Nonsuch, Warner's King and Bountiful. Good early pears include William's Bon Chrétien, Beth, Onward, Merton Pride, and Gorham.

OCTOBER

Month planner
• Store top fruit.
• Prune currants and gooseberries and take cuttings.
• Prune blackberries and hybrids.
• Prepare ground for planting trees and order trees.
• Tidy up strawberry beds and mulch with compost, cover perpetual strawberries to extend the season.

Pest and disease control
• Mow fallen fruit leaves with a rotary mower after spraying with liquid seaweed. This helps worms to

Bunyard's September favourite, Worcester Pearmain

digest the leaves and any scab spores they are carrying.
• Apply greasebands to apple and pear trees (and the stakes!) to trap winter moth and March moth.
• Spray against bacterial canker.
• Prune out canker on apples and pears, burn prunings and disinfect tools.
• Cut out and burn diseased raspberry canes. Hoe around new canes to expose overwintering pests to birds.
• Spray currants with soft soap or quassia to catch overwintering aphids.

Harvest

Fruity choice: the dessert apple St Edmund's Pippin, described by Bunyard as 'quite the best early russet with its pale yellow flesh, very juicy and fine flavoured'.

Pick autumn raspberries, late strawberries, blackberries, plums, apples and pears. Dessert apples to eat now include: Lord Lambourne, Jester, Mother, Ribston Pippin, Egremont Russet, Greensleeves and Sunset as well as the dessert apples shown for September. As for culinary apples, Golden Noble and Howgate Wonder are maturing nicely and the September choices are still going strong. The majority of the dessert pears picked in September are now ripe and include: Bristol Cross, Beurre Hardy, Beurre Superfin, and Louise Bonne of Jersey.

NOVEMBER

Month planner

• Ventilate the fruit store at night and inspect fruit for damage.
• In cold areas bundle up stems of blackberries, hybrid berries and figs to keep the frost out.
• Finish pruning cane fruits, currants and gooseberries.
• Prune apples and pears for fruit and shape.
• Root prune trees that are over-vigorous (see December).
• Plant trees and bushes.

• Pot up some strawberries and raspberries for forcing later in the year.

Pest and disease control

• Hang fat or peanuts in fruit trees to attract birds that will then go on to eat the aphids. It's like giving them chips and them then wanting fish, the combination of carbohydrate and protein.
• Prune out canker on top fruit, burn diseased prunings and disinfect tools.
• Grease band trunks and stakes to trap winter moths.

Harvest

Fruity choice: the well-known dessert apple Cox's Orange Pippin, described by Bunyard as the 'Château d'Yquem of apples' with its spicy, nutty, pear-like, honeyed aromatic flavour.

The late-keeping dessert apples Idared, D'Arcy Spice, and Sturmer Pippin can be picked now, but apart from Idared should be stored until Christmas to mature. Others picked earlier should be ready from the store now and include many really tasty apples such as Falstaff, Jupiter, Elstar, Fiesta, Kidd's Orange Red, Spartan, Gala, Orlean's Reinette, Jonagold, Suntan and Ashmead's Kernel, as well as several listed for October. Most of the good cookers will be ready from store from now until Christmas if not Easter and include: Warner's King, Golden Noble, Bountiful, Howgate Wonder, Blenheim Orange, Bramley's Seedling, Newton Wonder, Dumelow's Seedling and Woolbrook Russet.

Lots more pears have ripened up and will taste nothing like the hard fruits that were put in store barely a month before. These include: Durondeau, Thompson's, Concorde, Conference, Seckle and Doyenne du Comice. Eat these now and save some of the apples until December because they store better.

WINTER

The trees may have gone dormant for the winter but this does not mean you can be the same. Now is the time to plant trees and prune young trees for shape and established trees for fruit (provided they are not grown as restricted forms, such as cordons).

Root-pruning

Over-vigorous apple and pear trees that do not produce much fruit can be checked by root-pruning. Dig out a 4 ft (1.2 m) circle round the tree to reveal the roots. Now it is time to stress the tree into producing more fruit. Cut through about half of the thick anchorage roots, avoiding the thinner, fibrous feeding roots. Some gardeners cut one side one year and one side the following year to prevent shocking the tree too much. Return the soil to the hole and stake the tree until the poor thing has recovered. In the next year water well, because the roots will be damaged and need some assistance.

Fresh soft fruit for Christmas

In the nineteenth century, before the invention of the deep freeze, gardeners had novel ways of keeping soft fruits going. Bushes were pruned to fit under beehive-like covers made of straw or rushes. These kept off the heat and light and were put on just as the fruit began to ripen, with gaps left open at the bottom to ventilate the fruit and prevent build-up of disease. The fruit could sometimes be kept on the bushes right up until Christmas. The same bushes were not covered for the next few years to allow them to recover from the lack of light over one season.

Cider

One way of preserving fruit and keeping the pruners happy is to make cider.

In the 1500s cider as we know it today was born. Lord Scudmore came up with the apple Scudmore Crab, also known as the Herefordshire Red Streak. The ciders that developed before this time were like apple wine, sweet and sickly. This apple, however, had the right bitterness because it was full of tannin. It was no good to eat or to cook with but made a very fine cider. By the 1600s several high-tannin varieties had been planted and the basis of the cider orchards of the south-west laid down. One variety, Hereford Broadleaf, contained so much tannin that it could be used to tan leather. Imagine what the cider did to your insides! By the 1800s cider was part of farming tradition in the West Country, Hereford and Worcester: it was given to farm workers as part of their wages. In those days they were paid very little and the cider helped them forget this fact; whether it helped speed up the work, who can say! Payment with cider was made illegal in 1887, but farmers still gave the cider to their workers as a gift for many years after that. Commercial cider-making was instigated by Sir Robert Neville Grenville and F. J. Lloyd, who both experimented with ways of making better cider. This started the National Fruit and Cider Institute at Long Ashton in 1903, which helped to build up commercial cider ventures throughout the south-west.

In the south-east, dessert and culinary apples that do not make the grade are termed 'cider' because they are taken off for processing into cider, juice and pies. In the south-west, cider-making is an art and uses only particular blends of cider apples – these are grouped into: bittersharps, which are high in tannin and are very acidic; bittersweets, also high in tannins and sugars; sharps; and sweets. All four types are blended together to give distinctive ciders. Many of the cider apple varieties we have today arose as chance seedlings (gribbles) that grew out of the pomice, the pulp resulting from pressing apples that was thrown into the field. The well-known Dunkerton's Sweet, a lovely sweet cider apple, was a pomice seedling discovered by Mr Dunkerton on his farm in Somerset.

Traditional cider apples have some wonderful names, such as Slack My Girdle, Foxwhelp, and Graniwinkle. The first cider of the year is made from the earliest cider apples, the Morgan Sweets.

Cider apples are not delicate and can be harvested off the ground: on larger farms they are literally hoovered up from September until Christmas. On smaller farms locals used to gather in the apples and turn them into cider. Some can remember the taste of the fresh juice straight from the press and the well-earned bread, cheese and mug of cider which came at the end of a pressing. Many farmers used to make cider at night, having used every hour of daylight out on the farm. The barns would be lit with candles and filled with the aroma of apples and the noise of grinding cogs.

Although cider-making is filled with mystique, it has very basic principles. Ripe apples are milled and pressed, and the juice is squeezed out. Cider is traditionally pressed by placing layers of pomice between layers of wheat straw, or cloths to build up a 'cheese'. The cheese is then pressed with a heavy weight over a few days. The apple juice is put in barrels, which are 'bunged down' after furious frothing and allowed to ferment using the apples' own natural yeast. It is then drunk over the next few months.

Why does it taste so good? Here are a few trade secrets from the dim and distant past:

• Equipment was thoroughly cleaned and gaps sealed with wool and cow dung. Very clean!
• Wooden implements were used, because cider dissolves metal. Using lead for repairs or 'sugar of lead' to sweeten the cider was said to cause 'Devonshire colic'!
• A couple of calf's feet were sometimes hung in the cask for a few days to help cider to clear.
• Uncooked beetroots have been added to colour the cider up.
• Raw parsnips have been added to stop it going off.
• Drunken mice which fell into the unbunged barrels also added body to the cider.

Cider-making in the West Country is not history but is alive and definitely kicking. Marcus Govier still makes cider with his traditional press out in the wilds. The visitors come, the cider flows and life goes on as it always has done. Cider is a lot stronger than it tastes! If you are on a cider foray in Somerset go on foot! Marcus makes 300 gallons (70 litres) a year, and when asked where he sells it replied, 'I don't sell it, I drinks it!'

At the other end of the scale comes Julian Temperley, a local entrepreneur with some of the largest private cider orchards in the country. In the seventeenth century cider was worth more than wine, and Julian aims to raise its profile again. For over 100 years his farm has made real Somerset cider, fermented in oak vats and sold draught from wooden barrels. Julian Temperley believes the cider industry must move on to survive. He is one of the few cider makers in the country making bottle-fermented sparkling cider. Not the fizzy cheap stuff but the champagne of ciders made by fermenting the cider for a second time in the bottle using a technique called *méthode champenoise*. They say this drink is light years away from traditional coarse cider. What is the difference? As Julian says 'Its all in the size of the bubbles.'

Cider drinkers swear that cider keeps them going and have passed on some useful tips:

• To relieve rheumatism, put some cider vinegar in the bath.
• Very few cider drinkers have ever suffered from typhoid – they say the cider kills the germs!
• Cider, drunk hot with ginger and burnt toast, was said to cure colds. It certainly kept you in bed to allow convalescence.

Cider brandy

Julian Temperley only makes cider until Christmas, but it doesn't stop there. Another innovation on the farm is Somerset Royal Cider Brandy, a lovely alternative to Calvados which really warms the cockles of your heart. The cider brandy, with its 42 per cent alcohol, is made by Fifi and Josephine, two old but experienced copper stills that Julian brought over from Normandy; the product is stored in oak barrels. Only the best young fresh dry cider is used, from late-maturing high-tannin apples grown in Somerset. The distillate from the stills is put into barrels, stored in

Julian Temperley's cider brandy stills, Fifi and Josephine

a bond and is ready after three to ten years. The distillery (to satisfy Customs and Excise) has window bars, double-locked doors, sixty-eight locks, security alarms and has to be over two miles away from the cider-producing enterprise. Cider brandy is now being brought out of the bond. On the first day of January, in the year 2000, Julian will bring out his ten-year-old brandy! There is also a small distillery operating in Hereford which produces cider brandy and cider liqueurs.

DECEMBER

Month planner
• Plant trees and bushes and prune top fruit except if frosty or freezing.
• Check stakes, tree supports and ties.
• Inspect fruit in store.

Pest and disease control
• Prune out canker on top fruits. Burn diseased prunings and disinfect tools.
• Check greasebands on top fruit and renew if clogged up.

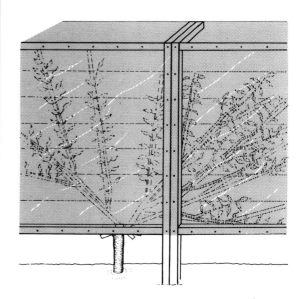

Plastic covers over the peaches

• Put plastic covers over outdoor peaches to prevent infection with peach leaf curl. This fungal disease carried by the wind and rain causes leaves to redden, blister and fall. The plastic cover totally prevents it, much better than spraying, and can be kept on to protect the blossom from frosts too.

Harvest

Fruity choice: the culinary apple Blenheim Orange, with its 'nutty warm aroma'. As Bunyard said, 'There is in this noble fruit a mellow austerity as of a great Port in its prime.'

Apples ready from the store in November will still be fine now. In addition some late-keeping cookers: Lane's Prince Albert, Crawley Beauty, Edward VII, Encore and Annie Elizabeth will be coming into season, as will the late pears Beurre, Alexandre Lucas, Josephine de Malines and Glou Morceau.

JANUARY

Month planner

• Plant and prune apples and pears unless it is really frosty.
• Inspect fruit store for rotten fruit.

Pest and disease control

• Protect fruit buds from birds such as bullfinches.
• Remove mummified fruit from top fruits and destroy to prevent the spread of brown rot.
• Renew greasebands to protect against winter and March moths.
• Renew fat in the trees to attract birds to eat aphids.
• Gently fork around soft and cane fruit to expose pests to birds.
• Remove lackey moth eggs, which look like bracelets girdling the branches.

Harvest

Fruity choice: the dessert apple Claygate Pearmain, with a strong aromatic and nutty taste.

If you have checked your fruit store regularly and not eaten all the fruits yet, all the varieties listed for December will still be edible.

FEBRUARY

Month planner

• Finish winter pruning and plant apples and pears unless it is really frosty.
• Inspect fruit store for rotten fruit.
• Feed fruit trees and bushes with potash.
• Prune autumn-fruiting raspberries and take out the tips of summer-fruiting varieties.
• Cloche some strawberries to get an early crop.
• Bring some potted raspberries and strawberries into the greenhouse for an early crop.
• Protect early blossom with polypropylene fleece or hessian.

Pest and disease control

• Renew greasebands and check apples and pears for canker.
• Hoe under trees in bare ground to expose pests to birds. At this time of year a few hungry chickens or bantams work wonders if they are allowed to scratch up in the fruit garden.
• Treat apple mildew by pruning affected shoots.
• Spray peaches against peach leaf curl with Bordeaux mixture.

Harvest

Fruity choice: the dessert apple Rosemary Russet, described by Bunyard as 'an aristocrat in every way', with the sharp, sweet taste of acid drops.

The dessert apples shown for November and December will just about be hanging on but it is now that the long-lasting qualities of the real late keepers Tydeman's Late Orange, Idared, Pixie, D'Arcy Spice and Sturmer Pippin really come into their own. The late culinary apples will still be going strong and a couple of pears, the dessert pear Olivier de Serres and the culinary pear Catillac, will be at their best.

Whether you have a fruit store or not, you can still enjoy the many fruit preserves that catch the flavours to savour at any time of year. And while you sit and sup your cider and eat your jams and pickles you can plan for an even more bountiful harvest next year.

Pickled Walnuts with Double Berkeley Cheese and Onion Tartlets

Walnuts are pickled complete with their shiny green casing before the shell inside has started to harden at the end of July. You can test for this by piercing the fruit with a pin.

Home-pickled eggs and pickled walnuts are familiar or perhaps nostalgic sights on the pub counter. These tartlets just make a little more ceremony of the classic cheese and pickle sandwich. The Double Berkeley cheese, which is made at Dymock in Gloucestershire, is ideal for this dish, as it has a lovely warm colour to contrast with the black walnuts and is firm enough to keep some of its body when cooked.

Makes 6 tartlets

Pastry
4 oz (100 g) 100 per cent wholemeal flour
2 oz (50 g) cold butter
approximately 3 tablespoons cold water to mix

Filling
2 medium-sized onions – red onions are very jolly
1 tablespoon sunflower oil
5 oz (150 g) Double Berkeley cheese or richly coloured orange cheese
5 oz (150 g) pickled walnuts
3 large eggs, beaten
double cream to make up to ½ pint (300 ml) with the eggs
freshly ground black pepper
sea salt (optional)

Mix the flour and the butter, chopped into small pieces, in a processor until crumbly but dry. Add the water gradually until the mixture forms a ball. Leave to rest in the fridge for 20 minutes.

Divide into 6 balls and roll out very thinly. Line 6 individual flat tartlet tins, about 4½ in (12 cm) diameter with removable base and bake blind. (Line each tin with greaseproof paper, fill partially with baking beans and bake for 10 minutes at 400°F (200°C, Gas 6). Remove the beans and paper and return to the oven to dry out for about 3 minutes.)

Meanwhile assemble the filling.

Slice the onions into thin rings and fry them in the oil until softened and very lightly coloured.

Cut the cheese into ½ in (3 cm) cubes, cut up the walnuts to match, and distribute between the tartlets. Beat the eggs and cream together and add the pepper, and possibly salt, depending on the savour of the cheese. Fill up the cases evenly and scatter the onion rings over the top.

Bake for 20 minutes at 350°F (180°C, Gas 4) until the filling has puffed up and browned. Serve warm with a salad or allow to cool for a starter, lunchtime snack or to take on a picnic. They look very pretty served on some walnut leaves.

Bottled Pears/Peaches/ Nectarines

There are some fruits which do not lend themselves to the freezer. The only way to preserve pears, peaches and nectarines seems to be to bottle them. Although there are methods using alcohol as a preservative, I use just a simple sugar syrup to keep the pure flavour of the fruit. This can always be reduced later, when perhaps something festive can be added if you wish. Choose pears which are just ripe, still firm and unblemished. They can be very deceptive and really need to be cut open to tell if they are suitable.

2½ lb (1.25 kg) dessert pears (Durondeau, Baronne de Mello, Comice, Conference)
juice of ½ lemon

Syrup
10 oz (275 g) granulated sugar
1 pint (600 ml) water

Peel the pears and slice in half. Scoop out the cores and put the pears into some water with the juice of ½ a lemon. Dissolve the sugar in the boiling water and cook for 3 minutes.

Pack the pears into very clean (I don't think many bugs can survive a modern dishwasher), warmed bottling jars and pour the hot syrup round them. Attach new rubber rings to the glass lids and place them on top of the jars. Set the bottles in a roasting tin in the oven at 300°F (150°C, Gas 2) for 1½ hours. Take out, tap to get rid of the bubbles, top up with boiling syrup if a lot of liquid has been lost, and very quickly screw down the rings. Leave to cool, then test for seal by removing the rings and feeling if the glass lid is tight. Clean off any stickiness, label, and store in a dark, cool place.

Peaches and nectarines can be bottled using the same method, but need to be skinned, stoned and halved first.

Greengage Jam

Greengages have the most exquisite flavour, oozing sweetness, made all the more rapturous because of the rarity of their fruiting to perfection in our climate. This year I have made jam from another gage, Coe's Golden Drop, using the method below. No water is used to dilute the concentrated flavour of the fruit.

Makes about 7 lb (3 kg)

6 lb (2.5 kg) greengages
3 lb (1.25 kg) sugar
juice of 2 lemons

Halve the greengages and remove the stones. Layer them in a bowl with the sugar, cover, and leave to macerate overnight in a cool place.

Put the fruit into a preserving pan or divide between 2 large stainless steel pans (or cook them in batches). The pan needs to be large, as the jam will boil up quite vigorously. Bring to the boil gradually so that the sugar dissolves and does not burn, add the lemon juice and boil without stirring for 20–30 minutes until setting point is reached. (A jam thermometer will register the correct temperature of 220–222°F (105°C) and then the jam will need to be cooked for about another 10 minutes.) Boil too long and the flavour will fade.

Ladle into clean, warm jars using a jam funnel. Label and store in a dark place if possible.

DAW Chutney

My grandfather had a vinegar brewery and, later, fruits farms and was always experimenting with new ways to use his products. DAW Chutney, so-called because it was 'Delicious, Appetizing and Wholesome' and which sported a jaunty jackdaw in profile on the labels of its green glass bottles, combined these interests.

Makes approximately 6 lb (2.7 kg)

4 lb (1.8 kg) tart apples
6 oz (175 g) onions
8 cloves garlic
¾ pint (450 ml) cider vinegar
12 oz (350 g) dates, stoned and chopped
6 oz (175 g) sultanas or raisins
12 oz (350 g) dark muscovado sugar
1 tablespoon pickling spice
½ teaspoon cayenne pepper
1 teaspoon coriander seeds
1 oz (25 g) piece fresh root ginger, quartered
sea salt (optional)

Peel, core and slice the apples. Peel and chop the onions and garlic. Tip both into a heavy-based saucepan containing half the vinegar and simmer for 10–15 minutes, until tender.

Add the dates, sultanas or raisins, sugar, pickling spice, cayenne pepper, coriander seeds and ginger, fresh if possible, since it has more zing and fragrance, and the remainder of the vinegar. Simmer all the ingredients together until the mixture is good and thick, about 20 minutes. Remove from the heat.

Extract the root ginger, season with salt if you wish and pot into warm sterilized jars. If the jars have metal lids, protect them with vinegar-proof paper and make certain the jars are sealed tightly, as vinegar evaporates easily and the chutney might become unappetizingly dry.

Opposite: DAW Chutney - Delicious and Wholesome

Roast Loin of Pork Stuffed with Apricots and with Apricot and Sage Sauce

Real home-grown apricots are scarce in England, and this is a case where the dried variety have an advantage in intensity of flavour over the fresh – and of course they are always available. Pork is a loyal partner of fruit – witness apple, prune, peach and pineapple – and apricots are no less successful. Free-range pig is now more available. Ask your butcher.

Serves 6

4 lb (1.8 kg) loin of pork – boned but including kidneys and skin (detached from the joint)
8 oz (225 g) chopped apricots
2 large shallots
1 oz (25 g) butter
1 tablespoon sunflower oil
1 stick celery
½ pint (300 ml) cider/white wine
½ pint (300 ml) chicken stock

1 sprig sage or some chopped leaves, or 1 teaspoon dried sage
tamari
freshly ground black pepper
sea salt
a few additional shapely apricots and sage leaves for garnish

Trim off the excess rib meat from the main fillet. This will be a sizeable amount, and can be used to make a casserole as well as helping to fortify the stock for the apricot sauce. Take a large skewer and push it through the centre of the fillet. Enlarge the hole with a wooden spoon handle and fill the cavity from both ends with the apricot pieces.

Soften the shallots in the butter and oil and add the celery, diced kidney and a little of the lean offcuts. Fry these until golden, pour in the cider and stock, add the sage and simmer until reduced by a third. Sieve out the stock and return to the pan with the remaining apricots. Cook again until the apricots are soft, whiz in a liquidizer, and pass through a fine sieve. Season with tamari and black pepper. Score the skin and lay in a shallow roasting tray. Press some sea salt into the cuts and bake in the top of the oven at 400°F (200°C, Gas 6) for 1–2 hours until crisp. This keeps well in a warm oven, so it is useful to cook this above some other dish earlier in the day if you have a hot oven switched on, say, for some bread.

Brush the pork with oil and roast at 400°F (200°C, Gas 6) for 30-40 minutes, depending on the size of the fillet. Put the meat to rest in a warm oven and deglaze the roasting tray with a little of the sauce. Sieve back into the saucepan and reheat just before serving.

Slice the meat to display the apricot heart, and serve with crackling pieces, rich fruit sauce and a garnish of sage leaves and apricots.

6
SOUR GRAPES

Britain has been intertwined with the vine for the past 1,800 years.

The Roman emperor Probus preferred English wine to continental wine and reinstated vine-growing in Britain after his predecessor, Domitian, had ordered the destruction of all the vineyards outside of Italy in 85 AD. Very fickle, these Romans!

By the time William the Conquerer had conquered, the Domesday Book listed over thirty-eight separate vineyards, all in the south of the country, but by the fifteenth century it had all come to a grinding halt. The problem, apart from French imports and the Black Death, was the climate, which changed from hot to cold and wet. Vines enjoy the same conditions as gardeners: a frost-free spring, a sunny, warm summer and a cold but not severe winter, so this didn't suit them at all.

Things do seem to be looking a little rosier now, as new varieties, better suited to the British climate have been developed. Who knows – now it is supposed to be getting hot again maybe there will be a major revival.

Although grapes have an excellent flavour, they tend to be grown mainly by experts and enthusiasts as they need the right weather conditions, lots of attention and, reputedly, lots of room. However, they really deserve a place in any garden. An average outdoor vine yields about 15 lb (6.8 kg) fruit, equivalent to a gallon (4.5 litres) of wine, and can be trained up a south- or south-west-facing wall, taking up vertical rather than horizontal space. Vines can also double up as ornamentals: trained over a pergola they make an attractive climber, providing shade for those hot, sunny summer days. Greenhouse vines serve a double role too. As well as providing dessert grapes they also offer a bit of welcome shade in mid-summer to plants growing underneath. Once you get the hang of training and pruning the vines, whether they be indoor or outdoor, they will reward you with fruit for forty years or more.

OUTDOOR GRAPES

Outdoor grapes grow best in the south and come in black or white. The white types are slightly hardier so are a better bet if you do want to grow grapes in the north. Grapes grown outside in this country are generally for wine although a few dessert varieties are available. The early varieties crop from late September and the lates up to late October.

Notable varieties

Madeleine Sylvaner White. Reliable, early variety that crops well. Suitable for northerly locations. For wine and dessert. Average flavour.

Siegerrebe White (actually more brown than white). Early variety. Good yields and medium vigour. Sweet-flavoured as a dessert grape and yields a spicy wine.

Precoce de Malingre White. Early, large berried variety of moderate vigour. For wine and dessert.

Madeleine Angevine White. Early, reliable, vigorous, heavy cropper. Suitable for northern locations but prone to mildew. Dessert and wine grape with a fair flavour.

Reichensteiner White. Early, mid-season. Good cropper with some resistance to botrytis. Average wine grape.

Cascade (= Seibel 13.053) Black. Mid-season, with compact bunches of small grapes. Wine grape with low sugar and high acid content. Vigorous and resistant to mildew.

Leon Millot Black. Mid-season, reliable, very vigorous, heavy cropper with small bunches. For dessert and wine. Resistant to mildew.

Muller Thurgau (= Riesling Sylvaner) White. Mid-season with heavy yields. Very popular grape. Needs good weather at pollination time. Excellent wine, and can also be used as a dessert grape.

Seyval Blanc (= Seyve Villard 5.276) White. Mid-season, reliable good cropper. Makes a light fruity wine. Resistant to powdery and downy mildew, therefore a favourite with organic growers.

Brandt Black. Late variety, vigorous heavy cropper. Good grape for the family garden, small sweet bunches loved by children and good autumn colour for amenity value. Not suitable for northern locations.

Chardonnay White. Late variety with moderate yields. Does well on light, chalky soils.

Planting

Vines are perennial climbers and need support. In their natural home, such as the forests of Transcaucasia, wild vines twine around and climb up the trees. This was one of the training methods adopted by the Greeks and Romans. Now, in gardens,

they are usually grown against a wall on a series of horizontal wires 12 in (30 cm) apart, or in the open against wires attached to end posts with straining bolts. They prefer a warm, sheltered location with a light to medium loam. Outdoor vines do not like waterlogged or very shallow alkaline soils, though they are fine on medium to deep soil over chalk.

As vines put on a lot of growth each year and are very deep-rooting, they need a really good start. Prepare the site well by breaking up any pans in the subsoil and incorporating generous quantities of organic matter into the topsoil. You should need only one vine in a small garden as they are very vigorous, although the serious wine-maker will want more.

Plant in autumn or very early spring, spacing 5 ft (1.5 m) apart if you do go for more than one. If the vine is young, with a stem under ¼ in (0.5 cm) in diameter, keep it well protected in the first winter by covering with horticultural fleece or keeping in a pot under cover until the late spring when the frosts have finished.

Training and pruning

Training vines is not as complicated as it seems, because the vines produce fruit on the current season's growth. When pruning, you need to develop a framework to support the new growth and have a simple system of replacing the new growths every year.

There are several ways of doing this. You can train them in the same way as the indoor types (see below), or on the Guyot system. This method was developed by Dr Jules Guyot in 1850, and if it has worked well for that long then it can't be bad. With the Guyot system, the one-year-old stems are trained horizontally as the framework and the grapes are borne on the fruiting laterals which grow up from them. It is a very easy training system once you get the hang of it.

When to prune? Carry out winter pruning in November if possible. The earlier the winter pruning is done, the earlier bud break takes place. Also, if you prune them in the spring they can bleed (exude sap) badly.

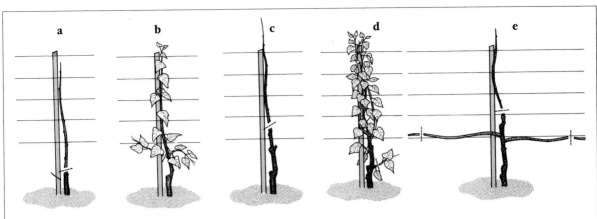

Pruning a vine on the double Guyot system

(a) Plant the vine next to a vertical post and cut it right back to 2 buds.

(b) As it grows in the spring and summer, train 1 shoot vertically up a support and cut back any side shoots to 1 leaf. This looks drastic but gets the plant well established, so don't expect any wine this year.

(c) When the vine has become dormant in November cut it back to about 20 in (50 cm), making sure you have left 3 good buds above the graft or above the ground if it is on its own roots. These buds will grow to become your one-year-old stems.

(d) In the second growing season, carefully tie in the 3 shoots that hopefully will have developed from these buds to a vertical post, and again pinch back all the laterals to 1 leaf. Do this as soon as they appear, to save the vine wasting its energy.

(e) When the vine becomes dormant again, get to work. Tie 2 of the shoots horizontally to the lowest wires on the supports, and cut the remaining vertical shoot back to 3 good buds again (*déjà vu?*)

(f) In the growing season the horizontally trained shoots will produce vertical cropping laterals that are secured in their upright position to wires. These should be thinned to 8 in (20 cm) apart and nipped back about 6 in (15 cm) above the top wire. Vines grow like Topsy once established, and the aim of pruning is to keep them under control so that they produce good bunches rather than little ones. The 3 buds on the vertical shoot will produce 3 shoots again. Think ahead; these are for next year. Tie 'em up to keep them out the way and cut any laterals they produce back.

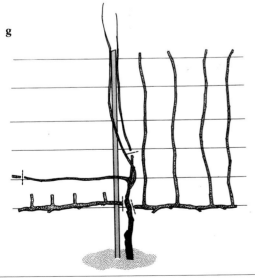

(g) In the dormant season, cut off the now two-year-old shoots along with their fruited laterals and train 2 one-year-old shoots in, horizontally, to the bottom wire to take their place. And the other shoot, well, you've guessed it - cut it back to 3 buds. In the growing season, repeat the same process as last year, and soon you will be able to do it automatically.

Allow only three or four bunches in the first year of cropping. This will let the vine get settled in and will enable it to produce healthier and heavier crops in the years to come. As a rule of thumb, allow a bunch per 12 in (30 cm) on a mature vine.

Jonathan Abbs has always wanted to make wine and started his first vineyard in his parents' back garden at the tender age of ten. It was not a passing phase, and in 1976, when he was twenty-three, Jonathan and his parents bought a farm near Sittingbourne in Kent. When he first saw the farm he had a feeling it was the right site for a vineyard because it was sheltered, caught the summer sun and had free-draining soil. He later found he had not been the only one to grow grapes here. The family discovered first the remains of a medieval vineyard, then the remains of a Roman vineyard on the site. The Abbs are still finding Roman coins and bits of pottery today.

In 1980 they produced their first vintage, 500 bottles from 4 acres (1.5 ha), and in 1983 had a bumper crop that produced 40,000 bottles. Jonathan Abbs grows many varieties including Muller Thurgau and Reichensteiner. He uses Pinot Blanc and Seyval Blanc to make a special sparkling wine by the *méthode champenoise* and calls it Canti, after a tribe that used to be in Kent before the Romans. So, if your child starts planting vines in your vegetable patch, watch out, a viticulturist may be in the making!

The Abbs used to use the Guyot system in their vineyard but had a catastrophe when it all blew down in the great storm of 1987. Jonathan decided to knock out every other row and start again on the Geneva double curtain system. Here the main stem is trained up like the trunk of a tree, with four long stems at head height providing a horizontal framework to support the fruiting laterals. The laterals grow down from the framework each year to give a curtain of grapes and leaves, hence the name. The Abbs like the

system, as they do not have to bend to prune or pick. This pruning method could be used in the garden to make an attractive cover for a pergola.

General care

Treat your vines as you would your family – keep them fed, watered and warm.

If there is a late frost cover them with horticultural fleece. In early spring, put an organic mulch around the base and feed with a general fertilizer at 2 oz per sq yd (6g per sq m). In the summer, water well in dry spells to help prevent mildew. A liquid seaweed feed can be applied every fortnight until the berries start to ripen, to provide potash for fruit development and help keep off fungal diseases.

Jasper patrol

One grower planted a willow hedge around his vines as a windbreak and next year found that his wasp problem had gone. The wasps had found an alternative food source to the ripening grapes, the honeydew that dripped out of the back of the willow aphid. If you don't fancy planting willows to keep off the wasps, try planting late-maturing grape varieties in the south and mids in the north. You can put stockings over the maturing bunches to keep off pests. Don't kill the wasps unless you can help it: earlier in the year, they eat vast quantities of pests.

A vine grown on the Geneva double curtain system

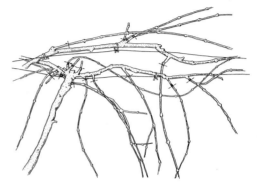

In the winter, after the grapes have been harvested, cut all the laterals back to a good bud.

Problems

The scourge of the vine used to be the vine louse, *Phylloxera vastatrix*, which came over to Europe from the USA in the 1860s and destroyed thousands of vineyards. Thanks to prompt action – grafting on to *Phylloxera*-resistant rootstocks and crossing with *Phylloxera*-resistant vines – the European vineyards made a comeback. Fortunately there is no problem with *Phylloxera* in the UK.

However, vines do get their fair share of problems. Yellowing leaves may be caused by lime chlorosis or magnesium deficiency. In the former case, increase the acidity of the soil by adding an organic mulch or grow a lime-tolerant variety such as Seyval. In the latter case give the vine a dose of Epsom salts. This will not act as a purgative on the vine but simply gives them the magnesium they need.

Vines can suffer from fungal diseases in June and July. Treat powdery mildew, which looks as its name suggests, with sulphur or by growing resistant varieties, and keep down botrytis, the grey mould, by careful pruning to keep the plant open and the air circulating.

Make your own wine

Use very ripe grapes – the riper they are the more sugar they will contain and the more alcohol they will produce. Crush the grapes with a stout stake or your (clean) feet to break the skins (but not the pips, as their acrid oil taints the wine). Next, press the pulp in a wine press and stand the juice overnight in a stoppered container at 50–60°F (10–15°C). After a day, siphon off the cleared liquid and measure its specific gravity with a hydrometer. This will tell you how much sugar you need to add, if any. Tables showing how much sugar to add are available from the shops that sell wine-making equipment.

Next, add a yeast starter, which needs to be prepared in advance. Two or three days before making the wine, press a pint of juice and sterilize it by heating to 160°F. Cool and add the appropriate yeast, such as a hock type or champagne type. Put in a sterilized bottle, plug with a wad of cotton wool and leave

---

Down on the allotment

You don't have to have a commercial vineyard to grow grapes for wine. All you need is an allotment, a few good vines, a bit of know-how and you're away. A group of allotment holders in south-east London produce 2,000 bottles of wine a year on less than 1 acre (0.4 ha) of suburban land. They all have their own individual plots and grow their own favourite varieties. They grow the grapes and make the wine as individuals because anything over ¼ acre (0.1 ha) counts as a vineyard and comes under EC regulations. Also, as profits must not be made from allotment produce, their friends can make a good guess at what they are getting for Christmas each year! One thing the allotment holders do together is exchange advice.

Over the river is a man who can pass on a few tips about vines. Mr Amatruda was brought up on a farm in Salerno, where he used to grow vines in the Italian sunshine to produce some excellent wines. He came to London fifty years ago and still grows vines, commuting daily by bus to his allotment. He certainly knows his grapes, and is very particular about how he grows them. One of his tips is to make sure that the soil under the vines is kept bare. This allows the soil to dry out at the surface, encouraging the vine roots to go deep into the soil to look for moisture. Despite the climate, Mr Amatruda usually manages to get a good crop. His son treads the grapes wearing very clean wellies (so as not to stain his feet), and the pulp is filtered through a muslin bag before fermentation in wooden barrels. Mr Amatruda uses no chemicals or sugar in his wine and the results are astounding, excellent-tasting wines year after year.

---

to get bubbling until you press the bulk of the grapes.

Put the grape juice (must), starter and half the sugar required in a demi-john and plug with a fermentation lock. Keep at 50°–60°F (10–15°C) to get a slow and steady fermentation. After three to four weeks siphon (rack) off the fermenting wine into a clean sterile demi-john to get rid of the sediment

Mr Amatruda on his allotment

(lees). Add the second half of the sugar before putting in the fermentation lock. After a month or two, rack off again to get rid of the lees. When fermentation has finished and the specific gravity reads about 995, meaning that all the sugar has turned to alcohol, rack off and cork it down to mature. It can be bottled after about eighteen months. If your wine does not clear, add a fining agent or put it outside for a night or two in frosty weather. This makes all the hazy bits shrivel up and sink to the bottom.

INDOOR GRAPES

Indoor grapes can be grown in a cold greenhouse, but a wider range can be grown in a warm one. Even a greenhouse as small as 8 x 6 ft (2.4 x 1.8 m) can house a vine, as long as you keep it well pruned. For best results plant the vine in a 'lean-to' and train it along the length of the house wall to take advantage of the heat that comes off the wall at night.

What to grow
There are three main types:

The Sweetwaters These are early, and tasty with thin skins. They grow well in a cold greenhouse and like early apples do not keep well.

Black Hamburgh Black. Good flavour, good cropper, good choice! Grows well in pots.

Buckland Sweetwater White. Good yields, fair flavour. Suitable for a small greenhouse.

Foster's Seedling White. Excellent flavour if eaten as soon as ripe. Good cropper.

The Muscats These crop slightly later and need heat and hand pollination. It is worth the effort, as they taste good.

Frontignan Both black and white. Early maturing with small tasty grapes. Good in pots.

Madresfield Court Black. Good flavour.

Muscat Hamburgh Black. Excellent flavour. Needs another grape to pollinate it.

Muscat of Alexandria White. Excellent flavour. The best of the Muscats.

The Vinous A firm favourite with the Victorians. These do not ripen until Christmas and need heat.

Alicante (Black Tokay) Heavy cropper with good flavour.

Lady Downe's Seedling Black. Excellent flavour.

The big Black Hamburgh

A magnificent Black Hamburgh grape vine grows at Hampton Court in London. The vine, planted in 1768, was producing over 2,000 lb (900 kg) of grapes a year by the nineteenth century. It is still going strong today and is there for all to see. The grapes are sold at harvest time and are delicious.

In the Victorian era, Richard Webb, from Calcot, near Reading, well known for breeding cobnuts and for his dislike of pruning, had a Black Hamburgh reputed to be the largest in England. The total length of its branches was in excess of 1,640 ft (500 m) and it produced about a ton of fruit a year.

Planting

With a cold greenhouse, plant the vine outside and train the stem inside, and with a warm greenhouse plant the vine inside. Good ground preparation is essential. Planted inside, the vine can be grown in a raised border to avoid waterlogging problems. Be-

fore planting put in horizontal wire supports, 12 in (30 cm) apart, starting about 3 ft (1 m) from the ground. Keep them about 12 in (30 cm) from the glass to prevent the leaves scorching and to allow air movement behind the vine. Plant the vine at the opposite end to the door, otherwise when it gets going you will not be able to get in to prune it! All vines need a cold period of dormancy to ripen the wood. If planted inside, open the greenhouse vents and doors in winter. If you keep frost-tender plants in the greenhouse in winter, either wave them goodbye or grow the vine in a large pot so that it can be moved outside.

Training and pruning

Indoor vines are usually grown on the rod and spur system. The rod, a thick stem used as the framework, is trained along the length of the greenhouse. The current season's fruit-producing laterals grow out at about 12 in (30 cm) intervals from spurs along the rod.

Vine titivation

To crop well, vines need a lot of attention. Although this is time-consuming, it is all quite simple. The jobs below are for a vine in a heated greenhouse – in a cold greenhouse they should be carried out three to four weeks later.

• **December** Gently scrape the old bark down to smooth brown bark. This keeps the vine clean and gets rid of overwintering pests, especially red spider mite.

• **January** Remove the old mulch and some of the old soil with a stiff broom and replace with fresh John Innes No. 3 compost.

• **February** When the sap starts to rise in the spring, it tends to rush to the end buds and cause them to burst into growth, leaving the ones further down dormant. If the main rod is untied from its supports and arched down, it slows down the sap, which allows the buds further down to get a look in. When the buds burst into growth the rod can be tied back up again.

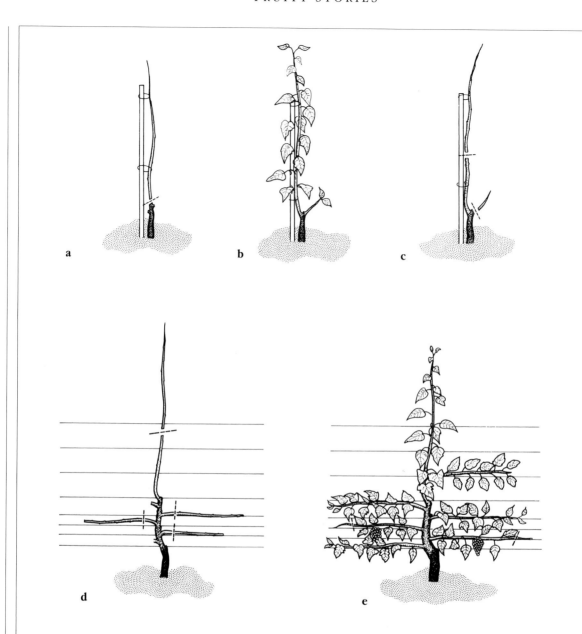

a   b   c

d   e

Formative pruning of indoor vines

After planting, the first step is to get the framework established.

(a) In November, cut the vine back by two-thirds. The harder a plant is cut back the more growth it will put on.

(b) In the growing season select a strong shoot and train it up towards the roof. If the vine has got its roots down into good fertile soil, the shoot can grow up to 10 ft (3 m). Tip other shoots back to 4 in (10 cm) to concentrate the energy into the one shoot. Some accident-prone gardeners retain 2 shoots, in case something untoward happens.

(c) In the second November, cut the selected framework shoot back hard again, by about two-thirds of the current season's growth, and take the laterals back to 1 bud.

(d) Continue the process , winter and summer, until the framework rod has reached the required length.

(e) After a couple of years train 1 or 2 laterals horizontally and allow them to fruit, pinching them out 2 leaves beyond the embryo bunch of grapes. This is just to give you a taste of things to come, but do not overdo it. If too many bunches are allowed to develop too early, the vigour and cropping ability will be damaged for years to come.

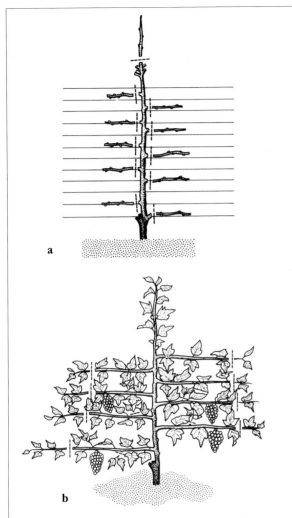

Regular pruning of indoor vines on the rod and spur system
(a) Once the framework has become established the pruning of indoor vines is very simple. Each November cut back the current season's growth on both the laterals and the main framework rod to 1 bud.
(b) Each summer, pinch back laterals with bunches to 2 leaves beyond the bunch and fruitless laterals to 5 or 6 leaves.

by tying it to the wire with a running noose knot and bringing it down over a period of a few days.

• **May** Help the grapes pollinate by giving the rods a little shake at midday. For the shy setters cup your hands round the bunch and gently stroke them – very sensual!

• **April to July** Pinch out laterals two leaves beyond the forming bunches of grapes, and to eight leaves if there are no grapes on that lateral. Pinch back all sub-laterals to one leaf. Also remove any tendrils as they form. Liquid feed with potash fertilizer every two to three weeks from when growth starts until the fruit starts to ripen. If growth is poor, apply a general fertilizer in spring.

In late spring and summer thin the bunches to give about 1 lb (500 g) of fruit for every 12 in (30 cm) of rod, to prevent the vine from overcropping and getting weak. Then thin the grapes in the bunches to allow room for the pick of the bunch to swell up to their full potential. Handling damages the bloom (which acts like a raincoat, keeping off water and fungal spores), so the tricky task is to thin the grapes without touching them, by using nail scissors and a small forked stick. If you are growing for show, shape the bunches like contestants in a muscle-man line-up, with firm, square shoulders and a thin waist. Support the top branches of the bunch (shoulders), by looping up to the wires with raffia. Cut away undersized berries and excess grapes in the middle of the bunch and space the outer berries to allow room for growth. Thin shoulders sparingly, as these need to stand firm when the bunch is harvested. Do several thinnings, and even after the bunches have reached perfection check regularly and remove diseased grapes.

Ripening grapes are prone to splitting, especially if water condenses on them. To avoid this, ventilate the greenhouse and avoid sudden air temperature changes.

When the grapes have coloured up they still need to hang on the vine for between two and ten weeks, depending on variety, to mature and let the sugars

• **April** In spring several laterals grow out from each spur; pinch them out to leave one per spur. Leave a couple of unwanted ones as back-ups for a while. The chosen lateral on each spur wants to grow upwards; you want it to grow horizontally so that it will produce more fruit and be manageable. The new laterals are very fragile and can snap very easily, hence the back-ups. Gently lower the lateral to the horizontal

The big show

The Royal Horticulture Society Autumn Show at the Westminster Halls in London attracts the crowds in early October each year. There are piles of apples and pears as high as the sky, but where are the grapes? Fight through the crowds and over against the wall you may spot them, all two entries! However, it is not quantity but quality that counts, and the bunches are in perfect condition. The strong competition is between His Grace the Duke of Devonshire, from Chatsworth, and His Grace the Duke of Marlborough, from Blenheim Palace. They and their gardeners are very keen dessert-grape-growers. Every year the Chatsworth and Blenheim greenhouses prepare for the show, and finally the head gardeners ride up to town and set up their treasured bunches. The coveted prize, £20! The gardeners have been known to call the Dukes within minutes of the result to give them the verdict. Who will win this year? Better go to the show and see.

Grapes on show

form. If they are for show and are ready before the deadline they can be kept in good condition, on the vine, for several weeks in a cool (45°F/7°C) dry atmosphere.

Potty about grapes

The Victorians loved to grow dessert grapes under glass. In some of the grander gardens the big greenhouses were even divided into sections so that grapes requiring different temperatures could be grown.

Their *pièce de résistance* was, however, the potted grape. This was brought to the table to impress guests by plucking grapes off the vine under their very noses. What better way to show off the expertise of the gardener than to bring the mountain to Mohammed.

The greenhouses at the Royal Horticultural Society gardens at Wisley often house potted grapes. Ray Waite, superintendent of the glasshouses, has the potting technique off to a fine art. The principle is very simple. In early spring layer a one-year-old stem (rod) horizontally over a series of pots filled with John Innes No. 3 potting compost and peg the buds on to the surface of the compost. Each bud or eye will hopefully send down roots and throw up a stem, which you can then tie to a cane.

Another way of doing it is to take a shoot from the previous year and pass it up through the drainage hole in the bottom of a pot filled with potting compost, with about 2 ft (60 cm) of stem protruding from the top. The stem will produce roots in the soil of the pot and grape-producing laterals above the pot. This method produces more grapes per pot than the first method.

If you do not have room to house a vine you can grow potted grapes by using 'coils', a type of cutting. Prune unwanted one-year-old growths off a vine and store 12 in (30 cm) lengths in sand over winter. In the spring coil the 'cutting' into a 24 in (60 cm) pot and secure the protruding stem with a cane. As with other cuttings, give the pot bottom heat to encourage rooting. The rooted cutting will produce laterals some of which support bunches of grapes.

With the first two methods, keep the baby plants attached to the parent during spring and summer and prune the laterals in the same way as an indoor vine. Water and feed the pots with a high potash fertilizer during the growing season. When the fruit has ripened, separate the potted grape from the parent over the course of several days, before taking the pot indoors for that all-important dinner party.

In a small greenhouse, grapes can be kept in pots

Ray Waite and the indoor vines at Wisley

the vine into a larger, say 9 in (22 cm) pot of John Innes No. 3 compost. This soil-based compost will ensure that the vine does not get top-heavy, and the high nutrient levels it contains will support the fruitful growth to come. At last the time has come to reap some rewards and grow some grapes. The fruiting laterals that develop from the top in the growing season can now be treated like any other indoor vine. That is, pinch out the tips at two leaves beyond the bunches and take sub-laterals back to one leaf. To prevent the laterals snapping under the weight of the fruit, tie them up to the cane in the middle like a maypole. From this year onwards, prune on the rod and spur system, treating the five or so laterals on the mop as the spurs.

Liquid feed the pot-grown vines regularly during the growing season and repot them every couple of years.

In the kitchen

Vines are very versatile and can be used in both savoury and sweet dishes. Wine transforms culinary dishes too, and even when you summer prune your vine the leaves can be used for dolmades.

permanently and trained as standards so they do not need horizontal supports. The framework is provided by a stout rod supported by a cane and the fruiting laterals grow as a mop at the top. Potted vines fit into a small space, fruit readily and can be taken outside in winter to get their cold fix. This method also enables several varieties to be grown even in a small space.

To grow vines as potted standards, pot up a healthy well-established rod in early spring and secure to a cane. When the rod has reached about 5 ft (1.5 m), prune back to a bud in November. In the following growing season allow about five new laterals to form a head at the top, pinching them out at six leaves, and remove any that sprout from the stem further down. Also remove any flowers that form to let the vine get well established. In the second and third years prune back the laterals on the head to one bud in November. In the spring move

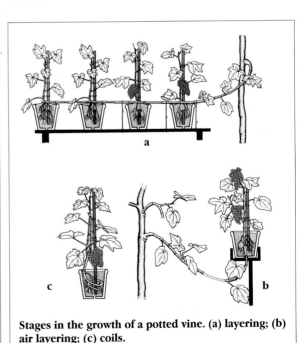

Stages in the growth of a potted vine. (a) layering; (b) air layering; (c) coils.

John Dory with Grapes

This grape dish is derived from the classic French dish Sole Véronique, and works well with any firm white fish. The grapes add freshness and succulent texture, point up the wine base of the sauce and look extraordinarily pretty.

Serves 6 as a main course

White wine sauce
1 shallot, chopped finely
7 fl oz (200 ml) fish stock
4 fl oz (100 ml) dry white wine
3 fl oz (75 ml) Noilly Prat
5 fl oz (125 ml) double cream
2 oz (50 g) butter, chilled and diced
parsley and chives, chopped
sea salt and freshly ground pepper

3 x 1½ lb (700 g) John Dory or firm white fish such as halibut or Dover sole
large black or green grapes
1 oz (25 g) butter

For the sauce, combine the first four ingredients in a large saucepan and boil down to half the quantity. Add the cream and bring to the boil again. Simmer gently until the sauce has thickened. Off the heat, gradually whisk in the pieces of butter, stir in the herbs and season.

While the sauce is cooking, skin and fillet the fish and lay the fillets on a shallow, buttered roasting tray. Brush with butter and grind a little black pepper over them. (The simplest stock can be made by covering the backbones of the fish with cold water or a mixture of water and white wine and a bay leaf and bringing the pot very slowly to the boil and then just barely simmering it for half an hour. Strain off and reduce down as necessary.)

Skin and halve the grapes and take out the pips.

Bake the John Dory for 10 minutes at 375°F (190°C, Gas 5), uncovered, until the fish is just firm to the touch. Just before serving, warm the grapes in the sauce and spoon around the fish.

Chicken Livers Fried in Red Wine

The red wine and butter dressing makes this simple starter quite special and ever popular. It could also be served as a light lunch dish or supper dish for 4 people, perhaps with some good husky bread and more red wine to drink.

Serves 6 as a starter

8 oz (225 g) organic chicken livers
1 tablespoon olive oil or sunflower oil
5 fl oz (150 ml) red wine
3 oz (75 g) butter, cut into 6 pieces
sea salt
freshly ground black pepper

Salad from selections of the following:
green salad leaves, e.g. lettuce, chicory, sorrel, spinach, watercress, rocket, purslane
chopped herbs, e.g., parsley, tarragon or chives
small pieces of something crunchy, such as radish, cucumber or green pepper
brown bread garlic croûtons or crisp dice of smoked bacon

Snip the stringy bits from the chicken livers and cut into 3 or 4 pieces. Heat the oil in a medium-sized frying pan and quickly fry the livers until brown on all sides. Add the wine and bubble for a minute. Lift the livers out of the pan and keep warm. Reduce the wine in the pan to about 2 tablespoons and stir in the butter. A fish slice helps to smooth out the lumps of butter. Season.

A quick way to make garlic croûtons is to toast 2 slices of bread and either spread with garlic butter, cut into dice and fry, or cut the toast into dice first and then fry in garlic oil. Either way, by toasting the bread first the croûtons do not soak up so much fat and crisp more quickly.

Make little heaps of salad on individual plates and arrange the chicken liver pieces on top. Pour some of the warm dressing from the pan over each helping, sprinkle on some croûtons or bacon bits, and serve.

Grape, Orange and Sweet Wine Tart

There is no season for this pudding, as the ingredients are always available, but perhaps it is more of a winter pudding when there is a lack of our own fresh fruit. It is colourful and festive and is very good made with tangerines and clementines at Christmas time.

Serves 10

Sweet pastry base
2 oz (50 g) 85 per cent wholemeal flour
1½ oz (40 g) unsalted butter
1 teaspoon icing sugar
about 1 dessertspoon cold water

Filling
2 leaves gelatine
12 oz (350 g) large black grapes (or green, not so dramatic)
6 medium oranges or equivalent in tangerines, etc.
7 fl oz (200 ml) Beaume de Venise or sweet pudding wine
1 oz (25 g) granulated sugar

Make the pastry and leave to rest. Roll it out very thinly and use to line a round fluted tart tin with a removable base.

Soak the gelatine leaves in cold water. Halve and pip the grapes. Segment the oranges and add the juice to the wine to make ½ pint (300 ml).

Warm a little of the wine and dissolve the soaked gelatine leaves and the sugar in this. Stir in the rest of the wine and orange juice. Put this to chill in the fridge.

Arrange the fruit pieces in the pastry case. When the jelly is beginning to set, pour it gently over the fruit. Chill until firm.

Serve with cream, vanilla ice-cream or the whole orange ice-cream on page 26.

Stuffed Vine Leaves

The attractive packaging of fresh red and green vine leaves make all the difference to these versatile vegetarian morsels, but the filling needs to be nicely spiced. A few chopped olives, mixed herbs or, for carnivores, some chicken or ham or diced cooked lamb, as in the traditional Greek recipe, can be added if you like.

Serves 6 as a starter, 4 as a main course

24–30 fresh vine leaves
4 oz (100 g) long-grain brown rice
2 oz (50 g) each of dried apricots and sultanas
2 oz (50 g) lightly toasted pine-nuts
1 teaspoon each ground cardamom, cumin and
  coriander seeds
2 tablespoons chopped fresh parsley
green virgin olive oil
zest and juice of ½ lemon
sea salt, freshly ground black pepper

Pick some fresh vine leaves about 4 in (10 cm) in diameter. Blanch them in a large pan of boiling water for 3–4 minutes, strain (saving the stock), and leave in a bowl of cold water to keep leaves separate.

Rinse the rice and cook in ½ pint (300 ml) of the vine stock for 25 minutes, by which time the rice grains should be cooked but still firm. NB: brown rice takes longer to cook than white.

Combine the rice with the fruits, nuts, spices and parsley, dress with a little oil, the lemon zest and juice, and season with salt and pepper.

Spread the leaves, snip off the stalks, and lay a heaped teaspoon of filling at the stalk end of each leaf. Roll up, tucking in each side to make cylinder.

Lay them snugly together in the bottom of an ovenproof dish, pour over the stock, and cook for 20 minutes in a low oven at 300°F (150°C, Gas 2). Take out of the oven and leave to cool and firm.

Brush with olive oil just before serving on their own or with a sweet pepper, tomato or leafy salad.

Celery and Grape Salad

The celebrated Waldorf Salad is an established favourite. As a mid-meal salad, I use a French dressing made with walnut oil, but as an accompaniment to a cold table or when serving with baked potatoes as a light supper dish, creamy yoghurt is a lighter echo of the original mayonnaise dressing. It is splendid served with cold meats, such as turkey leftovers after Christmas.

Serves 6

1 head of celery
6 oz (175 g) grapes, preferably black
2–3 dessert apples (Cox's or a Russet variety)
3 oz (75 g) shelled walnuts
watercress to garnish

Dressing
5 tablespoons walnut oil, 1 teaspoon cider vinegar
sea salt
freshly ground black pepper
  or 6 tablespoons thick natural yoghurt

Cut the celery crossways into small, neat slices, including all the fresh green leaves. Halve the grapes and remove the pips.

Just before serving, core and slice the apples, leaving the skin on, and cut into ½ in (1 cm) dice. Toss all the ingredients in the chosen dressing and snip some watercress over the top.

Opposite: Stuffed Vine Leaves

7
OLD AND WILD

Wild fruits once formed an important part of our diet. Some of them still do. Blackberries are so popular that 'to blackberry' has become a verb in the English language. It is comforting to know that we picked blackberries in Neolithic times and are still picking them today: some things never change! Some of our native fruits, such as the wild raspberry and wild cherry, may have ended up in the garden through selective breeding. The wild crab is also thought to be an ancestor of our cider apple and the sloe a relation of the plum.

Then there are the wildings: not quite wild but happy accidents, throwbacks of cultivated varieties grown up from discarded plum stones and apple cores. The Pershore Yellow Egg, once an important plum in the canning industry, was found growing wild in Tiddesley Wood in Pershore, while the Newton Wonder apple was said to have been discovered on a pub roof in Derbyshire, coming out of the thatch. Even though breeders have deliberately crossed fruits to produce new varieties, the old chance seedlings still take the biscuit as far as taste is concerned: the Cox, from 1825, nutty, honeyed and pear-like; Worcester Pearmain, with a taste of sweet strawberries; and D'Arcy Spice, from 1785, with its hot, spicy nutmeg-like flavour. So next time you throw an apple core into the hedgerow you may have set the ball rolling towards the discovery of a new variety.

Most of our cultivated fruits, however, came from natives of other areas, around the Caucasus and Turkestan. Here woods of wild pears, apples and cherry plums dominated the landscape. The local people selected the best varieties and took them to their gardens, and from there over the years the fruits travelled south to the Fertile Crescent. Further selections were made as the fruits made their way up across Europe, and now thousands of years later some of these plants have made it into our own gardens. So all our fruits have wild beginnings.

Despite all the well-known garden fruits it is sometimes pleasurable to put aside the large apples and pears for a moment and go back to your roots. With the wild fruits you get a rest from pruning, a good walk, a lot of fun, a taste of history, and free food. So go out into your communal garden, the countryside, and get picking.

Hawthorn
(*Crataegus monogyna/C.oxyacantha*)

If a plant has been used by man for a long time it acquires many names. Hawthorn is no exception, and is also called: agald, agarve, agase, agog, bird's eggle, bird's meat, chaw, hag, halve, harve, hippertyhaw, haw, hazels, gazels, halves, hagthorn, ladies meat hazle, heethen-berry, heg peg, hogail, hogarve, hoggan, hoggosse, may-fruit, pig-all, pigberry, pixie pears, cuckoo's beads and chucky cheese. Raw, the fruits taste like raw potatoes. Cooked with crab-apples to make a jelly, they make an excellent accompaniment to cheese. A cure for sciatica called the Duke of Monmouth's recipe was made of ripe haw berries and fennel roots mixed with syrup of elderberries. Research is now looking into the use of hawthorn berries as a cardiac tonic. The plant rather than the fruit has found its way into the garden and is used as a rootstock for medlars.

Dog rose
(*Rosa canina*)

The rose-hip is famous for its high Vitamin C content and the syrup it produces. Name follows fame and they certainly have a lot: buckie berries, choops, dogjobs, hagisses, hedgespeaks, hedge-pedgies, hipsons, hiopes, huggans, itching-berries, nippernails, pig's noses, and soldiers. The field rose, *Rosa arvensis*, and the sweet briar, *Rosa rubiginosa* , have rose-hips too.

Rose-hip syrup has been said to cure all ailments, from coughs and colds to diarrhoea and dysentery. The rose-hip is a false fruit: the real fruits are the little hairy objects inside it. These are still used commercially to make itching powder, and this is why you have to clean the pans and the jelly bags several times when making the syrup.

> In the Second World War, rose-hip syrup production became a commercial concern. Volunteers collected the berries for 'Operation Rose', in one year managing to collect 344 tons. The Rose-Hips Products Association treated freshly ground rose-hips with boiling water to destroy an enzyme which they found broke down the Vitamin C in the fruit. The rose-hip juice was then concentrated under reduced pressure to make syrup. Doctors during the war discovered that patients with fracture cases recovered more quickly when they received rose-hip syrup. Another discovery was that rose-hips collected from Scotland contained more Vitamin C than those from Cornwall.

Barberry
(*Berberis vulgaris*)

This large shrub with its yellow flowers, oval sharp-toothed leaves and vicious spiny stems was cultivated for its fruits until the nineteenth century. The berries were used for wine and medicinally against fevers, to treat typhoid, scurvy, sore throats and liver conditions such as jaundice. It is from these fruits that the delicious *confiture d'épine vinette*, for which Rouen is famous, is prepared. The red berries, which ripen in July, make a tart jelly and taste good candied or pickled. (See the section on poisons, page 129.)

Bilberry
(*Vaccinium myrtillus*)

This small shrub, with its purple fruits covered in grey bloom, is common on acid heath and moorlands. The fruits are sometimes called 'blaeberries', meaning bluish, but you may know them by names such as huckleberries, wortleberries, whinberries, trackleberries, hurtleberries, brylocks, cowberries, crowberries, hartberries or wimberries. Although the berries are laborious to pick, people have done it for years. Why? Because the bilberries, with their acidic, tart but sweet taste, are irresistible, raw or cooked! They have their medicinal virtues too, and were once used to treat scurvy, diarrhoea and urinary complaints. Nowadays, homeopathic bilberry tablets are sometimes used by diabetics.

Elderberry
(*Sambucus nigra*)

The elder is surrounded by superstition and some gardeners will not cut down an elder tree in case they are pursued by bad luck.

Raw elderberries are poisonous, but once cooked the cyanide they contain breaks down and they can be transformed into drinks, jams, jellies and even dried currants. Elderberries are used in Pontack's sauce, a famous spicy, vinegary sauce for meats. The recipe came from Pontack's restaurant in Lombard Street and was very popular with retired military gentlemen. To make the sauce, pour 1 pt (500 ml) of claret over 1 pt (500 ml) of elderberries and put in a low oven overnight. Decant the liquid, and boil for 10 minutes with a teaspoon of salt, a piece of mace, 40 peppercorns, 12 cloves, a finely chopped onion and a pinch of ginger. The sauce improves with time and was said to be best if bottled and kept for seven years before use!

As for non-culinary uses, elderberries were once used as a pH indicator (the juice going green with alkalis and red with acids) and as a Roman hair dye (to produce bright purple hair). In the past the elder was used to cure many ailments, from scurvy to toothache, and from rheumatism to syphilis. One seventeenth-century book by the German physician Martin Blochwich, explained how parts of the elder could be used to cure no less than seventy different diseases!

Sorbus and sea buckthorn: free and tasty

The Sorbus tribe

The fruits from these naturalized trees once formed part of our diet. Even its name hints at culinary uses, 'sorb' meaning 'drink down'. The best-known sorbus is the rowan (*Sorbus aucuparia*), with its large clusters of small orange berries. Also known as cares, cock-drunks, dog-berries, and quicken-berries, these fruits make good wine and an excellent jelly to accompany game or lamb. And if you had a sore throat you could always gargle with the wine, as they were supposed to be good for that too. The main setback is getting to the berries before the birds eat them. The Latin name *aucuparia* comes from *auceps*, a fowler, meaning a catcher of birds.

The fruits of the related wild service tree, *Sorbus torminalis*, which ripen in September, can be bletted and eaten like medlars. In medieval England they were known as chequers, and there may be a link with the fermented drink that can be made from the fruits and the pub name Chequers. 'Service' may have come from the Spanish *cerevisisa*, *mea*ning fermented drink. The fruits of the whitebeam, *Sorbus aria*, can also be bletted. Known as 'chess apples' in the north of England, the fruits were eaten with wine and honey in the seventeenth century. All in all, Sorbus has many connections with alcoholic beverages, and maybe that's why you so often see the trees in pub gardens.

Juniper
(*Juniperus communis*)

Another boozy berry, the juniper is well known for its connection with gin, made from the volatile oils extracted from the black ripe fruits. The name gin comes from *genevrier*, the French for juniper. The berries take two to three years to mature and ripen in September and October. As well as flavouring gin they add a tasty nip to gamey meats, and the oils they contain stimulate the gastric juices as well as acting as a diuretic. This property has made the berries valuable for the extraction of essential oils used in the treatment of kidney and digestive complaints. Externally, a tisane of bruised fruits can be used to speed up the healing of wounds and as a liniment for rheumatism. Sheep seem to know what is good for them – they eat juniper berries, which helps to cure dropsy.

Sea buckthorn
(*Hippophaë rhamnoïdes*)

This shrub with its orange berries is not to be confused with the other buckthorns, which are poisonous. The berries, which are tart when raw, taste good when made into ice-cream, jelly, juice and sweet and savoury sauces. They also contain an essential oil used in the pharmacy industry. The Scottish Crop Research Institute have their eye on the sea buckthorn as a possible new crop for the cottage industry. It has potential, because it grows on windy sites, tolerates salty soil, and has a high Vitamin C content and a good colour. They are thinking of tweaking its genes to get rid of the spikes. In years to come the sea buckthorn could appear next to the pots of raspberries and strawberries in your local garden centre. Another fruit brought in from the wild.

POISON: KEEP OFF

Many hedgerow fruits, even ones the birds can eat, are poisonous to us, so take care. Teach children about the dangers of poisonous berries as soon as they can walk and talk.

Ligustrum spp. Privet berries are very toxic but had many non-culinary uses in the past, from making dye to lamp oil. This is obviously not recommended today.

Euonymus europaeus The amazing bright pink and orange berries of the spindle are poisonous, although they were once used in folk medicine as a purgative. They didn't do insects a lot of good either, and used to be dried, powdered and rubbed into the scalp to treat headlice.

Berberis vulgaris Cultivated forms of berberis are a

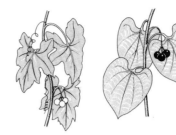

White and black bryony are poisonous.

lot more toxic than the native form and can cause vomiting and diarrhoea.

Sambucus nigra Raw elderberries are very poisonous, containing cyanide-producing glycosides. In 1983, raw elderberry juice poisoned a group of people in California within fifteen minutes of drinking it. Several of them were flown to hospital but all fortunately recovered.

Tamus communis/Bryonia dioica Both black bryony (*T. communis*) and white bryony (*B. dioica*) are very toxic. Black bryony can cause severe blistering and burning of the mouth and digestive system.

Viscum album Mistletoe from lime or poplar trees is more poisonous than that from apple trees. Be careful with your Christmas decorations. Mistletoe, holly and ivy are all poisonous.

Hedera helix Ivy berries are toxic and, although eaten by some birds, have killed chickens that have sampled them.

Ilex aquifolium Even two or three holly berries can be very poisonous.

Rhamnus cathartica, Frangula alnus The berries of both buckthorn (*R. cathartica*) and alder buckthorn (*F. alnus*) cause vomiting and diarrhoea and can be fatal. Victorians made syrup of buckthorn as a purgative, and disguised the disgusting taste with sugar and ginger. It is now considered far too toxic to use in this way. An ointment prepared from the berries was used by herbalists to treat warts. The berries can be used as a dye, yellow when unripe and green when ripe.

Taxus baccata All parts of the yew are poisonous except the fleshy red part of the fruit, which still contains poisonous seeds.

Other fruits poisonous to a greater or lesser degree include: *Symphoricarpus rivularis* (snowberry) *Fagus sylvatica* (beech nut) *Aesculus hippocastanum* (horse chestnut) *Atropa belladonna* (deadly nightshade) *Solanum dulcamara* (woody nightshade) *Solanum nigrum* (black nightshade)

If a wild fruit is not listed above, it does not mean that it is not poisonous.

PLUMS

(Prunus domestica)

Plums were one of the first fruits to be tamed. The cultivated plum did not arise in Britain, but is thought to be a natural cross between the cherry plum and the sloe, which probably took place in the Caucasus, real plum country! Before the plum arrived in this country, Britons ate the native sloe. The plum's family tree is a little akin to the local rabbit population. Here are a few of the relations:

The sloe or blackthorn
(Prunus spinosa)

The sloe, also known as bullens, heg-pegs, hedge-picks, hedge-speaks, slags, snags, winter kecksies, and winter picks, is one of our native woodland fruits. It also grows wild in Europe and Northern Asia. Raw sloes do very peculiar things to the mouth but are delicious when cooked and give a superb flavour to gin. The sloe contains alkaloids and stimulates the digestive juices, so sloe gin makes a good after-dinner drink. To make it, prick 8 oz (200 g) sloes, put in a bottle, and add 1 pint (500 ml) of gin,

6 unpeeled almonds and 2 oz (50 g) castor sugar. Swirl each day until the sugar dissolves and decant after 6 months. One keen sloe gin enthusiast puts the sloes out for the birds after decanting. The birds love them, but they get a bit sozzled and sometimes cannot fly!

The bullace
(Prunus insititia)

The bullace, also known as bully-broom, bullie, bolas, bullion, wild damson, and mirabelle, has become naturalized in Britain. The fruits develop their full flavour if picked after the frosts and make good wine and preserves. The bullace is less thorny than the sloe and has straighter branches, with brown rather than black bark. It also has larger leaves and fruits. Bullace flowers open after the leaves, while sloes come into blossom before they come into leaf.

The damson
(derived from Prunus insititia)

The damson, a descendant of the bullace, is named after Damascus, where it has been grown since before the Christian era. The small purple fruits have a similar but less drastic effect on the mouth than sloes and can be made into the most delicious dishes, such as the glorious damson crumble.

A damson makes an excellent garden tree, being compact, very hardy and resistant to pest and disease. Pick the fruits when they are ripe, tender and sweet. Damsons were once grown commercially in Kent, Norfolk and Shropshire. At Goldstone Hall in Market Drayton, Shropshire, they still celebrate their local fruit with an annual damson feast which has damsons in every course, including roast Shropshire goose with baked apple and damson pickle. Another local delicacy is damson cheese. In the 1980s the King of Nepal came to Britain and ordered 2 cwt (100 kg) of Market Drayton damson cheese to go with the roast lamb they were having for a banquet!

Old damson trees in the Lake District have recently had a reprieve – the Countryside Commission has given a grant to restock the orchards which are such a striking landscape feature. Originally the variety known as the Westmoreland prune was picked for jam, but now local publicans are using them to flavour beer.

The cherry plum or myrobalan
(*Prunus cerasifera*)

The cherry plum is known only in cultivation and has fruits that can be red, yellow or black. For centuries the fruits have been used in savoury and dessert dishes. You may see cherry plums in old hedgerows because they were often planted around orchards as windbreaks.

The domesticated plum
(*Prunus domestica*)

Thanks to introductions from the Romans, Henry VIII's fruiterer, nurseries, and research stations, we now have over 300 varieties of plum in this country. These can be grouped into plums and greengages. The plum itself is oval, while the greengage is rounder and also usually sweeter and tastier. Another difference: when picking ripe plums, the stalk usually stays on the tree, while with gages and damsons it comes off!

Noteworthy cultivars

One of the joys towards the end of summer is biting into a sun-ripened plum fresh off the tree: superb. To extend the season, grow a few different varieties to prolong the tastes as long as possible. Plums are either self-fertile, or not! If they need a partner Victoria is useful for mid-season, early and late flowerers, Denniston's Superb for early flowerers, and Oullin's Gage for late flowerers.

Dessert plums

Herman	Mid- to late July	A heavy-cropping blue plum. Self-fertile.
Early Laxton	Late July	Red tinged yellow fruits, good flavour. Susceptible to bacterial canker. Partially self-fertile.
Opal	Early August	Good flavour, red fruit, heavy cropper. Self-fertile.
Blue Tit	August	Compact, good flavour, heavy cropper. Self-fertile.
Victoria	Late August, early Sept.	Reliable, heavy cropper. Introduced in 1840, this plum was found as a chance seedling in a garden in Alderton in Sussex. Originally known as Sharp's Emperor, it was renamed Denyer's Victoria after being sold to a nurseryman in Brixton in 1844. It is self-fertile, heavy-cropping and has become very popular.
Laxton's Delight	Mid-Sept.	Good flavour. Partly self-fertile.
Coe's Golden Drop	Late Sept.	Very tasty , large yellow plum. It needs a bit of warmth to get a good crop. Some say that Golden Drop can be kept for twelve months if suspended by its stalk on a piece of string. If you try this, put a bowl underneath just in case! Self sterile.

Cooking plums

Early Rivers	Late July	Small blue plums. Heavy cropper. Good flavour. The first introduction from the Thomas Rivers nursery, raised in 1820. Partly self-fertile.
Czar	Early August	Heavy-cropping blue plum. A cross between Early Rivers and Prince Engelbert made by Rivers nursery. It was named after the Czar of Russia, who was visiting England at the time. Self-fertile.
Warwickshire Drooper	Mid-Sept.	Yellow fruit, good flavour. Alias Magnum or Magnum Bonum. Self-fertile.
Marjorie's Seedling	Late Sept.	Vigorous blue plum, heavy cropper, good flavour. One of the few successful seedlings discovered this century, in Berkshire in 1912. Self-fertile.

Marjorie's Seedling, a vigorous cooking plum

Dessert gages

Gages often split if it is too wet. If you live in an area of high rainfall, plant them in a sheltered spot but not in a frost pocket.

Count Althann's Gage	Late August	Good flavoured red fruit. Raised in Bohemia by Count Althann in the 1850s. Self-sterile.
Early Transparent	Late August	Yellow fruit, good flavour. Has see-through skin and when ripe with the sun behind it you can see right through to the stone. Beautiful. Self-fertile.
Denniston's Superb	Late August	Very good flavour. Self-fertile.
Cambridge Gage	Early Sept.	Excellent flavour but not a good cropper. Partly self-fertile.
Jefferson	Early Sept	Nice-tasting green plum. Raised by a judge in New York in 1825. Self-sterile.

The greengage

The greengage is a very well-travelled fruit that seems to have changed its name wherever it has been. Starting in Armenia, it travelled to Greece and Italy where it was called Verdocchia. When Queen Claude, wife of Francis I, introduced it into France, she renamed it Reine Claude. During the revolution, when royalty were not exactly popular, it was temporarily renamed Prune Citoyenne (the citizen's plum!). Then, in the eighteenth century, a Mr John Gage sent it to his brother Sir Thomas Gage in England and unfortunately it lost its label on the way. The unknown plum was nicknamed the green Gage's plum by a gardener.

Damsons

Farleigh	Mid-Sept.	Small tree, good flavour. Many wild damson seedlings have bigger and better fruits than the parents. Have a look round , maybe you can get a seedling named after you. Self-fertile.
Prune	September & October	Heavy cropper, excellent flavour. Also called the Westmoreland, Cheshire or Shropshire plum depending on who wants to claim it for their own. The prune plum from Bedfordshire hangs on the tree well after the leaves have fallen. It was once used to make into dye for German army uniforms. Self-fertile.

The plum collections

Brogdale Horticultural Trust holds the National Collection of plums with 336 varieties planted over 3.6 acres (1.47 ha). Like Noah's Ark they are in pairs, and include dessert and culinary plums, damsons and bullaces. Plums are not as robust or long-lived as apples and pears and have to be moved after about forty years. The plums at Brogdale were moved to their present site in the 1970s and now it is time to move them all again before some succumb to the dreaded plum pox (Sharka), an aphid-transmitted virus disease. To safeguard the collection, David Pennell and his colleagues are budding healthy, virus-free material on to clean rootstocks to replace and replant the entire collection. What a long job!

Fingerprinting plums

Plums have stones like our fingerprints, each one being unique to a particular variety, with a distinct shape, size and surface pattern. Brogdale Horticultural Trust have as many boxes of plum stones as they have plum trees. They have been used not only to help identify plums but also to piece together parts of history. The flagship of Henry VIII, the *Mary Rose*,

Patricia Hegarty in the walled garden at Hope End

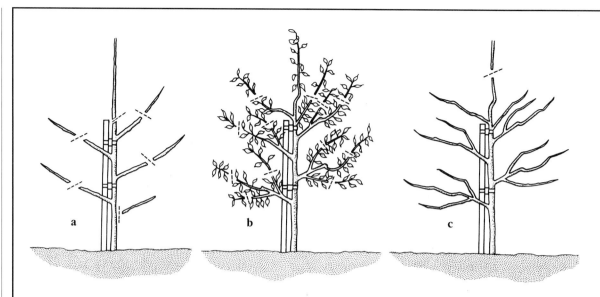

The stages in pruning a pyramidal plum
Plums trained as pyramids, which look a bit like a sparsely branched Christmas tree, make an ideal free-standing tree.

(a) In the first spring after planting, prune the leader back to a bud 4 in (10 cm) above the top feather, and cut the feathers back to one third of their length, to a bud that faces downwards to keep the branches as horizontal as possible.

(b) In late July shorten branch leaders to 10 in (25 cm) to downward-facing buds and laterals to 6 in (15 cm).

(c) Do not touch the main leader in the summer but cut it back to a third of its length the next spring. Cut back to a bud facing in the opposite direction to the one the previous year, to maintain the pyramid shape.

which sank in 1545, was raised in the 1980s. On board were over 100 plum stones in a basket. Using the stones from Brogdale, Wye College painstakingly worked out the types of plum in the basket. There was a greengage, a Catalonia, bullaces, and two sorts of cherry plum. Next time you eat a plum pie, and put the stones on the side of the plate, tinker, tailor, soldier, sailor could take on a whole new meaning!

Plums, care and attention
Plums need a sheltered site that escapes the spring frosts, with a well-drained, moisture-retentive soil that is slightly acid. Plant trees to be trained as pyramids or bushes 13 ft (4 m) apart, half standards 20 ft (6 m) apart and the big standards 25 ft (7.5 m) apart. One keen fruit gardener has trained his plum round the outside of his dining-room window to maximize use of space. It is a beautiful sight in the spring when in blossom, and in late summer he can just lean out of the window and pick plums straight off the tree.

Often your tree may not behave like the pictures in the textbook. Don't be frightened to tame it; there are ways to make it conform. If a branch is growing too vertically, tie it down, or if too low, tie it up. Alternatively cut off the offending branches to laterals or buds facing in the required growth direction. All this is done in the growing season, not the winter. Remember, you are in control.

Pests and diseases, and a few curative wheezes
Trap winter moths with greasebands and plum fruit moths with pheromone traps. Plum leaf-curling aphid can be controlled with insecticidal soft soap. One of the main problems on plums is silver leaf disease, a nasty fungus that gets in through pruning cuts in the winter. The symptoms are silver leaves, brown stains inside the branches and dieback. If it is very bad, bracket fungi develop on the bark which are brown and fluffy on the top and purple underneath. To avoid infection, do not prune plums be-

tween mid-September and the end of February, and always disinfect tools after you do prune. If your plums have silver leaf, cut back the branches to beyond the brown internal stains. You may be tricked by false silver leaf, where the foliage goes silver without any dieback or internal staining. This is due to irregular watering and malnutrition and can be treated with a foliar feed of liquid seaweed. Another disease, bacterial canker, causes the tree to exude orange gum from dead areas on the stem. The affected branches either produce small yellow leaves or do not come into leaf at all. To treat, prune out and spray with Bordeaux mixture.

Thinning and storing

If your plum crop looks as though it is going to be heavy, thin the plums at the beginning and end of July. This allows the ones left to develop a fuller flavour and helps to prevent the tree from becoming a biennial bearer.

Fresh dessert plums are delicious and juicy but last only a few days when picked ripe. They can be stored in a cool place for two to three weeks if picked just before ripening with the stalk attached.

CHERRIES

Both the sweet cherry and the acid morello cherry have ancestors in the wild woods of Britain: *Prunus avium,* the sweet, mazzard or gean, and *Prunus cerasus,* the wild, sour cherry. The sweet and the acid got together too, and produced the Duke, the sterile mule of the cherry world.

Richard Harris, fruiterer to Henry VIII, introduced many new cherries from Flanders when he planted up England's first fruit collection on 105 acres (42 ha) at the Teynham orchards in Kent in 1533. As the King had cherries, everyone wanted them, and soon new orchards were planted up to supply the demand. The orchard at Teynham soon became the basis of Kent's infant fruit industry, the garden of England in the making.

Mr Butt still grows cherries on the orchard site near Teynham. He has some large old trees and goes

Cherry facts

A local custom in Yorkshire was to stand beneath a cherry tree singing: 'Cuckoo, cherry tree, come down and tell me how many years I have to live.' Everyone then took it in turns to shake the tree, and the number of cherries that fell gave the length of your future life.

Cherries are associated with love and romance. 'So we grew together, like to a double cherry, seeming parted but yet an union in partition, two lovely berries moulded on one stem. So with two seeming bodies but one heart.' (Shakespeare, *A Midsummer Night's Dream.*) Soppy old thing!

Kirsch, the cherry liqueur, comes from Kirsche, the German for cherry. This in turn comes from *karshu,* the name given to the first cultivated cherries in Mesopotamia in 8 BC.

The Scythians who lived just north of the Black Sea around 5 BC used to protect their cherries from frost by tying felt around them.

Our wild cherries were often used as rootstocks for the imported types.

Cherry stalks were once used as an astringent and a tonic by soaking 1/2 oz (15 g) of stalks in 1 pt (500 ml) of water. They were used for bronchial complaints, for anaemia, and to regulate the bowels.

Hot cherry stones were once used in bed-warming pans.

Our wild cherries were once made into cherry beer and drunk with Kentish tart as an Easter treat.

Cherries do not last very long. But if the Queen wanted cherries, she got cherries. A fruiting tree was once covered with a damp canvas to retard the cherries so that Elizabeth I could have them a month after all the others had gone.

Riddle me, riddle me ree.
A little man sat in a tree.
A staff in his hand, a stone in his throat.
If you read me this riddle I'll give you a groat.

up his 40 ft (12 m) cherry ladders in June and July to pick the fruits as his grandfather did before him. Once up, the cherry ladders, so tall and heavy, didn't come down again until all the harvest was picked. Mr Butt still grows many of the old varieties, such as Merton Glory, Roundalls, Gaucher and Bradbourne Black.

Although the cherries are there, the market has nearly gone. Mr Butt sometimes takes his cherries to Covent Garden at six in the morning to find that cheap imports have already beaten him to it. His neighbours' farms have already gone and have been replaced by housing estates. The only remnants of the industry are the street names: Amber Close, Morello Close and Roundall Close, all cherry varieties. To keep his old trees, Mr Butt has had to apply for a grant from the Countryside Commission. Over 70 per cent of the traditional Kent cherry orchards have gone. Although beautiful, especially when in blossom, the trees were huge and difficult to harvest, and bacterial canker, virus diseases, frost and birds had almost caused them to throw in the towel. In Kent nowadays, many of the large trees have been replaced by smaller ones, grafted on to Colt rootstocks. As well as being easier to reach, they mature more evenly, can be netted against birds and come into fruit when they are younger. The cherries are still not as uniform as imports, or as big, but you can't beat the flavour.

Cherries for the garden
All the following cherries are self-fertile, so you won't need to find them any partners.

Sweet cherries
Delicious, dessert fruits

Sunburst	Early July	A black cherry with good flavour.
Stella	Late July	Red tasty fruits. Tree a little vigorous.
Compact Stella	Late July	Just like Stella, only smaller. Liable to revert back to original.
Cherokee	Early May	A black cherry, previously and correctly known as Lapins.

Duke

A cross between sweet and acid, with a taste half-way between the two.

May Duke	Mid-July	Compact tree. Partly self-fertile.

Acid cherries

Great in pies, wines, jams and for bottling.

Morello	Compact tree that tolerates shade.
Nabella	Good flavour.

Cherry care

Sweet cherries need the sun and acid ones can cope with shade. They both prefer deep, fertile, free-draining but moisture-retentive soil with a pH 6.5–7.5.

Sweet cherries (and Duke cherries) produce fruit on short spurs on two-year-old or older wood. They are best trained as pyramids (as described for plums) or fans (as described for peaches). Established fans, you will be glad to hear, need little pruning. Every spring cut out crossing or broken branches. Rub out buds facing towards or away from the wall in April. Pin back the side shoots in July and shorten them to four buds in September.

Acid cherries can also be trained as fans or pyramids, but as they fruit mainly on one-year-old wood they need to be pruned annually like peaches. The aim is to think a year ahead and prune to obtain new shoots that will crop the following year. Some acid cherries are weak-growing so occasionally a few older shoots need to be cut back to about 4 in (10 cm) from the base to stimulate new growth and prevent the centre becoming bare. Pruning should be carried out in March or April, when sap has started to rise, to decrease the risk of bacterial canker.

The main pest of cherries is cherry blackfly, which can be treated with insecticidal soap. Cherries, like plums, are prone to bacterial canker and silver leaf; avoid winter pruning and treat as for plums.

The taming of the stone fruits

Some landowners share their orchards with the wildlife, and get as much joy from the birds as they do from the fruit. Others see the birds as a threat to their livelihood. Birds love cherries, and at harvest-time guns, drums, car horns and noisy motor bikes are sent out into some orchards to keep our feathered friends away.

In the garden, one way of growing cherries and looking after your wildlife is to put the cherry in the cage and let the birds go free. To get the cherry into the cage is the first problem. The Colt rootstock which is semi-vigorous gets the tree down to 20 ft (6 m) but a little taming is also required. Root growth and therefore shoot growth can be restricted by growing cherries in large pots. Growth can be further restricted by tying down the main branches (festooning), and summer-pruning unwanted laterals to six or seven leaves. Always stick to the self-fertile types so that you will need only one tree.

Many of you will be familiar with towering plum trees, with delicious-looking plums well out of reach. The trees look great in orchards and large gardens, but what about the small gardens of today? The 'pixys' at the bottom of the garden have the answer. Plums and gages can now be grafted on to a dwarfing rootstock called Pixy. These dwarf trees can be trained as pyramids or even cordons in regimented rows alongside the raspberries. The plums Blue Tit and Victoria, both of which are self-fertile, make good cordon trees and can be pruned in the same way as apple cordons. (See Chapter 8, page 156). Summer pruning restricts growth, encourages fruiting, and with plums helps to control silver leaf disease which enters through winter pruning cuts. It seems the Pixy has solved more than one problem… and you can reach the fruit!

OLD BUT NOT FORGOTTEN

Three old fruits that you are more likely to happen across in a grand old garden than in a supermarket or a fruit cage are the medlar, mulberry and quince. They have all fallen from twentieth-century favour because they need a lot of time and effort: not for pruning and training, because they are easy to grow, but to prepare the fruit ready for eating. Nevertheless, they are steeped in history, and give you something that is just that little bit different.

THE MEDLAR
(Mespilis germanica)

The medlar is an odd fruit, with a tropical or even medieval look about it. Although it comes from Persia, its name derives from the Greek *mesos* meaning half and *pilos* meaning a ball. It has got some slightly more descriptive names such as *cul de chien* and old English equivalents that are best left to the imagination!

Medlars need little pruning and crop reliably from an early age. The fruits are picked in November, and stored calyx down in a single layer on newspaper. They are then left to blet, that is to soften and mellow (but not rot) for several weeks. Some say that you should eat them when they are decayed, but like a good Stilton it depends whether you like it fresh or crawling out of the fridge! When properly bletted the fruit is sweet and grainy. They can also be baked with butter and cloves for a few minutes and served like baked apple. It does take a while to get the hang of eating them: there is a lot of skin and pips to dispose of to get to the flesh. If you don't like getting bits stuck in your teeth go for medlar jelly, a lovely accompaniment to meat and game. Old herbals recommended medlars as a cure for looseness of the

The medlar

bowels, quite the opposite to most fruits. If you would rather use kaolin and morphine and don't like the taste of the medlar, the tree is still worth growing as an ornamental. It has pretty pinkish white blossom in May and June, bright red and yellow autumn foliage and rich brown gnarled and twisted bark. The medlar, being in the rose family, is related to quince, pear and hawthorn. It is often grafted on to one of these to control the size: on a quince rootstock it will reach 12 ft (4 m) and on a pear rootstock 15 ft (5 m). It has several long-lost relations in the British hedgerow, a thorned variety found wild in Southern England and an oriental cousin, the Japanese medlar or loquat.

If you want a medlar there are several varieties to choose from. The Nottingham is a reliable cropper with small, well-flavoured fruits. The Dutch, with its weeping habit has fruits half the size of an apple, while the Large Russian and Monstrous, as their names suggest, have large fruits well worth sinking the teeth into.

THE QUINCE
(Cydonia oblonga)

Do you have a strange apple or pear tree that has dark, leathery leaves, pinkish, white flowers 2 in (5 cm) across that blossom in June and beautiful looking inedible fruits? Well, you may have a quince. Quinces have apple- or pear-shaped fruits which are hard, tart, gritty and aromatic. Once cooked they turn into something else altogether – they are delicious. Good for pies, as an accompaniment for the Sunday roast, and for the well-known quince jelly. The word

To have or not to have

In a Somerset garden stood a large medlar tree. Every year a gypsy came to the garden, without invitation, picked all the medlars and left again. One year the woman stopped coming and the tree died right back. It has recently thrown up a new branch and has started to grow again, but the gypsy has not returned.

Others are not so keen on the medlars as to scrump them from another's garden. Anderson, writing on the foods of China, described the taste of the fruit: 'The medlar... is said to be at the best an acquired taste (and at worst reminiscent of raw sewage).' Each to his own!

marmalade does not come from oranges at all but from the Portuguese for quince, *marmalo*.

The quince originated in Central and Southern Asia but has been in Britain since the thirteenth century. The quince was the golden apple presented to Aphrodite by Paris, a symbol of love, marriage and fertility. The fruit was used as a cure-all as well as a love token. Quince flesh steeped in water was used as a laxative and to cure diarrhoea depending on which herbal you went to. The seeds are poisonous, containing prussic acid. If you grow one, make sure you remove the seeds before making any dishes from them.

There are many good varieties to choose, including Maliformis, an apple-shaped quince, and Champion, with its large pear-shaped fruits. Although the trees are said to be self-fertile, they crop better when they cross-pollinate.

The tree will grow best in the south and Midlands and needs a moist soil. To formative prune the young tree, remove half of the current season's growth each winter for the first three or four years to build up a framework. As with a bush-shaped apple tree, keep the centre open. Once the tree has a suitable framework no further pruning is necessary except to cut out dead, diseased or crossing-over branches.

Pick the fruits in October, before any hard frosts, and store in straw-lined trays in a single layer. Don't mix them with other fruits, such as apples, which will taint the flavour. They are ready to use after four to eight weeks when they ripen from green to yellow.

THE MULBERRY
(*Morus nigra/Morus alba*)

Mulberries are easy to grow, attractive, have few pest and disease problems and bear heavy crops of fruit for a long season.

The black mulberry (*Morus nigra*), grown for its delicious fruits, has stout shoots, fat buds and rough leaves, whereas the white mulberry is more of a decorative tree with slender shoots and smoother leaves which are sometimes used to feed silkworms. The fruits are very insipid.

The mulberry has long been dubbed the wisest of trees (Pliny the Elder, AD 23–79) because it avoids cold weather. It drops its leaves as soon as autumn arrives and does not come out again until after the last frost has passed in the spring. Gardeners used to say; 'When the mulberry leaf is as large as a crow's foot, then you may be sure that the weather is settled.' It certainly springs into life with a bang – the buds, which can be heard cracking open, can come out within twenty-four hours.

Mulberries for the garden

Black mulberries normally make a tree some 30 ft (9 m) high by 20 ft (6 m) across and will bear fruit when they are only about four years old. They are fairly hardy but may need protection from cold winds when young. If you are stuck for space they can be trained as espaliers on a wall or grown in pots where they can be pruned like a dwarf bush apple. (see Chapter 1, page 13). Mulberries fruit in late August and early September and try to make a real mess when they do it. To save the fruits and the lawn from getting ruined, put a net on the ground just as they start to fall and gather them every few days. To propagate mulberries a big cutting is needed! Take a truncheon (a piece of branch 6 ft (1.8 m) long and 6 in (15 cm) across), and push it in the ground the right way up in the autumn. Smaller hardwood cuttings can also be taken from the tips of the tree. To grow them from seed, gardeners used to rub a ripe fruit into an old well rope (not a thing you often come across in the local garden centre!) and bury it in the garden.

Mulberries don't only taste good, they do you good: Gerard said that ripe mulberries cured constipation while unripe ones are good for diarrhoea, (presumably in between they are just right), and that the juice cured mouth inflammations. But all these fruit cures are not just a thing of the past. Scientists recently extracted a chemical from mulberry tree roots which they hope may be of use in treating diabetes, cancer and HIV. Maybe James I's trees will prove fruitful after all.

Our old fruits may have something to offer us for the future and our wild fruits, such as the sea buckthorn, may become the commercial crops of tomorrow. If more people could taste these older fruits in beautiful desserts they would very probably spring up in a lot of gardens.

Mulberry trees are very long lived

The Stuart silk industry

Silk and wealth have always gone hand in hand. Silk comes from the cocoon of the silkworm that feeds on white mulberry leaves. The Chinese managed to keep the secret of silk under their hats for 3,000 years, but by the fourteenth century Chinese whispers had reached Europe and everyone was into sericulture (the rearing of silkworms). In Stuart times, James I got on the bandwagon and decided to plant mulberry trees around the country to create a silkworm industry and increase the country's revenue. He had been advised that the black mulberry would be more suited to the British climate and ordered 100,000 mulberry trees from France. Although he did manage to make his wife, Queen Anne of Denmark, a silk dress, the venture was a huge flop. The silkworms preferred the leaves of the white mulberry and the silk importers preferred the King to keep out of their hair. Nevertheless many of the trees were planted and some of the originals are still with us nearly 400 years on. If you know of an old mulberry tree you can work out its age with a tape-measure. The age of the tree is roughly equivalent to the circumference of the trunk in inches, 3 ft (1 m) above the ground.

Damson Richmond Cakes

Damsons are ideal for sauces and to enliven custards, milk puddings and strong ice-creams. The potency of the damson is unimpaired even after several months in the freezer. Shropshire is famous for its damsons, notably the Shropshire Prune, and it is one of the few fruit trees to prosper in the Lake District, where damsons are a popular ingredient in the regional cooking.

Makes 6-7 individual tarts

1 lb (450 g) damsons
2 tablespoons water
sugar to sweeten

Pastry
3 oz (75 g) wholemeal flour
2 oz (50 g) cold unsalted butter
1 teaspoonful icing sugar
1 egg yolk, cold water
light, tasteless oil, e.g. sunflower, for the moulds

Filling
4 oz (115 g) whole sweet almonds
2 oz (50 g) unsalted butter
3 oz (75 g) fine demerara sugar
1 teaspoonful wholemeal flour
2 egg yolks, beaten
grated zest of 1 well scrubbed lemon
juice of ½ lemon
2 oz (50 g) curd
few drops of natural almond essence

To make the pastry, rub the butter into the flour, stir in the sugar, then mix together with the egg yolk and water. Grease 6 or 7 brioche moulds and line them with the pastry.

Put the damsons and water in a saucepan and simmer slowly for 15-20 minutes, until soft.

While the damsons are cooking, blanch the almonds by pouring hot water over them. Leave for a few minutes, drain and remove the skins. Grind the almonds. Cream the butter and sugar together until light and fluffy and mix with nuts and remaining ingredients.

Preheat the oven to 400°F (200°C, Gas 6) and put in a baking sheet.

Pick the stones from the cooked damsons and sweeten to taste. Put a layer of damsons in the bottom of the pastry cases. If you have leftover fruit, serve it by the side of the tartlets.

Fill up the pastry cases with the almond mixture and bake on the preheated baking sheet for 20 minutes, until the filling has risen and turned golden. Serve on their own or with thick Jersey cream.

Mulberry and Apple Upside-Down Pudding

A little variation on the classic apple pudding. The mulberries stain the apple and the caramel topping a very grand deep purple – you do not need many mulberries, their taste is so distinctive. Any of the early Worcester apples are ideal for this pudding, as their season coincides with the mulberries.

Serves 6

Rich pastry
3 oz (75 g) wholemeal flour
1 tablespoon icing sugar
2 oz (50 g) chilled unsalted butter in small pieces
2 tablespoons cold water

Filling
6 dessert apples
3 oz (75 g) demerara sugar
1 oz (25 g) unsalted butter
up to 8 oz (225 g) mulberries (a handful will do)

Whiz the flour, icing sugar and 1 oz (25 g) butter to make a crumble. While whizzing add the water, until the pastry gathers into a ball. Refrigerate for 20 minutes. Pull the pastry ball into about 5 parts and drop into the processor with the rest of the chilled butter. Whiz quickly – the butter does not have to be completely amalgamated. Dust the pastry ball with flour and refrigerate again.

Peel core and slice the apples. Divide the sugar and butter between 6 individual dariole moulds or a small cake tin, and set either on the hot surface of a solid top cooker or on a baking tray in a moderately hot oven, 400°F (200°C, Gas 6) to caramelize.

Take off the heat and pack the moulds with the apple slices interspersed with mulberries. Build up just above the rim of the moulds, as the fruit will sink in

cooking. Sprinkle over a little more sugar if the apples are too sharp.

Roll out the pastry and use one of your moulds to cut out a 'lid' for each one. Place this on top of the fruit, but do not try to seal it round the edges. Put on a baking sheet and bake at 400°F (200°C, Gas 6) until the pastry has browned, usually about 20 minutes. Keep the puddings warm, and turn out to eat with custard, cream or vanilla ice-cream.

Victoria Plum and Oatmeal Crumble

Everyone loves a traditional English fruit crumble, starting with the early rhubarb and gooseberries, moving through the black currants and cherries and ending with a flourish at the end of the season with plums and apples.

Serves 6

2 lb (900 g) Victoria plums, halved and stoned
4 oz (100 g) sugar
cinnamon stick

Crumble
4 oz (100 g) 100 per cent wholemeal flour
4 oz (100 g) organic porridge oats
5 oz (150 g) demerara sugar
3 oz (75 g) unsalted butter, at room temperature
1 teaspoon ground cinnam

Put the plums into a 3 pint (1.75 litre) ovenproof dish, sprinkle on the sugar and add the cinnamon stick.

Make the crumble by combining the dry ingredients and lightly rubbing in the butter by hand or using a processor. Add the cinnamon and cover the plums lightly with the crumble mixture.

Bake at 350°F (180°C, Gas 4) for 30-40 minutes, until the top is slightly brown and crunchy.

Best served with hot custard.

Medlar Jelly

To make the strongest, ruby-coloured and most flavoursome jelly, pick the medlars when they are just beginning to ripen, but are still firm and a warm, russety green, usually mid- to late October. Once they become bletted, that is soft and brown, the jelly will not be such a bright colour, the flavour will fade and it will not set so easily. However, you can eat them raw at this stage: just peel off the skin with your fingers and scrape the soft fesh off the pips with a teaspoon. The taste is like sweet, rich dates.

Serve this beautiful, bright jelly, with its slightly dry tannic undertones, with roast game or cold meats. It also goes well in old-fashioned sweet pastries like Maids of Honour.

Makes about 3 lb (1.3 kg) jelly

4 lb (1.8 kg) medlars
6 pt (3.6 l) cold water
2 lb (900 g) granulated sugar
juice of 2 lemons

Cut the medlars in two; put them in a large stainless stell pan and cover them with 4 pt (2.4 l) of the water. Bring to the boil and simmer for 45 minutes to an hour, to break down the fruit. Strain the fruit through a jelly bag.

Because medlars are rather a dry fruit and you will only achieve a small, but intensely-flavoured amount of juice from the first cooking, I like to process the pulp a second time to extract the utmost flavour and some more volume before throwing it away. To do this, return the strained pulp to the saucepan and add the remaining 2 pt (1.2 l) of water. Simmer for at least 20 minutes. Strain this through the jelly bag to join the first batch of juice.

You should now have about 2 pt (1.2 l) of strained juice. Do not worry if this is a slightly brown colour. Put this into a deep stainless steel pan or special preserving pan, and add the sugar and lemon juice. The pectin content of medlars is quite high and the jelly will probably set well without the addition of lemon juice, but it will help guarantee a good result.

Warm the liquid to dissolve the sugar completely and then boil until setting point is reached. This is 220-222°F (110°C) registered on a jam thermometer, when a blob of juice should wrinkle on a cold saucer or the droplets congeal on the edge of a wooden spoon and spot slowly from a thread of syrup. Continue cooking and testing until this happens. You will see the jelly miraculously clear and brighten as it is heated.

Tip the jelly into small, warm, clean jars before it starts to thicken, filling them well. Seal with circles of waxed paper or baking paper, screw on the lids tightly and store in a cold, dark place.

8
FORBIDDEN FRUIT

The fruite of apples do differ in greatness,
   form, colour and taste;
some covered with a red skin, others yellowe
   or greene, varying indefinitely according to
   the soyle and climate;
some very great, some little and many of a
   middle sort;
some are sweet or tastie or something sower;
most be of a middle taste between sweet and
   sour.
(John Gerard, 1597)

There are as many varieties of fruit out there as there have always been, but where are they? Can we get hold of them, or are they forbidden fruit?

Over the years wars, fashion, politics, climate, establishments and individuals have all affected the types of fruit we eat and the fruits that make up the landscape. The exciting thing is that history is still being made today and we are making it; what we buy, grow and eat affects the future of fruit varieties and the orchards we see around us.

A POTTED FRUITY HISTORY

Our ancestors were content eating the wild fruits, until the Romans came along and revolutionized our palates as well as the road system; they introduced many cultivated fruits to Britain, including vines, cherries, mulberries, chestnuts, walnuts and the well-loved apple.

In the Dark Ages, when everyone seemed more intent on fighting than on pastoral activities, the fruit scene went very quiet and was kept alive only in quiet corners behind monastery walls, both before and after the Norman invasion. The Normans, incidentally, were quite a fruity lot and brought over a few tips, especially on how to make a good drop of cider, rekindling an interest in the soil. This grew steadily over the next few hundred years but then, what with the Black Death and the climate cooling down, a damper was put on things for a while.

The Italians in the Renaissance really brought fruit back to the tables, for the rich at least! They rediscovered art and food and turned the garden into an outdoor room. Here they grew beautiful fruits and presented them at the end of lavish outdoor feasts, as an edible art form, either straight off the tree or transformed into candied sweets and conserves. The Tudors were impressed by Renaissance fashion, and Henry VIII was as keen on fruit as he was on wives. Grand gardens were planted Italian style, with some twiddly Tudor bits put in. Fruit trees graced the ornamental gardens, as few flowering shrubs were around at the time. Trained to fit in with the style, they were harvested to decorate the tables of the rich. Henry VIII's orchards at Teynham in Kent soon became the nucleus of fruit production; others came to see the range of varieties and take grafts for their own gardens. Orchards and market gardens sprang up around Kent, which had everything going for it: good soil, proximity to a large market and a mild climate. The fruity scene had further improved with the introduction of printing, and the first practical

Showing off

Every year on the first Tuesday in October fruits make their way to London, not to the market-place but to be admired. The Royal Horticultural Society have held an annual exhibition of British-grown fruit ever since 1895 – a real celebration of our fruity heritage.

There are over 300 varieties of apple at the show, each with its own distinctive taste, colour and shape, from the strawberry flavour of the early Worcester Pearmain to the nutty, warm aroma of the late Blenheim Orange.

How did the shows start? In the mid-1800s there were many fruits and countless varieties to choose from. The wealthy Victorians grew hardy fruits in their walled gardens, alongside peaches and grapes in the glasshouse. When improved sea transport made exotics readily available, the gentry returned to their apples and as usual the middle classes followed suit and started to buy apples too.

Up until now the nurseries had concentrated on supplying a wide range of varieties to satisfy the Victorian gentry's quest for novelty. They were not equipped to supply a few standard good doers to the commercial growers to supply the market. In contrast, the Americans had concentrated on the commercial side with a few varieties of quality apples, quadrupled their exports between 1875 and 1879, and were making a fortune. The government, and the growers, knew something had to be done to get people to buy home-grown apples, but what?

The Royal Horticultural Society fruit committee, led by Dr Robert Hogg, the great Victorian pomologist, decided to launch a major campaign to sort out all the hundreds of varieties on offer. Another aim was to select some for the commercial market and save the British fruit industry. The Apple Congress was mounted in 1883 to bring order to chaos. Within a three-week period nearly every fruit-grower in the country was contacted and asked to bring their fruits to London. The response was astounding. The fruits arrived at the

RHS's Great Vinery at Chiswick and members stayed up all night sorting them out. By the morning, when the Congress was opened to the public, there were 1,545 labelled varieties on the tables. Growers and gardeners descended upon London to compare their own varieties with those on display and filled in question-naires to choose the best apples for the commercial market. They chose the Cox's Orange Pippin for its flavour and the Bramley as a fine culinary apple, thus placing our two finest apples on the road to stardom.

Breeders and nurserymen started to concentrate on what the market wanted and large orchards of Cox's and Bramleys were planted in all the fruit-growing areas. By 1895, when the Royal Horticultural Society held its first exhibitions of British-grown fruit at the Crystal Palace, the number of orchards in the Thames Valley alone had doubled to cover 5,000 acres (2,000 ha).

So the commercial growers had to specialize in an attempt to survive, but fortunately the fruit collections, nurserymen and private gardeners kept the varieties alive. So now everything is rosy, or is it?

handbook on fruit-growing, written by Mascall in 1572, helped to explain a thing or two to gardeners and aspiring gardeners.

Horticulturally, the seventeenth century was a very fruity era. Plant-hunting became the vogue, and fruits as well as ornamentals flooded in. Tradescant brought over Roman peaches and Algerian apricots to grace the gardens of the large mansions. In the Interregnum, Cromwell's agents attempted to keep fruit-growing alive by ordering mass planting of fruit trees throughout the land for rich and poor alike. When Charles II was restored to the throne this policy continued and orchards were planted up as a new agricultural crop. Things were also on the move in the garden. Dwarf rootstocks and the real art of pruning arrived from France, when it was discovered that trees could be 'clipped' to encourage fruiting as well as for shape. The cordon had been born! Closer spacing meant more trees and with more choice the season could also be extended, starting with tiny Jenetting apples in July and going through to the Deux Ans, which stored until May. Dwarfing trees were very fashionable and were planted up in huge geometric parterres in grand gardens.

By the mid-1700s gardening fashion had changed: sweeping green landscapes were in and the edible fruits and vegetables were trotted off to the walled garden. The gardeners on the private estates got into trained trees, cold frames, and competition to see who could get the most varieties for the longest period of time. Fashion spread and everyone, wanting to emulate the tastes of the gentry, demanded fruits too, in as many shapes and forms as possible. Nurseries were set up to supply the demand. Things were not so rosy for the commercial growers: canker and woolly aphid were rife, and competition, in the form of red, shiny apples, had started to arrive from America.

At the beginning of the nineteenth century Thomas Andrew Knight, president of the newly formed London Horticultural Society, had a cunning plan. He believed that plants had only a certain life span, and that cuttings or grafted material aged at the same rate as the parent, eventually to succumb to death and disease. He started a programme to breed new young healthy fruits from seed. As it happened his theory was completely wrong, but he had started the fruit breeding industry and since then no one has looked back. The famous nurseries of Laxton's, Keen's, Rivers, Bunyard's and Pyne's continued to bring out new varieties and the fruit avalanche was well under way. One of the initial aims of the London Horticultural Society, which became the Royal Horticultural Society in 1861, was to improve the range and quality of all produce, both in the private garden and the market place and also to provide a centre for pomological research. In an attempt to catalogue and experiment they collected and planted up a huge fruit collection in Chiswick and in 1826 published a catalogue of 3,825 fruit varieties. After the 1883 apple congress, the cox was chosen as the main commercial apple.

And now?

Unfortunately, that's not the end of the story. The Cox's may have tasted good but was found to be very susceptible to disease. In the 1920s lime-sulphur came to the rescue, and this helped a great deal with the control of disease. The research stations then moved in to try and iron out all the other problems.

We now have cold storage, improved fruit nutrition, detailed breeding programmes, dwarfing rootstocks, intensive planting, mechanical harvesting, integrated pest control and apples that don't go off. But there are still problems due to the large amounts of cheap apple imports from Europe and America. Supermarkets and the big shops demand perfection and continuity which the British growers are ill equipped to meet, due partly to our climate.

A grubbing-out scheme was introduced in 1994 to all EU countries to reduce overproduction of culinary and dessert apples in Europe, particularly in the southern Member States and France. To qualify for the grant of £4,600 per hectare (£1,900 per acre), trees had to be less than twenty years old, have a density of more than 400 trees to the hectare (160 per acre) and be capable of producing a full, healthy crop. Another stipulation was that after removing the trees the land was to remain free of fruit trees for fifteen years. UK growers, who did not contribute to the surplus, should have benefited from reduction of imports as it should have meant less competition. However, being in the EU, the UK growers were entitled to the grant as well, and by 1 December 1994, they had put in 284 applications to grub 2,568 hectares (6,343 acres) representing 13.2 per cent of our total orchards, at a cost of £12 million. The money will give some growers the opportunity to retire, others to square up with the bank, and others to change to a more profitable venture. Overall in Europe the grubbing grant applications represented 7 per cent of the total crop. In Britain, some growers were even grubbing older trees without the grant because they could not make a living. All very sad, leading to the demise of many a good old tree.

Who Knows What to Do?

Due to our cool climate Britain produces some of the best-tasting apples in the world, and orchards form part of the traditional English landscape. Also, hidden out there we have hundreds of apple varieties all with their own distinct flavours, to take us from August to the following June. How can we save our rural landscapes, help the fruit industry and get hold of the range of tasty varieties that are still out there? We have here not one quest but three!

The Landscape

As well as getting grants to pull trees out you can also get grants, albeit a lot smaller, to put trees in. Somerset County Council started off one scheme by grant-aiding the planting of traditional standard cider trees. Now other counties have taken it up. In Kent traditional cobnut plats are being replanted and in Hereford and Worcester 5,000 apple trees have been put in in the last five years, including old local varieties such as Stoke Edith Pippin, Pitmaston Pine Apple and Worcester Pearmain. One catch: you have to be able to see the trees from a public right of way, as the schemes are designed to enhance the landscape. Small farmers wanting to restore their farm orchards to make cider have taken up the grants as well as landowners wanting to recreate traditional landscapes. The Countryside Commission's grant scheme, Countryside Stewardship, has also helped to conserve old traditional orchards helping with tree replacement, and old orchard maintenance.

Common Ground is an organization that works to encourage people to value and enjoy their own surroundings. When they realized the plight of the old orchards in 1989 they launched one of their many successful projects: the 'Save Our Orchards' campaign. Since then many traditional orchards have been saved, new ones planted, old varieties found and community orchards created. Success stories include:

• *Carhampton, Somerset* Villagers awoke one morning to find that a planning application had been submitted to build on the only green area in their village, an old orchard. The villagers set up a 'Save Our Orchards' committee. They raised a petition, put up posters and called in the media to draw attention to their plight. The planning application was withdrawn and the villagers still have their orchard.

• *South Hams* is a picturesque area between the sea and the wilds of Dartmoor peppered with remnants of orchards, reminders of old local farms and their tradition for growing cider. The local people have had their own Save Our Orchards campaign since 1989 and have managed to replant many orchards and found several old local varieties. They are still looking for the Grand Sultan and the Sugar Loaf apple. Have you got one in your garden?

• *Derbyshire* A community orchard in Langley Mill put out a plea for a lost local variety called Mrs

Orchards as landscapes

An 'ort yeard' originally referred to a vegetable garden that was enclosed to keep out animals but then became the term for a collection of fruit trees. Traditional orchards consist of widely spaced large trees under which soft fruits were grown or animals grazed. Figures suggest that we have lost two-thirds of our traditional orchards in the last thirty years, amounting to some 150,000 acres. Some counties have suffered more than others. Gloucestershire, the home of the perry pear, has lost 75 per cent of its traditional orchards in the last fifty years, Kent has lost 85 per cent of its traditional orchards and two-thirds of the total orchard cover in the last forty years, and poor Devon, famous for its cider, has lost 90 per cent of its traditional orchards in the last thirty years (Figures from Common Ground and the County Councils).

In losing an orchard we lose far more than fruit. There is the genetic diversity to consider, as the orchard may have contained old rare varieties such as

A traditional West Country cider orchard

the Keswick Codlin or Cornish Honeypin. Then there is the habitat value. Old orchards are often excellent for wildlife, being long-lived and never sprayed. They support wild flowers such as early purple orchids, cowslips and hay rattle, wildlife such as hares and badgers, and many birds and insects. An apple tree may come second only to the oak in the amount of wildlife it supports. The traditional orchard is also good for us, creating a beautiful landscape with its welcoming spring blossom and fruits of autumn.

Coombe Florey perry pear orchard

In Coombe Florey lie the remains of some 16,000 productive pear trees which until recently were a delight to behold, particularly when blossoming in springtime. In August 1992, this 120 acre (50 ha) pear orchard (one of the largest in the country) was felled with its fruit because the new owner could get better returns from subsidised arable crops.

Wilmott. The variety was found alive and healthy in a nearby village. In addition, they found Mrs Wilmott's seventy-seven-year-old granddaughter, Adalene Langton, who came to the community orchard and told everyone what it was like back in her grandmother's day.

• *Lewisham* once in the Garden of England, is now in the heart of London. The Borough Council has redressed the balance by creating a demonstration orchard on an old allotment site. With the help of local groups, volunteers and schoolchildren they have planted many old Kent varieties, such as the apple Kentish Fillbasket, as well as local plums, cherries, cobnuts and even peaches. As a multicultural borough they have also planted a loquat, a Chinese quince and an Asian pear.

These orchards, although in the main not commercial concerns, are essential. They keep people in touch with their environment and help to educate others as well as conserve the landscape and the old varieties.

TRADITIONS, OLD AND NEW

As the apple has been at the core of things for so long it is steeped in folklore, especially of a more romantic nature. Greek lovers used to play 'ball' with an apple and kiss it before they threw it to their partner. Those still looking for 'the apple of their eye' could tell if they were going to be lucky or not by spitting apple pips at the ceiling. If they stuck they were in with a chance. The Celts had a custom which they hoped would even reveal the name of their future partner. A long strip of apple peel thrown over the left shoulder was supposed to fall in the shape of their initials. A partner's faithfulness was also tested by putting named pips on the edge of the fire and saying: 'If you love me, bounce and fly, if you hate me, lie and die.' The lover was said to be faithful if the pip burst noisily in the fire's heat.

The apple has been regarded as a holy or magical tree from very early times. King Arthur was taken to the Arthurian paradise, Avalon, the apple vale, to heal his wounds; in ancient Ireland the apple tree was one of the three things that could be paid for only by a living object, the other two being the hazel tree and the sacred grove. Many omens and charms were associated with the apple – autumn blossom was a bad omen: 'A bloom on the tree when the apples are ripe, is a sure termination of somebody's life.' On a happier note, if the sun was seen to shine through the trees on Christmas morning, it was the sign of a good crop and good luck for the owner of the tree.

Wassailing, from the Anglo-Saxon *waes hael*, meaning 'health be to you', is thought to be associated with fertility rights and probably a Celtic ceremony. Some say it dates from Roman times, as part of their festival for praising and encouraging Pomona, the goddess of fruit trees. On 6 January, the new twelfth night, the wassail song rings out:

> Here's to thee old apple tree.
> Stand fast root, bear well top,
> Pray God send us a yuling crop.
> Every twig, apple big.
> Every bough, apple enow.
> Sacks full, bins full, fill bushel boxes full.
> Hurrah, boys, Hurrah!

Was it a ghostly song from our pagan past? No, it was late twentieth century in a flourishing, commercial orchard. The Charlton's Orchards team have wassailed for the past thirty years, ever since the family came to the orchards. Toast is hung in branches to attract the robins, the good spirits of the orchard; the trees are doused in cider to put back in what has been taken out. To ward off evil spirits, the villagers and farm workers link hands round a tree in the orchard, chant rhymes and make as much noise as possible. A bonfire made from the prunings keeps everyone warm while they sample the local cider and taste the fruits of their labours. Why do they wassail? They say they do it to get a good yuling, a good crop, and chase away evil spirits. They have had favourable crops for the last few years and dare not stop now.

Seriously, it is a good event to get together all the people who have worked on the farm during the year and thank them for their efforts. As they say: 'Tongue in cheek we take the wassail very seriously.' Everyone at the wassail was tucking in to their favourite apples, and voices rang out in the cold night air: 'I'll have a Court Pendu Plat', 'An Ashmead's Kernel for me', 'Save me an Orlean's Reinette.' These local people knew their apples. Do you?

Every 21 October a celebration of our much loved fruit, the apple, occurs in all sorts of places, from schools to restaurants and from village halls to the Houses of Parliament. All sorts of things go on, including apple games, apple meals, apple story-telling and apple identification. The first apple day was held at the Old Apple Market in Covent Garden in 1990. It was conceived by Common Ground as a celebration and to raise the apple's profile. It worked: up to a hundred events are now held every year from Land's End to John o' Groats.

THE INDUSTRY

In the south-west, commercial growers are making a living, conserving the landscape and keeping old traditions alive by planting cider trees. Cider apples are still produced traditionally on large standard trees, often with livestock grazing beneath.

Julian Temperley, owner of the largest private cider orchards in the country, makes cider brandy, cider champagne and traditional cider. He thinks grant schemes to plant trees are well intentioned but feels that they are looking to the past and setting up the fruit industry as a museum. He believes that there is no pride in a museum society and that as well as having a glorious past the cider industry has an exciting future. His cider orchards are living landscapes that are economically viable and therefore self-sustaining. They are still working today as they always have done.

The large cider companies are also encouraging local farmers to plant more cider apple trees so that they can increase the percentage of English apples in the bulk-produced ciders. If you ask for cider you will help the growers and help save the landscape.

Dessert fruit is grown more intensively, giving a very different landscape. One commercial grower in Kent said that if every person ate one more English Cox each the industry would be saved. Others believe that grubbing-out money could go into something more positive, such as juicing plants to provide a product that could be sold all year round.

Despite the move towards specialization and intensification in an attempt to survive, a few commercial orchards, particularly the smaller ones, have gone the other way – for diversity. Crapes Fruit Farm in Essex grows over 150 varieties in 15 acres (6 ha) and Charlton's Orchards grow a wide range of different plums, pears, damsons, quinces and twenty-five varieties of apples on their 35 acre (14 ha) site on the Somerset levels, including some old traditional varieties such as Court Pendu Plat, Orlean's Reinette, and Ashmead's Kernel. They sell from their farm shop, which is full of the most beautiful apple aromas, from larger greengrocers and by mail order. So the varieties are out there, it is just a matter of finding them. The supermarkets have noticed that the consumer is on the lookout for taste and are now stocking a wider range of traditional English apples. It's up to you. If you ask for the apples you will help the growers and help conserve the varieties.

VARIETY

Fruits, especially apples, come in a wide range of flavours as distinct as different wines or cheeses. Maybe you have tasted one in an old garden or on Apple Day or read a passionate description in an old book. From the Thomas Rivers cooking apple described by Bunyard as having a 'distinct pear flavour with an almost quince-like acidity' to the wonderful description of Ashmead's Kernel from Morton Shand, which makes you want to rush out and sink your teeth into one immediately: 'What an apple, what suavity of aroma. Its initial Madeira-like mellowness of flavour overlies a deeper honeyed nuttiness, crisply sweet not sugar sweet, but the succulence of a well-devilled marrow bone. Surely no apple of greater distinction or more perfect balance can ever have been raised anywhere on earth.'

There are over 2,000 varieties of apple in the UK National Collection. Today only nine dominate our commercial orchards, although over the country there are fifty or sixty that are commercially grown, many of which are regional varieties. Regional identity is part of our heritage. You should be able to tell a county by its fruit, from the cider apples of the south-west to the pears of Gloucestershire, from the plums of Hereford and Worcester to the Garden of England, where dessert apples, cobnuts and cherries flourish. Individual varieties may also taste better on home ground, where they are suited to the climate and soil. D'Arcy Spice does best in its native Essex, with its low rainfall; enthusiasts say Blenheim Orange apples taste best from the old trees growing in north Oxfordshire. There are many local varieties in old gardens, and experts can tell whereabouts in the country they are by the fruits they see growing. If local growers could supply local outlets, we could travel to anywhere in the country and know where we were by the fruits and foods on the shelves.

What grows where?

Bedfordshire

Apples: Laxton's Fortune, Lord Lambourne.
Pear: Warden.
Plum: Fotheringham.
Local dish: Bedfordshire clangers, a dumpling with meat at one end and apple at the other.

Berkshire

Apples: Charles Ross, John Standish.
Pear: William's Bon Chrétien.
Plum: Marjorie's Seedling.
Local industry: vineyards.

Buckinghamshire

Apples: Arthur Turner, Langley Pippin.
Plum: Aylesbury Prune.

Cambridgeshire

Apples: Chiver's Delight, Emneth Early.
Plum: Cambridge Gage.
Local dish: Huntingdon Fidget apple pie.

Cheshire

Apples: Arthur W. Barnes, Lord Derby.
Gooseberry: Montrose.
Local dish: pork and pippins pie.

Cornwall

Apples: Scilly Pearl, Cornish Gilliflower.
Plum: Kea.
Local dishes: baked mackerel with gooseberry sauce, West Country apple tart.
Local industry: early strawberries.

Cumbria

Apples: Keswick Codlin (discovered in the ruins of Gleaston Castle).
Damsons: Witherslack damsons.

Derbyshire

Apples: Newton Wonder.

Devonshire

Apples: Devonshire Quarrenden, Allspice, Star of Devon.
Cider apples: Tremlett's Bitter, Sweet Alford, Ponsford.
Plum: Dittisham Ploughmans.
Cherries: Dun, Large Black, Small Black, Bottlers, Mazzard.
Local industry: cider apples. Cider apples and cherries were once landmarks of the Tamar Valley.

Dorset

Apples: Melcombe Russet.
Cider apple: White Jersey.
Plum: Bryanston.

Essex

Apples: D'Arcy Spice, Discovery, George Cave, Sturmer Pippin, Queen.
Blackcurrant: Carter's Champion (a chance seedling).
Local industry: vineyards.

Gloucestershire

Apples: Ashmead's Kernel, Catshead.
Cider apples: Old Foxwhelp, Must, Forest Styre.
Plum: Blaisdon Red.
Local industry: apples and perry pears.
Local drink: perry.
Home of the perry pear, such as High Pear, Thorn and Moorcroft.

Hampshire and the Isle of Wight

Apples: Beauty of Hants, Hambledon Deux Ans, Howgate Wonder.
Plum: Angelina Burdett.
Local industry: vineyards and early strawberries.

Herefordshire and Worcestershire

Apples: King's Acre Pippin, Pitmaston Pineapple, Worcester Pearmain.
Cider apples: Brown Snout.
Pears: Elton, Black Worcester.
Plum: Pershore Yellow Egg, Purple Pershore.
Local industry: plums, cider and dessert apples.
Local dish: plum jam.
Local drinks: cider, perry and fruit juices.

Hertfordshire

Apples: Brownlee's Russet, Golden Reinette, Lane's Prince Albert.
Cherries: Alba Heart, August Heart, Smoky Heart.
Pear: Conference and Fertility.

Kent

Apples: Beauty of Kent, George Neal, Warner's King (locally Killick's apple).
Plum: Diamond.
Cherries: Nutberry Black, Kentish Red.

Damson: The Farleigh.
Raspberry: Lloyd George (a chance seedling).
Local dish: cherry huffkins, ripe cherry tart, apple and hazelnut layer.
Local drink: cherry beer, cherry brandy, cider and apple juice made from dessert apples, fruit wines from elderberry to gooseberry.
Local industry: dessert apples, cherries, cobnuts, vineyards, and soft fruits.

Lancashire and the Isle of Man

Apples: Duke of Devonshire, Lord Suffield, Mank's Codlin. Gooseberries.
Local dish: Eccles cakes.

Leicestershire and Rutland

Apples: Annie Elizabeth, Dumelow's Seedling.

London and Middlesex

Apples: Rev. W. Wilks, Fearn's Pippin, Hounslow Wonder.
Local industry: soft fruits.

Lincolnshire.

Apples: Ellison's Orange, Peasgood Nonsuch.

Norfolk

Apples: Dr Harvey, Golden Noble, Norfolk Beefing, Norfolk Royal.
Pear: Robin.
Cherry: Caroon.
Local dish: Norfolk biffin, baked Norfolk Beefing apples.
Local drink: Norfolk cyder, spelled with a 'y', made from cooking apples.
Local industry: vineyards.

Northamptonshire

Apples: Barnack Beauty, Lord Burghley.
Aynho is known as the apricot village – every garden used to grow them.

Northumberland

Apples: Mrs Lakeman's Seedling.

Nottinghamshire
Apples: Bramley's Seedling, Bess Pool.

Oxfordshire
Apples: Blenheim Orange.

Shropshire
Apples: Princes Pippin.
Wild damsons.
Local dishes: Shropshire fidget pie.

Somerset and Avon
Apples: Beauty of Bath, Hoary Morning, Camelot.
Cider apples: Dunkerton's Sweet, Chisel Red, Dabinett.
Pear: Beurre d'Avalon.
Local dish: Somerset apple cake.
Local drink: cider and cider brandy.
Local industry: cider apples and early strawberries.

Suffolk
Apples: Lady Henniker, St Edmund's Pippin.
Plum: Coe's Golden Drop.
Local drink: cyder, spelled with a 'y', made from cooking apples.
Local industry: vineyards.

Surrey
Apples: Claygate Pearmain, Cockle Pippin, Cox's Orange Pippin.
Plum: Mitchelson's.
Local industry: vineyards.

Sussex
Apples: Alfriston, Crawley Beauty, Egremont Russet.
Plum: Victoria, discovered as a chance seedling in Alderton.
Local industry: vineyards.

Warwickshire
Apples: Wyken Pippin.

Wiltshire
Apples: Roundway Magnum Bonum.

Yorkshire
Apples: Ribston Pippin, Yorkshire Greening (Goose Sauce).
Pear: Wyedale.
Plum: Winesour.
Local dish: the open fruit tart.
Fruity facts: sailing ships from Whitby used to take apples on voyages for their Vitamin C.

Wales
General
Apples: Baker's Delicious.
Cider apple: Frederick.

Monmouthshire
Apples: Monmouthshire Beauty.

Radnorshire
Apples: Cummy Norman.

Scotland
Angus
Apples: Tower of Glamis.

Fife
Apples: Lady of the Wemyss.

Galloway
Apples: Galloway Pippin.

Lanarkshire
Apples: Cambusnethan Pippin.

Midlothian
Apples: James Grieve.

Moray
Apples: Beauty of Moray.

Peeblesshire
Apples: Stobo Castle.

Perthshire

Apples: Bloody Ploughman.

Ross and Cromarty

Apples: Coul Blush.

Roxburghshire

Apples: Golden Pippin.

Stirlingshire

Apples: Stirling Castle.

Strathclyde

Pears: Ayrshire Lass.

Tayside

Local fruit: raspberries.
Local dish: Dundee cake and Dundee marmalade.

THE NATIONAL FRUIT COLLECTIONS

We still have our range of fruit varieties, thanks to the people who have had the foresight to set up collections. The National Fruit Collections, first established in Chiswick, moved to Wisley in 1921 and then to Brogdale Farm, Faversham, Kent, in the early 1950s.

Despite being closed by the Ministry in 1990, Brogdale soldiered on and with help from the Duchy of Cornwall and Swale Borough Council bought the site and saved it from closure. Now their vital work can continue. The Brogdale Trust work with MAFF and Wye College to conserve the diversity of temperate fruit species, collect genetic material for use in breeding programmes, and maintain the collections which form an important part of our heritage. They continue to search the world for new and old fruit varieties and evaluate new fruit cultivars from around the world for use in the amateur and commercial markets. They are now building on their fruity heritage by developing a range of gardens to show the complete history and culture of fruit gardening and fruits from around the world.

In 1995 they had 3,869 different cultivars/varieties of fruit comprising:

2,009 dessert and culinary apples.
75 cider apples
90 ornamental apples
10 apricots.
272 cherries
14 peaches
336 plums and their relations
41 ornamental Prunus
495 dessert and culinary pears
20 perry pears
16 quinces
4 medlars
41 hazelnuts
55 vines
391 varieties of bush fruit

And many of the people who work there can tell you which variety is which!

There are other large National Fruit Collections around the country, which is vital in case one collection is lost due to unforeseen circumstances. These include strawberries at Horticulture Research International, East Malling, citrus, figs and greenhouse grapes at Read's Nursery in Norfolk, perry pears at the Three Counties Showground, gooseberries at Granada Arboretum and Rougham Hall Nurseries and rubus (raspberries and relations) at Aberdeen College. RHS Wisley also have a large temperate fruit collection.

The collections are vital to remind us of our past and to take us into the future.

GROW YOUR OWN

If you can't get the varieties you want in the shops and want to try some old favourites, grow your own. Nurseries are now stocking more and more unusual and old fruit varieties. New gardens today tend to range from small to minuscule, but there are ways

Saving the Bramley

The original Bramley tree is still standing in Southwell in Nottinghamshire, grown from a pip planted by Mary Ann Brailsford 160 years ago. The tree has been given tender loving care over the years but is now getting very old. Every Bramley apple tree today is a grafted cutting of a grafted cutting taken over many generations; some of these may have mutated over the years. Scientists from the University of Nottingham have now produced Bramley trees that are genetically identical to the original by using tissue culture. This will conserve the genes if the original dies and also show whether grafted Bramleys have changed over the years.

and means of fitting a quart in a pint pot. You can maximize use of space by careful planning and by using every square inch. Even the Victorians with their huge walled gardens were very thrifty in the garden and have lots of tips that can be used on the pocket-handkerchief plot. They grew morello cherries and red currants on north-facing walls, late flowering apples on east-facing walls, apples and pears on west-facing walls and peaches on south-facing walls.

To go up the wall, train fruit trees as cordons, espaliers or fans. Cordons are single-stemmed trees usually grown at an angle of 45°, and espaliers are made up of a main trunk supporting several tiers of horizontal branches. Apples, pears, plums, gooseberries and red and white currants are all suitable for training as cordons, fans or espaliers because they produce their fruits on spurs on the older wood. Plant top fruit cordons 2½–3 ft (75–90 cm) apart and soft fruit cordons 12–15 in (30–37 cm) apart. Fans have 6–10 ribs radiating out from a short trunk, and are a suitable shape for peaches, nectarines and morello cherries. These trees all fruit on one-year-old growths, and the fan shape enables old growths to be cut out and new ones tied in each year.

Trained trees have many virtues: they fit into a small space, are easier to pick, and are less likely to get mildew because they have more air movement around them and the sun can get to all parts of the plant. By fitting more apple and pear trees into a small space you can also make sure that you have

Training cordon gooseberries

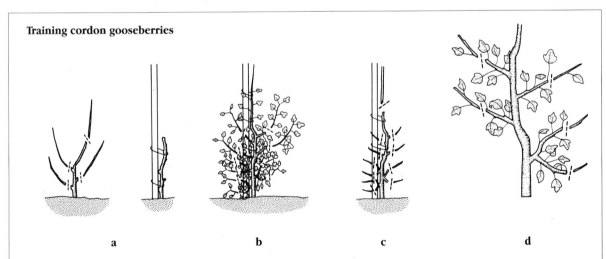

a   b   c   d

(a) In the first winter after planting, cut the leader back by half and cut all the laterals back to 1 bud.
(b) In the summer, around early July, cut back the new growth on the side shoots to 5 leaves to encourage fruiting spurs. Do not summer prune the leader. The cordon should be supported by fastening it loosely to a cane.

(c) In the second winter prune the current season's growth of the leader back to 6 in (15 cm). Cut the current season's growth on the laterals back to 1 in (2.5 cm), to a bud.
(d) In the second summer prune the side shoots to 5 leaves as in the previous summer.

There are many ways of growing fruit in limited spaces

enough varieties to get good cross-pollination. Trained fruit does need support. Horizontal wires strung across a fence or wall on vine eyes are needed, or between straining posts if they are free-standing. Do it properly right from the start and use heavy duty (14–16 gauge) galvanized fencing wire, pulled taut between straining bolts. Fix wires 6 in (15 cm) apart for fans, 18 in (45 cm) for cordons and 15–18 in (37–45 cm) for espaliers.

Gooseberries and red and white currants tend to be grown as vertical cordons and will produce almost as much fruit as a bush.

Apples and pears can easily be grown as oblique cordons, which slows down growth and encourages fruiting. Always choose a tree on a dwarfing rootstock and ask the nursery if the variety is suitable for growing in a restricted form. Follow the same guidelines as for gooseberries with the following changes:

• Plant the tree at a 45° angle facing north and make sure the graft union faces upwards to prevent the scion from rooting.

• Do not prune the leader in the first winter.
• Cut laterals back to four buds in the first winter.

Plums are worth trying as cordons on the dwarf rootstock Pixy. These are trimmed in June and July back

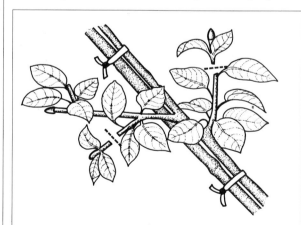

Regular pruning of the apple cordon
In the first and subsequent summers cut laterals longer than 9 in (22 cm) back to 3 leaves ignoring the basal cluster. Cut back sub laterals to one leaf beyond the basal cluster. Each July cut back the current season's growth on the leader to 1 in (2.5 cm).

to five leaves of the current season's growth, and after cropping all the laterals are cut back to three leaves of the current season's growth.

To really slow down growth and create an attractive low fruiting hedge, apples can be grown as stepover trees. The trees, on M27 rootstocks, are trained horizontally on a single wire, 5 ft (1.5 m) apart to give a hedge of about 18–24 in (45–60 cm) high. Plant the maiden tree next to a straining post and secure to the post with a tree tie. Then, very gently, bend the tree over horizontally and attach to the wire using chain-lock tree ties. After planting cut back

The stepover apple tree

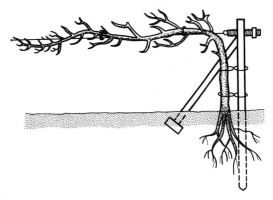

bud. Cut off the vertical stem to a strong bud, with two opposite just beneath, as close to the next wire up as possible. The next summer repeat the whole process on the next tier up, and carry this on each year until you get the number of tiers you want.

For free-standing trees or bushes in a small space,

The oblique apple cordon in winter

the leader by a quarter to an upward-facing bud and cut back any feathers (side shoots) to three buds. At the end of the summer tie the new growth, which has hopefully come from the cut-back leader, on to the horizontal wire to extend the length of the trained tree. After this prune just like an apple cordon (see above).

Pears make beautiful espalier trees. After planting against supporting wires, cut back to three strong buds near the bottom wire. In the summer when the shoots grow, train one straight up, two at 45° angles from the central stem and remove any others. The following winter lower the two side branches carefully to the horizontal and tie in to the bottom wire, then prune them by one third to a downward-facing

The espaliered pear

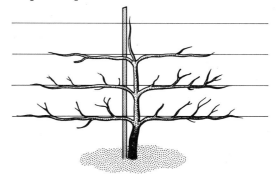

choose non-vigorous varieties on dwarfing rootstocks and/or grow in pots to restrict the root growth. Grow family trees, where more than one variety has been grafted on to one tree. To encourage fruiting and restrict growth still further you can summer prune and even tie down the branches on some trees. Trees can be trained as a dwarf bushes, spindles or dwarf pyramids.

The model fruit garden shown overleaf gives some idea of what you can fit in to a space, 30 ft x 30 ft (10 m x 10 m). Use varieties that will benefit each other by cross-pollination and benefit you with the best flavour, best resistance to pest and disease and give you

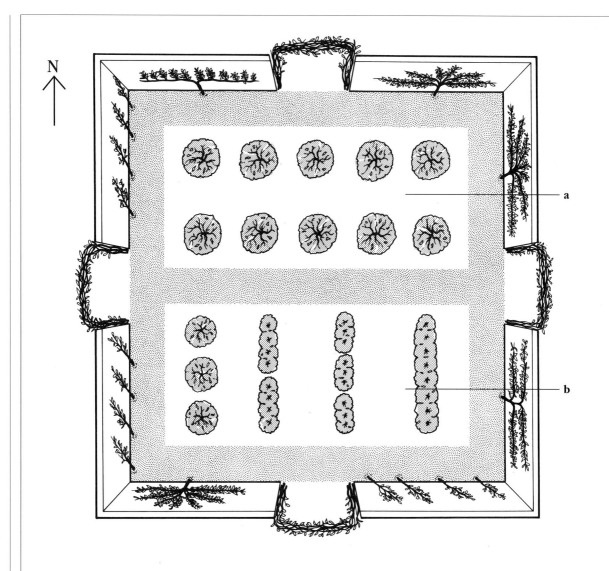

N

a

b

Plan of a Model Fruit Garden

The north-facing wall: fan-trained morello cherry, cordon red currants and gooseberries (Whinham's Industry), and a thornless blackberry over the arch.

The east-facing wall: 4 late-flowering apple cordons (to avoid the frost), 2 cordon cooking plums on Pixy rootstock, 2 cordon mid-season dessert plums on Pixy and a loganberry or tummelberry trained over the arch.

The west-facing wall: espalier pear, fan-trained self-fertile sweet cherry on Colt rootstock and a tayberry trained over the arch.

The south-facing wall: fan-trained peach, outdoor vine trained on the Guyot system and a vine over the arch.

Bed A: 5 pears and 5 apples trained as dwarf pyramids or spindles. Spaced 4ft (1.2m) apart within the row and 6ft (1.8m) apart between the rows. Grafted on to the dwarf stocks, M27 for the apples and Quince C for the pears.

Bed B: A row of Autumn Bliss raspberries (6ft (1.8m) between the row and 15in (37cm) within the row), a row of 3 early, 3 mid-season and 3 late-summer-fruiting raspberries (spaced as autumn fruiters), three compact Ben Sarek black currants (spaced 4ft (1.2m) apart), 4 cordon gooseberries and 4 cordon red or white currants (spaced 5ft (1.5m) between the rows and 12in (30cm) within the rows for gooseberries and 15in (37cm) for red and white currants).

Rows of strawberries can be fitted in between the soft fruits or fruit trees wherever the space is available.

as long a season as possible. Many of the answers lie in these pages; now over to you to make what you want of it. As well as being good for you when you eat it, preparing and planting up a fruit garden will keep you fit too.

Wisley have some other good ideas for the model fruit garden. Anyone keen on fruit who is a member of the RHS should join the Fruit Group for fruity lectures, visits and demonstrations.

The ornamental fruit garden

If you don't have room for a separate fruit garden, mix the fruit with the ornamentals. Have a fruit tree, with its beautiful blossom and coloured fruits, as a lawn specimen or train it into an arch. Train apples as stepovers around a flower border or herb garden. Put red currants, with their jewel-like fruits, in a mixed border and use cane fruits as a living fast-growing fence. Grow fruit trees and bushes in attractive terracotta pots and bring them on to the patio when the fruit is ready to pick. On hot summer afternoons you can sit under a pergola shaded by a vine, picking fresh grapes and sipping home-made fruit juices.

The permaculture fruit garden

Permaculture is a garden design system that can act like a natural ecosystem. The fruit garden, for example, is planted like a natural woodland where all the trees and shrubs produce an edible crop. The tall trees consist of well-spaced standard fruit trees, with a lower tree layer of nut trees and fruit trees on dwarfing rootstocks. Shade-tolerant gooseberries and red currants grow beneath this as a shrub layer, and cane fruits and vines use the taller trees as supports. Prepare the ground well before planting and mulch annually with well-rotted compost and comfrey leaves to provide potash, other nutrients and to suppress weeds. To maximize production, prune the plants well and protect them from pests and diseases. The fruits grow as they do in their natural habitat, the wild fruit forests of the Caucasus. This woodland fruit garden is a good low-maintenance system that would suit busy weekend gardeners.

The garden as part of the landscape

If you are more concerned about landscapes and wildlife than fruit varieties there is something you can do on this score too. Your garden is not an island – you are part of the whole, part of the landscape, even if you live in the middle of a city.

At the beginning of the century a keen fruit enthusiast, Dame Henrietta Barnett, insisted that each garden in Hampstead Garden Suburb was planted with a fruit tree. Now seventy years later there are still forty varieties of these old trees here, an orchard spread across suburbia. They connect local people together. If you and your neighbours all planted a fruit tree you too could create an orchard, an aesthetic, productive, living landscape, even in the middle of a city.

THE FOOD YOU EAT IS THE LANDSCAPE YOU CREATE

If you seek out and grow the old varieties and buy home-grown fruits you can go some way towards helping to save our old fruit varieties and the landscape. And when you have got the fruits you can use them in a wide range of recipes to savour the flavour and to give you a taste of local distinctiveness and history. But most of all, enjoy your fruit gardening and enjoy your food, and pass on some of your own fruity stories.

Apple Quince and Honey Suet Crust

This is a marvellous dish for the colder months and is a light version of the traditional suet pudding. Only 3 oz (75 g) of suet is used for the pastry, which is finely rolled and filled with plenty of fruit. The pastry is too fragile to support the filling if it were to be turned out, so I just cut wedges out of the bowl.

The quince turns a delightful coral-pink when it is cooked and imparts an indescribable fragrance, which wafts from the basin when the lid is lifted. Quinces, like apples, overwinter well if stored in a cool place. They can also be sliced and frozen quite successfully.

I find a boilable plastic 2 pint (1 litre) pudding basin with a snap-on lid indispensable and very practical for steamed puddings, if more mundane than the traditional china bowl and cotton cloth, complete proof against sogginess.

Baked custard is the natural and perfect accompaniment for steamed puddings, especially when it is made with real free-range eggs and fresh, raw creamy milk.

Serves 6

Pastry
3 oz (75 g) fresh beef suet
6 oz (175 g) wholemeal flour
2–3 tablespoons iced water

Filling
1 lb (500 g) cooking apples
1 large, ripe quince
4 heaped tablespoons honey
pinch of powdered ginger
3 whole cloves

First make the pastry. Use a processor to grate the suet. Add the flour, whiz for a moment and then add the water. As soon as the pastry is amalgamated and leaves the sides of the bowl, stop the machine. Leave the pastry to rest for at least 30 minutes.

Peel, core and slice the apples and quince. Roll out the pastry fairly thinly. Put a dollop of honey in the bottom of a 2 pint (1 litre) pudding basin and line the basin with some of the pastry, making sure you have enough left over for the lid. Fill with layers of fruit, honey and spices. Re-roll the pastry for the lid and fit it on the pudding. Snap on the basin lid and steam steadily in a covered saucepan for at least 3 hours. Keep topping up the water from a boiling kettle and make sure the water never stops boiling or drops below halfway point.

Serve steaming hot, with baked custard or cream.

Roast Duck Breast with Gooseberry Sauce

Gooseberries have a special place as the first fruits of summer. Their fresh tartness is splendid with duck when there are no apples around. I like to keep some whole gooseberries in the sauce to add texture. They also freeze extremely well.

Ducks and chickens growing plump on the grazing beneath the orchard trees have always been part of the rural landscape, and ducks fatten particularly well in the rich, lush grass of Herefordshire where I live. This is one of our favourite dishes.

Serves 4

1 coffeespoon honey
2 x 4 lb (1.8 kg) organic ducks, including giblets
sea salt
1 oz (25 g) flour
½ pint (300 ml) red wine
½ pint (300 ml) duck stock
2 bay leaves
tamari
sea salt
freshly ground black pepper
1 lb (500 g) gooseberries, fresh or frozen
sugar to taste

Dilute the honey in a little warm water and paint the duck skin (not too much honey or the skins will blacken). Rub in a little sea salt. Roast the ducks, uncovered, for 45 minutes at 400°F (200°C, Gas 6). Tip off the roasting juices into a bowl and leave to cool and settle.

When the ducks have cooled a little, carve off the breasts and legs. Put the carcasses into a large pot, with the giblets except for the liver. (The liver is too special to use for stock; keep it to make a paté with any meat left over, e.g. from the legs.) Cover with water and boil, covered, for approximately 45 minutes to make stock. Keep about 1 pint (600 ml) stock, and strain the rest into a clean pan and reduce to ½ pint (300 ml).

Peel the skin and fat off the breasts, discard the fat and cut the skin into ½ in (1 cm) strips. Fry these until crisp and keep warm on a dish lined with kitchen paper.

Make the gravy by using 1 oz (25 gm) duck fat to make a roux with the flour. Stir in the ½ pint (300 ml) each of stock and wine and simmer with the bay leaves to reduce by half. Add any duck jelly beneath the dripping. Pass through a very fine sieve and adjust the flavour with a little tamari, salt and pepper.

Cook the gooseberries until soft but still whole, pass two-thirds through a coarse sieve and sweeten to taste. You may feel like nipping off the tops and tails of the whole gooseberries with scissors if you are a perfectionist but they usually soften quite well in the cooking.

Quickly warm the duck breasts in the remaining stock, keeping them pink. Serve them with the crisp skin strips scattered over the meat and the gooseberry sauce with the whole gooseberries in it. Pass the gravy round in a sauceboat.

Lemon Lamb

The marinade in this recipe tenderizes the lamb and allows the spices to impregnate the meat. English lamb from the West country and Wales is beautifully tender anyway, so will not need to steep long. I often use perry, made traditionally from the perry pears of Gloucestershire and Herefordshire, instead of stock. This lightens the recipe and complements the fruitiness of the lemon.

Serves 6

3 lb (1.4 kg) boned leg of lamb
4 tablespoons olive oil
6 cloves garlic, finely chopped
2 lemons, well scrubbed
1 teaspoon ground cumin
2 teaspoons ground coriander
½ teaspoon ground ginger
2 medium-sized onions, finely sliced
2 tablespoons wholemeal flour
hot chicken stock or perry
½ lb (225 g) fresh mushrooms, sliced
sea salt
freshly ground black pepper
4 lemon twists
fresh root ginger to garnish (optional)
fresh flat-leafed parsley to garnish
brown rice and toasted, flaked almonds to serve

Cut the lamb into 1 in (2.5 cm) cubes. Put into a bowl with the oil, garlic, the rind of 1 lemon, cumin, coriander and ginger and marinate for about 2 hours, turning the mixture quite often.

Remove the lamb with a slotted spoon, reserving the marinade, and brown the lamb on all sides in a heavy saucepan or casserole. Add the reserved marinade and the onions and scatter with the flour. Brown for a further moment or two and pour on enough chicken stock or perry to cover. Bring to simmering point over a moderate heat. Remove from the heat.

Preheat the oven to 300°F (150°C, Gas 2). Make a tight seal for the lamb by putting a sheet of aluminium foil over the pan and cover with the lid. Bake for about 1 hour, or until the lamb is tender, adding the mushrooms after 40 minutes. Remove from the oven.

If the meat and mushroom juices have made the sauce too thin, remove the meat, keeping it warm, and reduce the sauce by fast boiling. Stir constantly, as the small amount of flour used will catch if it can. Strain through a fine sieve. Add lemon juice to taste. Season with salt and pepper. Garnish with lemon twists, very fine shavings of peeled ginger root if liked, and flat-leafed parsley. Serve with brown rice and toasted flaked almonds.

Cranachan with Raspberries

Eating cranachan or cream-crowdie round the table with the family was the traditional Scottish way of celebrating harvest home. Crunchy oatmeal is combined with cream and crowdie – a soft cheese made from naturally soured milk – and berried fruits, particularly brambles and blaeberries, gathered by the children from the hedgerows.

Raspberries, which flourish so well in Scotland, are a natural partner with this simple but exquisite dish. Flaked porridge oats are probably easier and quicker to toast, but are not so authentic in taste and texture as the coarse oatmeal. Toasted muesli could be an up-to-date alternative. Sour cream or yoghurt can be hung up in muslin and allowed to drip as an alternative to crowdie to give the required sharpness.

bowl of 1 part double cream to 2 parts crowdie
bowl of pinhead oatmeal toasted slowly in the oven
bowl of fresh raspberries or fresh soft fruits
heather honey or sugar
whisky

Mix in your own bowl to taste.

Morello Cherry and Rice Pudding

From the tall cherry trees of Kent in the east to the orchards of Herefordshire and Worcestershire in the west, the billowing white blossom of the standard cherry tree is dwindling each spring, vanishing completely or being replaced with smaller, less graceful, dwarf stock which are easier to harvest. But the slighter morello tree can grow in every garden and is happy gracing a north wall. The dark red fruit is strong, sharp, freezes well and makes lovely desserts, jams and relishes. Below is a simple child's pudding which is also elegant enough for a dinner party.

Serves 6-8

6 oz (175 g) brown short grain rice
1 pint (600 ml) milk
5 fl oz (150 ml) double cream
4 oz (100 g) granulated sugar
1 vanilla pod
1½ lb (675 g) morello cherries
sugar to taste
natural almond essence

Rinse the rice and put it into a casserole with the milk, cream, sugar and vanilla pod. Cover tightly and cook at 150°C (300°F) for about 1½ hours or until the rice has swelled and all the liquid has been absorbed. Note that brown rice can take a little longer to cook than white.

Stone the cherries or not, depending on who is going to eat the pudding – children like to count the stones and it does take a lot of time – and simmer gently until the juice runs. Sweeten the fruit and strain off the juice. (The stones can be cracked and some kernels put in a muslin bag and cooked with the cherries instead of using almond essence.)

Grease individual moulds or a single dish and layer the rice and half the cherries. Leave to cool and set.

Turn out the mould(s) to serve. Thicken the cherry juice slightly with a little cornflour (1 teaspoon per ¼ pint (150 ml), add a drop of almond essence and use the sauce and the remaining cherries and a few cherry leaves to decorate the pudding. Hand round a jug of cream.

Glossary

Apex The tip of a stem, the uppermost stem on a system of branches.

Biennial A plant with a life cycle of two seasons. Biennial bearers produce fruit every other year.

Biological control The control of a pest by another living organism.

Bush tree Pruned as an open-centred shaped tree with 2–2.5 ft (60–75 cm) of clear stem.

Central leader The central, upright stem of a tree.

Cordon A single-stemmed tree bearing spurs, sometimes planted at a 45° angle.

Dormant buds Buds that have formed but have not become active.

Espalier A tree trained with a vertical main stem and tiers of horizontal branches.

Eye A growth bud, especially with vines.

Extension shoot One year's vegetative growth.

Feather The side shoots of a vigorous maiden produced in the first year of growth.

Framework The basic structure of a tree.

Frost pocket A low-lying area susceptible to ground frost.

Fruit buds Large, rounded buds that produce flowers and fruit.

Grafting A method of propagation where a scion is united with a rootstock.

Half-hardy A plant that cannot survive the winter without protection.

Hardy A plant that can survive the winter outdoors.

Heel in To store plants temporarily with their roots covered with soil in a trench.

Hybrid A plant produced by crossing two species or forms of species.

John Innes compost A good-quality soil-based compost containing slow-release fertilizer.

Lateral Side-shoots produced by the leader.

Leader The terminal shoot of a tree or branch that determines the main direction of growth.

Loam An average soil with a good mixture of sand and clay.

Maiden A one-year-old (grafted) tree.

Maiden whip A one-year-old tree with no feathers.

Pan A hard layer beneath the soil surface.

Perennial A plant that lives for three or more seasons.

pH The scale used to measure acidity (1–7) and alkalinity (7–14). pH 7.0 is neutral.

Rootstock The root system and stem of a tree used for grafting.

Rod The main woody stem of a vine.

Runner A rooting stem that grows along the surface of the soil.

Scion The shoot or bud of a tree used to graft on to a rootstock.

Sport A plant that differs genetically from the typical growth of the plant that produced it. ·

Spur A slow-growing short branch system that carries clusters of flower buds.

Spur-bearer A tree that produces most of its growth on spurs.

Stopping Nipping out the growing point of a shoot.

Sucker A shoot growing from a stem or root at or below ground level.

Tip-bearer A tree that produces its fruit at the tip of the previous year's growth.

Triploid Has 1½ times the normal number of chromosomes and needs to be pollinated by two partners.

Union The junction between the rootstock and scion.

Vegetative bud A small narrow bud that gives rise to a shoot.

Further Reading

Harry Baker, *The Fruit Garden Displayed*, Cassell/RHS, 1991.

Joan Morgan and Alison Richards, *The Book of Apples*, Ebury Press, 1993.

F. A. Roach, *Cultivated Fruits of Britain. Their Origin and History*, Blackwell, 1985.

Also:
Mrs M. Grieve, *A Modern Herbal*, Penguin.

Harry Baker, *Fruit, RHS Encyclopaedia of Practical Gardening*, Mitchell Beazley.

Rosanne Sanders, *The English Apple*, Phaidon, Oxford.

Jack Woodward, *Pruning Hardy Fruits*, A Wisley Handbook, RHS.

Harry Baker and Ray Waite, *Grapes Indoors and Out*, A Wisley Handbook, RHS.

Stefan Buczacki and Keith Harris, *Collins Shorter Guide to the Pests, Diseases and Disorders of Garden Plants*, Collins.

Useful Addresses

Brogdale Horticultural Trust
Brogdale Road
Faversham
Kent
ME13 8XZ

If you want to know anything about fruit, this is the place to come. Holder of the National Fruit Collections, host guided walks of orchards and new demonstration gardens, run day schools and demonstrations. Have a Fruit Plant Centre. Run a Friends of Brogdale Membership scheme for newsletter, advice information line on Friday afternoon, and free entry to Brogdale.

Countryside Commission
4th Floor
71 Kingsway
London
WC2B 6ST

The Fresh Fruit and Vegetable Information Bureau
Bury House
126–128 Cromwell Road
London

The Heligan Manor Gardens Project
Heligan
Pentewan
St Austell
Cornwall

Restoration of nineteenth-century gardens, with walled gardens, jungle gardens, Italian garden, and the all-important pineapple pits.

Henry Doubleday Research Association
Ryton Gardens
Ryton on Dunsmore
Coventry
CV8 3LG

A large organic demonstration garden with a wide range of fruit (in season) and demonstrations of organic pest and disease control.

Kentish Cobnut Association
Mrs V. Coleman
Clakkers House
Crouch
Borough Green
Kent
TN15 8PY

Ministry of Agriculture, Fisheries and Food
The Plant Variety Rights Office and Seed Division
White House Lane
Huntingdon Road
Cambridge
CB3 0LF

RHS Wisley
Wisley
Woking
Surrey
GU23 6QB

As well as wonderful displays of ornamental plants, Wisley has a superb model fruit garden, and a large fruit collection.

The National Collections

Both Brogdale Horticulture Trust and RHS Wisley have extensive fruit collections. The research stations, such as East Malling (now Horticulture Research International) and the Scottish Crop Research Institute, also house large fruit collections. In addition:

Actinidia: G. E. Bland, Bristol Zoological Gardens, Clifton, Bristol BS8 3HA.

Rubus: B. Gilliland, Aberdeen College, Clinterty Centre, Kinellar, Aberdeen AB5 0TN.

Gooseberries: Dr R. Benton, University of Manchester, School of Biological Sciences, Williamson Building, Oxford Road, Manchester M13 9PL. The collection is at Granada Arboretum, Jodrell Bank.

Gooseberries: K. N. Harbutt, Rougham Hall Nurseries, Ipswich Road, Rougham, Bury St Edmunds, Suffolk IP30 9LZ.

Grapes: Reads Nursery, Hales Hall, Loddon, Norfolk, NR14 6QW.

Specialist Fruit Nurseries

J. C. Allgrove, The Nursery, Middle Green, Lampley, Slough, Berks SL3 6BU. Traditional varieties of fruit trees.

Aylett's Nurseries Ltd, North Orbital Road, St Albans, Herts AL2 1DH. Traditional varieties of fruit trees.

Blackmore Wholesale Nurseries, Blackmoor, Liss, Hants GU33 6BS. Wide range of top and soft fruit.

Chris Bowers and Sons, Whispering Trees Nurseries, Wimbotsham, Norfolk PE34 8QB. Wide range of top and soft fruit.

Brogdale Plant Centre, Brogdale Horticulture Trust, Faversham, Kent. Wide range of top and soft fruit.

Buckingham Nurseries, Tingewood Road, Buckingham MK18 4AE. Wide range of top and soft fruit.

H. P. Bulmers, The Cider Mills, Plough Lane, Hereford HR4 0LE. Cider apple trees.

Burncoose and Southdown Nurseries, Gwennap, Redruth, Cornwall TR16 6BJ. Not specialist, but interesting fruit varieties.

Copton Ash Gardens, 105 Ashford Road, Faversham, Kent ME13 8XW. Wide range of top and soft fruit.

Cranmore Vine Nursery, Yarmouth, Isle of Wight. Vines.

Castle Rising Plant Centre, The Hirsel, 38 Church Road, Wimbotsham, Norfolk PE34 3QG. Good range of unusual plums.

Deacon's Nursery, Godshill, Isle of Wight PO38 3HW. Wide range of top and soft fruit.

Eden Nurseries, Rectory Lane, Old Bolingbroke, Spilsby, Lincs. Traditional fruit trees.

Family Trees, PO Box 3, Batley, Hampshire. Organically grown fruit trees.

The Fruit Garden, Mulberry Farm, Woodnesborough, Sandwich, Ken CT13 0PT. Old varieties of tree fruit.

Highfield Nurseries, The Nursery, School Lane, Whitminster, Gloucester GL2 7PL. Wide range of top and soft fruit.

Keepers Nursery, 446 Wateringbury Road, East Malling, Kent ME19 6JJ. Good range of unusual plum trees and other top fruit including cobnuts.

F. P. Matthews Ltd, Berrington Court, Tenbury, Wells, Worcs. Traditional fruit trees.

Morrey and Son, Forest Nursery, Kelsall, near Tarporley, Cheshire. Traditional top fruit.

Ken Muir, Honeypot Farm, Weeley Heath, Clacton-on-Sea, Essex CO16 9BJ. Soft fruit.

Notcutts Nurseries, Ipswich Road, Woodbridge, Suffolk IP12 4AF. Cobnuts.

Philip House, Family Trees, Curdridge, Botley, Southampton. Traditional fruit trees.

P. J. Nurseries, 26 Church View, High Street, Oakington, Cambridge. Traditional top fruit.

T. A. Redman Ltd, Elms Farm, Ancton Lane, Middleton-on-Sea, Bognor Regis PO22 6NJ. Cider apple trees.

Reads Nursery, Hales Hall, Loddon, Norfolk NR14 6QW. National collection of grapes and figs.

R. V. Roger Ltd, The Nurseries, Pickering, York YO18 7HG. Traditional fruit trees.

Saint Bridget Nurseries, Old Rydon Lane, Exeter EX2 7JY. Traditional top fruit.

Scotts Nurseries Ltd, Merriott, Somerset. Wide range of top and soft fruit.

W. Seabrook and Sons Ltd, Little Leigh's Hall, Little Leighs, Chelmsford, Essex CM3 1PG. Traditional top fruit.

Clive Simms, Woodhurst, Essendine, Stamford, Lincs PE9 4LQ. Nuts and unusual fruits.

Thornhayes Nursery, St Andrew's Wood, Dulford, Cullompton, Devon EX15 2DF. Cider apple trees and top fruit.

Triscombe Nurseries, Triscombe, Bagborough, near Taunton, Somerset. Traditional fruit trees.

Trees for Life, 3 Westdene, Gaddesden Row, Hertfordshire HP2 6HU. Fruit trees.

Taunton Cider Company, Norton Fitzwarren, Taunton, Somerset. Cider apple trees.

J. Tweedie Fruit Trees, Maryfield Road Nursery, Maryfield, near Terregles, Dumfries DG2 9TH. Wide range of top and soft fruit.

Welsh Fruit Stocks, Bryngwyn, via Kington, Hereford HR5 3QZ. Soft fruit.

INDEX